MW00387012

TASTE OF THE
TERRITORY

*A Collection of Recipes Featuring
the Flair And Flavor Of Oklahoma!*

PUBLISHED BY
SERVICE LEAGUE OF BARTLESVILLE
BARTLESVILLE, OKLAHOMA

Founded in 1958, Service League of Bartlesville is a nonprofit, tax-exempt organization. Using the voluntary services of its members, the League developed and maintains a Youth Canteen, provides college scholarships for graduating high school seniors and upperclassmen, and contributes money, time, and resources to a variety of community endeavors.

Photography: Jerry Poppenhouse   Design: Joe Willams

Cover photo: The Tallgrass Prairie, located west of Bartlesville in Osage County, spans 36,000 acres and is owned and operated by the Nature Conservancy. Formerly the Barnard Ranch, the land is being carefully conserved to retain the fragile ecosystem originally shaped by the forces of climate, fire and grazing. The prairie supports a wide range of plant, bird and animal species. In 1993 a herd of 300 bison was introduced and eventually 2000 of these magnificent animals will roam freely throughout the preserve.

Printed in the USA by

WIMMER
The Wimmer Companies, Inc.
Memphis

2

CONTENTS

 *Denotes lighter fare*   *Denotes recipes with particular flair*

Indian recipes designated with tribal seals.

Ranch recipes designated with ranch brands.

PREFACE

Two distinct territories created Oklahoma, a state rich in resources, lore and people. In 1866, Indian Territory formed what is now the eastern third of the state. It was home to the Plains Indians and other tribes relocated by the government.

The remainder of the state—the unassigned lands—became Oklahoma Territory after the great land run of 1889. In 1907 Indian Territory and Oklahoma Territory joined, making Oklahoma the 46th star in the blue firmament of the U.S. flag.

The colorful town of Bartlesville, 50 miles north of Tulsa, is located just across the border of old Indian Territory. As a result it has a rich heritage derived from many influences. The land itself gives generously, providing a good life for its people. There is fertile loam for farming and ranching, plentiful water from rivers, and underneath it all, the oil which has played a pivotal role in Bartlesville's development.

Indians, cowboys and outlaws, immigrants from around the globe, entrepreneurs and oil pioneers—all left their indelible brand on this small corner of Oklahoma, creating Bartlesville, a community with a unique blend of cultures.

APPETIZERS

WOOLAROC—a 3600-acre wildlife
refuge and world-renowned Western art
museum, once the ranch of Frank Phillips,
founder of Phillips Petroleum Company.

A LAND SO RICH

It is easy to envision the Indian Territory of the 1800s—rolling hills framing expanses of grass tall enough to hide buffalo, streams clear enough to reflect summer thunderheads ready to burst.

And there were the native plains tribes of Commanche, Kiowa, Cheyenne, Arapaho, Pawnee and Osage. They shared the land with the monolithic monster which meant their survival. Buffalo provided fresh meat in summer and dried meat in winter. Its skin gave them robes, leggings and tunics. Tallow for candles was made from buffalo grease, and bones became the tools necessary to sustain life.

The Plains Indians were later joined by the Choctaw, Chickasaw, Cherokee, Creek and Seminole, the eastern "Civilized Tribes" which were forced from their home lands by white settlers. Beginning in the 1830s these tribes were marched across the continent to Indian Territory, a trek that became known as "The Trail of Tears." In 1867 the first Delaware Indians arrived from Kansas, also victims of more than three centuries of forced migration.

The native and displaced tribes lived together in the crowded territory, sometimes amicably, sometimes less so. But the fertile land was rich enough to sustain them all—so rich, in fact, that they were unable, once again, to keep their land for themselves.

Curry With The Fringe On Top

Yield: 3 cups

1 cup Monterey Jack cheese, shredded
1 cup Swiss cheese, shredded
1 cup Cheddar cheese, shredded
2 tablespoons minced green onion
12 stuffed green olives, minced
½ cup mayonnaise
1 teaspoon curry powder

✦ **Mix** together all ingredients and chill several hours before serving.
✦ **Serve** on cocktail rye bread topped with a slice of stuffed olive.

Also good in pita bread. Cut the round in half and fill each half with the spread. Carefully cut each half into 3 or 4 wedges.

Wildfire Chile-Cheese Dip

Yield: 10 to 12 servings

1 cup mayonnaise
1 (3 ounce) package grated Parmesan cheese
12 ounces Monterey Jack cheese, shredded
2 (4½ ounce) cans chopped green chilies, drained
2 (11 ounce) cans Mexicorn, drained
1 (4 ounce) jar chopped pimiento, drained

✦ **Mix** all ingredients together and put into a greased 2 quart casserole dish.
✦ **Bake** at 350° for 30 to 40 minutes or until hot and bubbly.
✦ **Serve** with large corn chips.

Oklahoma Olé •

Yield: 24 servings

2 large avocados, mashed
⅓ teaspoon garlic powder
⅛ teaspoon garlic salt
1 tablespoon lemon juice
2 tablespoons mayonnaise
1 cup sour cream, room temperature
2 (8 ounce) jars medium hot picante sauce, well drained
1 large onion, chopped
¾ cup chopped ripe olives
3 medium tomatoes, chopped
1½ cups Cheddar cheese, shredded

✦ **Mash** the avocados with the garlic powder, garlic salt, lemon juice and mayonnaise and spread in an 8x11 inch serving dish.
✦ **Spread** sour cream over avocado mixture.
✦ **Layer** picante sauce, onion, ripe olives, tomatoes and cheese on top of sour cream.
✦ **Refrigerate** until ready to serve.
✦ **Serve** with crackers.

GREEN COUNTRY CHILI CHEESECAKE

Yield: 20 servings

1 cup tortilla chips, finely crushed
3 tablespoons butter or margarine, melted
2 (8 ounce) packages cream cheese
2 eggs
8 ounces colby or Monterey Jack cheese, shredded
1 (4½ ounce) can chopped green chilies
Dash Tabasco
1 cup sour cream
GARNISH
Red or yellow peppers, sliced
Scallions, chopped
Olives
Salsa

♦ **Combine** crushed chips and butter and press in the bottom and sides of a 9 inch springform pan. Bake for 15 minutes in a 325° oven.
♦ **Beat** cream cheese and eggs well; mix in shredded cheese, chilies and pepper sauce. Pour in pan over tortilla crust and bake 30 minutes.
♦ **Spread** sour cream over the top while the cheesecake is still warm. Cool completely before removing from pan.
♦ **Chill** and garnish.
♦ **Serve** with tortilla chips.

POCO PEPPER SNACKS

Yield: 10 to 12 servings

2 (3 ounce) packages cream cheese
1 cup grated Cheddar cheese
4 tablespoons chopped green chilies
4 tablespoons chopped ripe olives
4 teaspoons minced onions
10 drops Tabasco sauce
1 can refrigerator crescent rolls (8 crescents)

♦ **Roll** out can of crescent rolls, pinch seams to make one piece of dough.
♦ **Mix** together cream cheese, Cheddar cheese, chilies, olives, onions and hot pepper sauce and spread mixture on the dough.
♦ **Roll** up dough like a jelly roll beginning with the long side.
♦ **Slice** and place on a greased cookie sheet.
♦ **Bake** at 400° for 10 minutes.

MEXICAN HOT DIP

Yield: 10 to 12 servings

1 bunch green onions, chopped
1 green pepper, chopped
1 medium tomato, chopped
¾ - 1 cup mild or medium picante sauce
8 ounces colby or Monterey Jack cheese, grated

♦ **Add** chopped onions, green pepper and tomato to picante sauce in a 9x9 inch square pan or a 9 or 10 inch pie plate.
♦ **Mix** half of the grated cheese with the picante mixture in the dish.
♦ **Top** with remaining cheese, cover with wax paper and microwave on high for 3 to 4 minutes.
♦ **Serve** with tortilla chips.

GOOD TIMES CHEESE ROLL

Yield: 12 to 14 servings

2 pounds Velveeta cheese, at room temperature
8 ounces cream cheese, at room temperature
1 (4½ ounce) can chopped green chilies, drained
1 (4¼ ounce) can chopped ripe olives, drained
3 green onions, chopped
1 (4 ounce) jar chopped pimientos, drained
¾ - 1 cup chopped pecans
Paprika
Cayenne pepper

♦ **Flatten** Velveeta with hands between sheets of wax or parchment paper or plastic wrap.
♦ **Roll** with a rolling pin until Velveeta is in a rectangle approximately 16x18 inches and fairly thin. (Leave paper in between cheese and surface at all times.)
♦ **Spread** softened cream cheese on flattened Velveeta.
♦ **Top** cream cheese evenly with chilies, olives, onions, pimientos and pecans.
♦ **Peel** off paper as you roll cheese "jelly roll" style.
♦ **Sprinkle** top of roll with paprika and cayenne pepper.
♦ **Serve** with crackers.

This recipe freezes well.

SHERRIED CHEESE BALL

Yield: 4 inch ball

1 (3 ounce) package cream cheese, softened
2 cups (8 ounces) Cheddar cheese, shredded
3 tablespoons mayonnaise-type salad dressing
2 tablespoons dry sherry
½ teaspoon Worcestershire sauce
¼ teaspoon garlic powder
¼ cup ripe olives, drained and chopped
3 tablespoons dried beef, minced
3 tablespoons fresh parsley, chopped

◆ **Blend** together all ingredients except olives, dried beef and parsley in a medium mixing bowl.
◆ **Stir** in olives.
◆ **Cover** and refrigerate for 2 hours or until firm.
◆ **Combine** dried beef and parsley in a small bowl and set aside.
◆ **Shape** cheese mixture into a 4 inch ball.
◆ **Roll** ball in the beef and parsley mix.
◆ **Cover** and refrigerate for at least 30 minutes before serving.

BLUE CHEESE BALL

Yield: 1 large or 2 small balls

4 (3 ounce) packages cream cheese
6 ounces blue cheese
2 (5 ounce) jars sharp pasteurized process cheese spread
2 tablespoons chopped onion
1 teaspoon Worcestershire sauce
½ teaspoon seasoned salt flavor enhancer
1 cup chopped pecans
½ cup chopped fresh parsley

◆ **Bring** all cheese to room temperature.
◆ **Add** the onion, Worcestershire sauce, seasoned salt and half of the pecans to the three cheeses.
◆ **Roll** into one large ball or two smaller ones.
◆ **Roll** in the remaining pecans and parsley after ball has hardened.
◆ **Serve** with crackers or corn chips.

BREAD POT FONDUE

Yield: 12 to 14 servings

1 (8-10 inch) round firm loaf of bread
2 cups sharp Cheddar cheese, shredded
2 (3 ounce) packages cream cheese, softened
1½ cups dairy sour cream
1 cup cooked ham or dried beef, diced
½ cup chopped green onions
1 (4½ ounce) can chopped green chilies, drained
1 teaspoon Worcestershire sauce
2 tablespoons vegetable oil
1 tablespoon butter, melted

♦ **Slice** off top of bread, reserve. Hollow out inside leaving ½ inch shell. Cut removed bread into 1 inch cubes. Reserve for toasting.
♦ **Combine** Cheddar, cream cheese and sour cream in a bowl. Stir in meat, green onion, chilies and Worcestershire sauce. Spoon into bread shell. Replace top of bread.
♦ **Wrap** the loaf tightly in several layers of heavy duty foil. Place on a cookie sheet.
♦ **Bake** at 350° for 1 hour and 10 minutes or until cheese is melted and heated throughout.
♦ **Stir** together oil and butter and toss bread cubes. Place on a cookie sheet and bake at 350° for 10 minutes or until golden brown.
♦ **Serve** fondue with toasted bread cubes, assorted fresh vegetables or chips and crackers.

Rye, pumpernickel or sourdough bread may be used.

 ## Marbled Tea Eggs

Yield: 24 servings

12 eggs
2 tablespoons salt
3 tablespoons soy sauce
2 whole star anise
4 teaspoons loose tea
　Soy sauce
　Minced fresh chives

♦ **Place** eggs in cold water, bring to a boil, reduce heat to low and simmer gently for 10 minutes.

♦ **Pour** out hot water and cover eggs with cold water.

♦ **Pick** up each egg and tap gently with the back of a spoon to cause tiny cracks. Return eggs to water.

♦ **Add** salt, 3 tablespoons soy sauce, star anise and tea to water covering eggs. Stir to mix.

♦ **Bring** eggs to a boil again then turn the heat very low. Cover and simmer for 2 hours.

♦ **Check** often to make sure water stays above eggs. Add more water if necessary.

♦ **Drain** eggs and refrigerate for 8 hours.

♦ **Peel**, slice in half, and serve yolk side down with a bowl of soy sauce sprinkled with chives for dipping.

Delicious with poultry or as a garnish for any salad.

SHRIMP MOLD

Yield: 16 to 20 servings

1 (10½ ounce) can tomato
soup
1 (8 ounce) package cream
cheese
2 envelopes gelatin
¼ cup cold water
1 cup mayonnaise
2 cups cooked fresh shrimp
(or canned)
¾ cup chopped green onion
½ cup finely chopped celery
1½ teaspoons Worcestershire
sauce
1½ teaspoons lemon juice
½ teaspoon Tabasco
½ teaspoon garlic salt
Pepper to taste

♦ **Dissolve** gelatin in cold water.
♦ **Heat** soup to boiling and blend
into gelatin.
♦ **Add** cream cheese and mix
until smooth. Cool.
♦ **Add** remaining ingredients.
♦ **Pour** into 2 medium sized
greased molds. Chill until set.

MINNIE'S SHRIMP DIP

Yield: 3 to 4 cups

1½ pounds shrimp, boiled and
chopped
1 small clove garlic, minced
1 small onion or 4 - 5 green
onions, chopped fine
1 bell pepper, diced
1 stalk celery, diced
1 cup Miracle Whip (do not
substitute)
1 (8 ounce) package cream
cheese
1 teaspoon sugar
Dash of Tabasco
Juice of 1 small lemon
Salt and pepper to taste

♦ **Mix** all chopped ingredients
together in one bowl.
♦ **Cream** together cream cheese
and Miracle Whip in a
medium bowl.
♦ **Add** chopped ingredients to
cream cheese mixture. Stir well
and chill.
♦ **Serve** with white tortilla chips.

HOT DILLED SHRIMP

Yield: 8 servings

2 pounds medium raw shrimp, peeled and deveined
¼ pound (1 stick) salted butter
1 tablespoon Worcestershire sauce
2 cloves garlic, minced
1 teaspoon dill seed
1 teaspoon dry dill weed
Juice of ½ lemon
1½ tablespoons capers (optional)

♦ **Rinse** and dry shrimp on paper towel. Refrigerate until serving time.
♦ **Melt** butter in a chafing dish. Mix in Worcestershire sauce, garlic, dill seed and dill weed.
♦ **Add** shrimp and sizzle until pink and curled.
♦ **Turn** heat to lowest setting and serve.

MARISCOS A LA MARINERA

Yield: 12 servings

3 dozen shrimp, cooked and cut in halves or thirds
½ cup fresh lime juice
2 medium tomatoes, diced
1 bunch green onions, chopped
1 large avocado, diced or cubed
3 - 4 serrano or jalapeño peppers, seeded and chopped
2 heaping tablespoons chopped cilantro
3 tablespoons olive oil
Salt and pepper to taste

♦ **Mix** all ingredients together and chill.
♦ **Serve** with tortilla chips.

Best if served within 2 to 3 hours.

Leave shrimp whole to serve as a salad on a bed of lettuce leaves.

IMPERIAL CRAB

Yield: 2½ cups

1 (8 ounce) package cream cheese (room temperature)
½ cup mayonnaise
¼ cup finely chopped onion
1 - 3 teaspoons horseradish
1 teaspoon dry vermouth or 1 tablespoon lemon juice
1 (6½ ounce) can crab meat, drained
1 (2¼ ounce) package slivered almonds

♦ **Mix** together all ingredients (except almonds) and pour into a greased baking/serving dish.
♦ **Top** with slivered almonds.
♦ **Bake** at 275° for 25 to 30 minutes.
♦ **Serve** at once with crackers.

Keep the dip warm on an electric warming tray.

To prepare as a spread use ¼ cup mayonnaise and 4 ounces cream cheese. You can vary this recipe by adding green peppers, green onions or a pinch of fine herbs.

MINI CRAB CAKES WITH SALSA MAYONNAISE

Yield: 36 mini crab cakes

CRAB CAKES
3 tablespoons butter
½ large celery stalk, finely chopped
3 large eggs, beaten
1 pound fresh lump crabmeat
½ cup diced roasted red bell pepper
1 cup shredded Monterey Jack cheese with jalapeños
Vegetable oil
1 small onion, finely chopped
1 jalapeño, seeded and minced
¼ cup sour cream
1½ cups Italian bread crumbs
½ cup chopped fresh cilantro

SALSA MAYONNAISE
1 cup mayonnaise
½ cup sour cream
½ cup picante sauce

♦ **Blend** salsa mayonnaise ingredients and chill.
♦ **Melt** butter and sauté onions, celery and jalapeño for 5 minutes in a large skillet over medium heat. Transfer to a bowl and let cool.
♦ **Add** eggs and sour cream and mix. Add remaining ingredients. Cover and chill for 1 hour.
♦ **Form** 1 heaping tablespoon of the mixture into 1½ inch cakes.
♦ **Heat** oil over medium heat and fry the cakes in batches for approximately 4 minutes each side or until golden.
♦ **Top** each cake with a dollop of Salsa Mayonnaise before serving.

13

WILD, WEIRD AND WONDERFUL

Yield: 8 to 10 servings

2 tablespoons butter
2 tablespoons toasted sesame seeds
2 tablespoons chunky peanut butter
2 tablespoons soy sauce
2 tablespoons sour cream
1½ cups finely minced scallions or onions
1 clove garlic, crushed
1 teaspoon grated fresh ginger (or powdered)
1 (7 ounce) can fancy white Albacore tuna in spring water, drained

♦ **Brown** butter in a skillet, add sesame seeds; stir until browned.
♦ **Mix** together all ingredients except tuna.
♦ **Flake** tuna and fold into the mixture. Refrigerate covered.
♦ **Serve** on light rye party bread or Triscuits.

ORIENTAL ANGEL WINGS

Yield: 30 wings or 10 servings

3 pounds chicken wings
½ cup sugar
½ cup water
½ cup soy sauce
¼ cup pineapple juice
2 tablespoons vegetable oil
1 teaspoon grated fresh ginger
½ teaspoon garlic powder

♦ **Remove** chicken wing tips and discard. Place remaining wings in a 9x13 inch Pyrex pan.
♦ **Stir** together the rest of the ingredients until sugar is dissolved. Pour over wings. Marinate for 8 hours in the refrigerator, turning occasionally.
♦ **Drain** marinade into a saucepan and bring to a boil.
♦ **Bake** wings at 350° for 30 to 40 minutes, basting frequently with marinade. Serve warm.

CRISPY CHICKEN WITH CREAMY HONEY SAUCE

Yield: 4 servings

SAUCE
1 cup mayonnaise
½ cup honey
2 tablespoons Dijon mustard
1 teaspoon sesame oil
½ teaspoon ground ginger

CHICKEN
4 chicken breasts, boned, skinned and cut into strips or nuggets
2 cups finely crushed potato chips
2 tablespoons sesame seeds

♦ **Mix** sauce and brush ½ cup on chicken strips or nuggets. Place the rest of the sauce in the refrigerator for about 1 hour before serving.

♦ **Coat** chicken with potato chips and seeds. Place on a greased cookie sheet.

♦ **Bake** for 7 to 9 minutes in a 425° oven; turn over. Bake for 4 to 5 minutes longer until light brown.

♦ **Serve** with the remainder of the sauce.

SESAME CHICKEN

Yield: 24 appetizers

1 pound chicken breasts, skinned and boned
1 teaspoon salt
2 tablespoons light soy sauce
2 tablespoons maple syrup
2 tablespoons dry sherry
½ teaspoon shredded fresh ginger root
½ teaspoon Chinese five-spice
2 tablespoons vegetable oil
2 tablespoons sesame seeds
Parsley
Chutney or plum sauce, if desired

♦ **Cut** each breast in half lengthwise.

♦ **Stir** together salt, soy sauce, maple syrup, sherry, ginger root, five-spice and oil in a shallow baking dish. Add chicken and turn to coat evenly. Cover and refrigerate at least 2 hours or up to 8 hours, turning occasionally.

♦ **Sprinkle** chicken with sesame seeds.

♦ **Bake** uncovered 15 minutes in a 400° oven or until chicken is done. Brush occasionally with marinade during baking.

♦ **Cut** chicken in chunks and serve warm or cold, garnished with parsley. Accompany with chutney or plum sauce if desired.

PRAIRIE PÂTÉ •

Yield: 14 to 16 servings

8 ounces Braunschweiger
1 (10½ ounce) can beef
  consomme
1 (8 ounce) package cream
  cheese
1 envelope gelatin
1 tablespoon Worcestershire
  sauce
½ teaspoon onion powder
½ teaspoon celery salt
½ teaspoon garlic powder

♦ **Dissolve** gelatin in a small
  amount of cold soup. Heat
  remaining soup and add
  gelatin mixture.
♦ **Pour** a small amount in the
  bottom of a mold and let
  congeal.
♦ **Blend** sausage, cheese and
  other ingredients. Slowly add
  soup and pour over congealed
  gelatin.

May be frozen.

KIELBASA KICKER

Yield: 6 to 7 dozen

1 (12 ounce) jar apricot
  preserves
2 tablespoons lemon juice
2 teaspoons Dijon mustard
½ teaspoon ground ginger
1½ pounds Kielbasa, cut into ¼
  inch pieces

♦ **Combine** preserves, lemon
  juice, mustard and ginger in a
  1½ quart saucepan.
♦ **Cook** mixture over low heat
  for 2 to 3 minutes, stirring
  constantly.
♦ **Add** Kielbasa and cook until
  sausage is heated.
♦ **Serve** warm.

*Serve in a chafing dish with
toothpicks. Could double the sausage
in the same amount of liquid if
necessary for a large crowd.*

DOWN HOME MEATBALLS

Yield: 5 to 6 dozen

MEATBALLS

1 pound ground chuck
½ pound ground pork
¾ cup fine bread crumbs
2 tablespoons grated onion
1 tablespoon ketchup
4 drops Tabasco
2 tablespoons Parmesan cheese
1 teaspoon horseradish
2 eggs, beaten
½ teaspoon salt
¼ teaspoon pepper
2 tablespoons butter, melted

SAUCE

½ cup ketchup
½ cup chili sauce
¼ cup cider vinegar
½ cup firmly packed brown sugar
2 tablespoons chopped onion
1 tablespoon Worcestershire sauce
4 drops Tabasco
½ teaspoons dry mustard
3 drops aromatic bitters (optional)
1 teaspoon salt
¼ teaspoon pepper
Chopped green onions

♦ **Mix** together all meatball ingredients and shape into 1 inch balls.

♦ **Cook** meatballs in a skillet over medium to medium high heat until browned on all sides. Drain well and set aside.

♦ **Combine** all sauce ingredients in a large saucepan. Stir well. Bring to a boil then reduce heat and simmer 10 to 15 minutes.

♦ **Combine** meatballs and sauce in a chafing dish and serve warm.

♦ **Garnish** with chopped onions.

ARTICHOKE ADVENTURE •

Yield: 20 servings

1 (4 ounce) jar diced pimientos, drained
1 (14 ounce) can artichoke hearts, drained and chopped
1½ cups mayonnaise
2 (4½ ounce) cans diced green chilies, drained
4 ounces shredded Monterey Jack cheese
¾ cup grated Parmesan cheese
Tortilla or corn chips

♦ **Reserve** 2 teaspoons pimientos for garnish.
♦ **Mix** pimientos, artichokes, mayonnaise, chiles, Monterey Jack cheese and ½ cup Parmesan cheese in a medium bowl.
♦ **Spread** mixture in a shallow 1½ quart baking dish. Sprinkle with additional Parmesan cheese and the reserved pimientos.
♦ **Bake** uncovered at 325° for 30 minutes or until bubbly.
♦ **Serve** with tortilla or corn chips.

May add 2 (6 ounce) packages frozen crabmeat.

SPINACH ARTICHOKE DIP •

Yield: 10 to 12 servings

1 (10 ounce) package frozen chopped spinach, thawed and squeezed dry
1 (14 ounce) can water packed artichokes, coarsely chopped and well drained
1 cup mayonnaise
2 green onions, chopped
1 package (3 ounces) shredded Parmesan cheese
½ cup grated Monterey Jack cheese
1 teaspoon Worcestershire sauce
4 drops Tabasco
½ teaspoon garlic powder
Juice of ½ lemon

♦ **Mix** together all ingredients except Monterey Jack cheese and put in an 8 or 9 inch pie pan.
♦ **Top** with Monterey Jack cheese.
♦ **Bake** at 350° for 15 minutes, then bake at 400° for 2 to 3 minutes.
♦ **Serve** hot with tortilla chips and salsa.

CRUNCHY CORN DIP •

Yield: 10 to 12 servings

2 (8 ounce) packages cream
    cheese, at room temperature
2 packages ranch dressing
    mix
2 (2¼ ounce) cans chopped
    ripe olives
1 (4½ ounce) can chopped
    green chilies
1 (11 ounce) can corn, drained
1 red bell pepper, chopped

♦ **Mix** all ingredients together
and chill one to two hours.
♦ **Serve** with tortilla or corn
chips.

May substitute Green Giant
Mexicorn and a green bell pepper
for the corn and red bell pepper.

SPINACH DIPPIN' SAUCE

Yield: 10 servings

2 - 3 jalapeño peppers, chopped,
        reserving some seeds
1 medium onion, chopped
2 tablespoons vegetable oil
1 (4½ ounce) can chopped
    green chilies
2 tomatoes, chopped
1 (10 ounce) package frozen
    chopped spinach, thawed
    and squeezed dry
1½ tablespoons red wine
    vinegar
1 (8 ounce) package cream
    cheese, softened
2½ cups grated Monterey Jack
    cheese
1 cup half-and-half
    Salt and pepper to taste
    Paprika

♦ **Sauté** peppers (with seeds)
and onion in oil until soft
(about 4 minutes).
♦ **Add** green chilies and
tomatoes. Cook, stirring
constantly for 2 minutes.
Remove from heat and transfer
to a mixing bowl.
♦ **Stir** in spinach, vinegar, cream
cheese, Monterey Jack cheese,
half-and-half, salt and pepper.
♦ **Pour** into a buttered 10 inch
round baking dish. Sprinkle
with paprika.
♦ **Bake** at 400° for 20 to 25
minutes or until hot and
bubbly.
♦ **Serve** with tortilla or corn
chips.

SPANAKOPITTA (GREEK SPINACH PIE)

Yield: 50 appetizers

3 (10 ounce) packages
chopped spinach
3 bunches green onions,
chopped
1 (24 ounce) large curd
cottage cheese
1 (16 ounce) box phyllo
dough leaves
1 small crumbled package
feta cheese
5 eggs, beaten
Salt to taste
½ pound margarine, melted
½ pound butter, melted

♦ **Thaw** phyllo dough at room temperature overnight or in the refrigerator for 1 day. Keep covered with a damp dish towel until ready to use.

♦ **Thaw** spinach and squeeze out excess water.

♦ **Sauté** onion in a small amount of margarine in a large skillet. Add spinach and mix until warmed through. Pour into a large bowl.

♦ **Add** cottage cheese, feta cheese, eggs and salt. Mix well.

♦ **Open** phyllo package, unfold to a single layer, and cover with a damp dish towel.

♦ **Melt** butter and margarine together in a saucepan.

♦ **Brush** sides and bottom of an 11x16 inch metal pan with butter using a large pastry brush.

♦ **Lay** one sheet of phyllo evenly in the bottom of the pan and brush sides and bottom with butter (do not let the butter pool). Repeat layering with butter until ½ of dough has been used.

♦ **Put** down Phyllo as follows: Place edge of phyllo in the center of the pan. Brush the half with butter then fold overhanging half back on itself and brush it with butter. Repeat with subsequent layers. This allows phyllo to be thicker in the middle and not so thick on the edges.

♦ **Pour** spinach filling on dough and spread.

Continued on next page

♦ **Layer** remaining ½ of dough and butter on top of the spinach filling. The last 3 - 4 sheets should be put on as one sheet. Butter the top.

♦ **Bend** edges toward the center with a knife to make a nice edge. Butter if necessary to prevent the phyllo from drying out.

♦ **Cut** the dough in diagonals both directions to make diamond shapes (use a very sharp knife).

♦ **Bake** uncovered at 350° until golden brown. At 50 to 60 minutes check the bottom by lifting a corner with a spatula. When the bottom is golden brown remove from the oven and serve.

If a 9x13 inch pan is used, cut phyllo to fit pan. Use about 1 cup less of the filling.

Best served hot. May be frozen after baking.

CHÈVRE STUFFED MUSHROOMS

Yield: 8 servings

8 large mushrooms, stems removed
Green grapes
6 - 8 ounces chèvre (goat cheese)
Fresh Parmesan cheese, grated
Melted butter

♦ **Stuff** as many large mushrooms as you wish to serve with chèvre (about ½ full).

♦ **Push** a green grape into the cheese. Sprinkle with Parmesan cheese. Drizzle with butter.

♦ **Bake** at 350° for 10 to 15 minutes.

Green olives may be used instead of grapes.

STUFFED MUSHROOM CAPS

Yield: 20 mushrooms

20 large mushroom caps
6 - 8 tablespoons melted butter
3 tablespoons minced green
   onions
1 tablespoon flour
¾ cup heavy cream
3 tablespoons chopped
   parsley
¼ cup grated white cheese
Salt and pepper to taste

♦ **Clean** mushroom caps and stems. Remove stems and save.
♦ **Brush** caps with melted butter and arrange hollow side up in baking dish. Season with salt and pepper.
♦ **Mince** mushrooms stems and sauté with chives in 4 to 5 tablespoons butter for 4 to 5 minutes. Lower heat and stir in flour for 1 minute. Add cream and simmer until thickened. Stir in parsley and seasonings.
♦ **Fill** mushroom caps with mixture. Top each with 1 teaspoon cheese. Drizzle with melted butter.
♦ **Bake** at 375° for 15 minutes on the middle rack of the oven.

VIDALIA ONION APPETIZER

Yield: 24 servings

MARINADE
5 - 6 thinly sliced Vidalia or mild
   sweet onions
2 cups water
½ cup white vinegar
1 cup sugar
DRESSING
½ cup mayonnaise
1 teaspoon celery salt

♦ **Marinate** onions for 4 hours. Drain.
♦ **Mix** together mayonnaise and celery salt and pour dressing over sliced onions.
♦ **Refrigerate** until serving time.
♦ **Serve** with crackers.

This recipe makes a nice side dish, especially with beef.

HOT BLACK-EYED PEA DIP

Yield: 8 servings

1 (15 ounce) can jalapeño
   black-eyed peas, drained
¼ cup chopped onion
¼ cup sour cream
3 tablespoons picante sauce
1 cup grated Cheddar cheese
Salt, pepper and Tabasco to
   taste

♦ **Mash** drained peas with a fork, leaving some whole. (Do not use a blender.)
♦ **Add** remaining ingredients and mix well.
♦ **Spread** mixture in a 1 or 1½ quart baking dish.
♦ **Bake** uncovered at 350° for 20 to 30 minutes or until bubbly.
♦ **Serve** hot with corn chips or tortilla chips.

BOWL GAME DIP

Yield: 10 to 12 servings

2 (15 ounce) cans black-eyed
   peas, drained
1 (15½ ounce) can white
   hominy, drained
2 medium tomatoes, chopped
1 bunch green onions,
   chopped
2 cloves garlic, minced
1 medium bell pepper
   chopped
1 - 2 jalapeño peppers, seeded
   and chopped
1 cup chopped fresh cilantro
1 (8 ounce) bottle lite Italian
   salad dressing

♦ **Mix** all ingredients together.
♦ **Chill** at least two hours before serving.
♦ **Serve** with large corn chips.

HUMUS •

Yield: 1 pint

7 ounces dried chick peas, soaked overnight
2 pints water
7 ounces tahini paste
2 cloves garlic, peeled, crushed
1 teaspoon sea salt
Juice of 1 large lemon
1 tablespoon fresh parsley
Pita bread, warmed

♦ **Simmer** chick peas 3 to 3½ hours or until soft. Drain, reserving liquid. Process in food processor, adding some reserved liquid if necessary to give a smooth even texture.
♦ **Mix** tahini, garlic and salt in a separate bowl. Add to chick peas. Process, adding lemon juice gradually.
♦ **Add** reserved cooking liquid sparingly to produce a mayonnaise consistency. Stir in parsley. Add more salt and lemon juice to taste.
♦ **Serve** with pita triangles.

Makes a great sandwich by spreading on thick bread with alfalfa sprouts, cucumbers, tomatoes and cheese.

TASTY TOMATO DIP •

Yield: 5 to 6 cups

1 (10¾ ounce) can cream of tomato soup
1 (3 ounce) package lemon jello
3 (8 ounce) packages cream cheese
½ cup water
1 cup chopped green peppers
½ cup chopped pecans
1 medium onion, chopped
1 cup mayonnaise-type salad dressing

♦ **Combine** soup, jello, cream cheese, and water in a pan.
♦ **Heat** until all ingredients are melted.
♦ **Blend** the mixture until smooth.
♦ **Cool** until lukewarm.
♦ **Add** peppers, pecans, onions and salad dressing and stir well.
♦ **Chill** until ready to serve.
♦ **Serve** with crackers or vegetables.

Harvest Garden Delight •

Yield: 4 cups

1 large cucumber, chopped
1 medium onion, chopped
½ cup chopped green olives
¼ cup (2 large) jalapeño
  peppers, chopped and
  seeded
1 large tomato, chopped

Dressing

¼ cup vinegar
1 teaspoon sugar
¼ teaspoon salt
1 teaspoon oil

♦ **Stir** together all chopped vegetables.
♦ **Mix** together dressing ingredients, pour over vegetables and toss.
♦ **Serve** with corn chips or crackers.

Caviar Mousse

Yield: 12 servings

4 ounces red caviar
3 tablespoons minced fresh
  parsley
2 tablespoons finely minced
  white onion
1 cup sour cream
¼ teaspoon pepper
1½ teaspoons unflavored
  gelatin
2 tablespoons water
½ cup whipping cream,
  whipped
Cucumber slices
Rye melba rounds

♦ **Combine** caviar, parsley, onion, sour cream and pepper in a non-metallic bowl and blend well.
♦ **Sprinkle** gelatin over water in a small pan. Stir over low heat until dissolved. Cool slightly.
♦ **Fold** gelatin and whipped cream gently into caviar mixture. Turn into a 2 cup non-metallic serving bowl and refrigerate until set.
♦ **Serve** with cucumber slices and melba rounds.

Always use non-metallic utensils and serving pieces when serving caviar. Stir gently so you don't mash caviar.

ANTIPASTO TRAY *

Yield: 12 to 14 servings

Hard salami, rolled
Provolone cheese, rolled
Red radishes
Celery sticks
Rutabaga sticks
Carrot sticks
Red bell pepper strips
Green bell pepper strips
Black olives
Cracked green olives
Calamata olives
Quarters of hard boiled
eggs
Pepperoncini salad peppers
Roasted red peppers
Fennel
Cheese tortellini, cooked,
chilled and lightly tossed in
olive oil and basil
Capers, large and salty (for
garnish)

♦ **Arrange** on a very large round tray a choice of any of the ingredients. Lay them in a pattern that radiates from the center like spokes of a wheel.
♦ **Sprinkle** the entire tray with drained capers.
♦ **Place** a whole artichoke or whole roasted heads of garlic in the center of the tray.
♦ **Serve** with a big basket of sliced Italian crusty bread and bagna couda.

BAGNA COUDA

Yield: 1 cup

½ cup unsalted butter
¼ cup olive oil
2 cloves garlic, finely minced
6 anchovies, drained and
  finely chopped or 2
  tablespoons anchovy paste

♦ **Heat** butter, oil and garlic over a low flame in a heavy pan. Stir well until blended.
♦ **Stir** in anchovies and heat gently on a low flame for 15 minutes. Do not overheat or it will separate.
♦ **Pour** into a chafing dish and keep warm over a candle or alcohol burner.
♦ **Serve** with sticks of celery, carrots, fennel, rutabaga, radishes and crusty Italian bread to catch the drips.

Serve with Antipasto Tray.

APPETIZER TWISTER

Yield: 8 to 10 servings

12 slices bacon, cooked and crumbled
1 cup mayonnaise
1 teaspoon paprika
2 teaspoons Worcestershire sauce
2 green onions, chopped
8 ounces sharp Cheddar cheese, shredded
1 (2½ ounce) package sliced almonds
Pepperidge Farm thin sliced white bread

♦ **Trim** crust off the bread and cut into triangles or rounds.
♦ **Mix** together all the rest of the ingredients in a medium bowl.
♦ **Spread** the mixture on the bread and place on a cookie sheet.
♦ **Bake** at 400° for 7 to 9 minutes.
♦ **Serve** hot.

Watch carefully while toasting.

HOT JARLSBERG SPREAD

Yield: 10 to 12 servings

2 cups thinly sliced onions
¼ cup butter or margarine
8 ounces Jarlsberg cheese, grated
1¾ cups mayonnaise
Paprika

♦ **Sauté** onion in butter for 5 minutes.
♦ **Combine** onions with cheese and mayonnaise.
♦ **Pour** mixture into a greased 9 or 10 inch pie plate and sprinkle with paprika.
♦ **Bake** at 350° for 25 to 30 minutes until bubbly and golden.
♦ **Serve** with sturdy crackers.

SOMBRERO SPREAD •

Yield: 12 to 14 servings

½ pound ground beef
½ cup chopped onion (reserve half for garnish)
¼ cup chili sauce
1½ teaspoons chili powder
½ teaspoon salt
1 (8 ounce) can red kidney beans with liquid
½ cup shredded sharp American cheese
¼ cup chopped stuffed green olives

♦ **Brown** meat and ¼ cup onion in skillet or chafing dish.
♦ **Stir** in chili sauce, chili powder and salt.
♦ **Mash** the beans. Add to chili mixture and heat through.
♦ **Garnish** with the cheese, olives and ¼ cup onion.
♦ **Serve** with corn chips or sturdy tortilla chips.

MANGO CHUTNEY SPREAD

Yield: 12 to 14 servings

1 (8 ounce) package cream cheese, softened
1 (3 ounce) package cream cheese, softened
2 tablespoons cream
1 cup golden raisins
½ cup chopped green onions
12 ounces lean bacon, cooked and crumbled
2 - 3 teaspoons curry powder
1¼ cups Major Grey's mango chutney
1½ cups cashews or peanuts, coarsely chopped

♦ **Blend** cream cheese with cream, half of the bacon, ¼ cup onion, curry powder, ¾ cup nuts, raisins and chutney. (Do not use a food processor.)
♦ **Press** mixture with spatula onto a serving platter to form a 1½ inch thick circle or square.
♦ **Spread** top with the remaining chutney and garnish with the rest of the bacon, onions and nuts.
♦ **Serve** with crackers.

CURRY IN A HURRY DIP •

Yield: 10 to 12 servings

1 pint mayonnaise
1 tablespoon Worcestershire sauce
3 tablespoons chili sauce
1 tablespoon grated onion
2 teaspoons curry powder
½ teaspoon salt
½ teaspoon garlic powder

♦ **Mix** together all ingredients and chill.
♦ **Serve** with assorted vegetables.

ROLE'S SALSA

Yield: 15 to 20 servings

1 (28 ounce) can whole tomatoes, coarsely chopped
½ bunch green onions, coarsely chopped
⅓ bunch fresh cilantro, coarsely chopped (or to taste)
1 teaspoon fresh minced garlic
1 tablespoon vinegar
½ teaspoon cumin
Juice of 1 lime
1 teaspoon salt
1 teaspoon pepper
1 - 2 jalapeños, seeded and coarsely chopped (to taste)

♦ **Mix** together all ingredients.
♦ **Serve** with warm tortilla chips or flour tortillas.

Add a jigger of tequila for fun.

Keeps in the refrigerator for about 10 days.

HOT PEPPER PECANS

Yield: 1 cup

1 cup large pecan halves
2 tablespoons butter or margarine
2 teaspoons soy sauce
½ teaspoon salt
½ teaspoon Tabasco (do not substitute)

♦ **Melt** butter in a shallow pan in a 300° oven. Spread pecan halves in a single layer in the butter.
♦ **Bake** 20 to 30 minutes, stirring several times until nuts begin to brown. Immediately pour nuts into a bowl.
♦ **Mix** together soy sauce, salt and Tabasco in a small bowl. Pour over hot pecans; stir carefully.
♦ **Spread** pecans on a double layer of paper toweling to cool. Store in a container with a tight fitting lid.

These make a great Christmas gift.

PECAN GROVE TIDBITS

Yield: 1 pound

4 tablespoons butter
1 tablespoon chili powder
¼ teaspoon ground cumin
⅛ teaspoon garlic salt
1 pound pecan halves
Salt to taste

♦ **Melt** butter in a large skillet. Add all spices except salt, mix well. Add pecans and stir to coat well.

♦ **Spread** nuts on a cookie sheet and bake for 20 to 30 minutes in a 300° oven, stirring frequently.

♦ **Remove** from oven and sprinkle with salt.

Wonderful with Margaritas!

ORANGE PECANS

Yield: 6 cups

2 cups sugar
½ cup orange juice
Grated rind of 2 oranges
6 cups pecan halves

♦ **Cook** the sugar and orange juice to form a soft ball.

♦ **Remove** from heat and add the orange rind and pecan halves. Stir to coat. Spread and separate on cookie sheet until cool.

♦ **Dry** thoroughly before storing in an airtight container.

PRALINE CRUNCH •

Yield: 8 to 9 cups

1 cup brown sugar, packed
¾ cup margarine
1½ cups pecan halves
2 cups Rice Chex
2 cups Corn Chex
2 cups Wheat Chex

♦ **Boil** brown sugar and margarine for 2 minutes.

♦ **Add** pecans and cereals. Mix and put into a roaster pan.

♦ **Bake** uncovered at 350° for 8 minutes. Cool on wax paper.

HONEY WALNUTS

Yield: 1 pound

4 tablespoons butter
4 tablespoons honey
1 pound walnut halves
   Salt to taste

♦ **Melt** butter and honey in a heavy skillet.
♦ **Add** walnut halves and mix well.
♦ **Cook** over medium heat, stirring often, until walnuts caramelize.
♦ **Pour** immediately onto a sheet of buttered foil and separate with a fork.
♦ **Sprinkle** with salt.

These are delicious in a spinach or green salad.

CRISPY CHESTNUTS

Yield: 8 to 10 servings

1 (9 ounce) can water chestnuts, drained
2 tablespoons regular or low sodium soy sauce
2 tablespoons Worcestershire sauce
4 tablespoons lemon juice
½ teaspoon seasoned salt
1 tablespoon garlic powder
1 pound bacon, thinly sliced or regular

♦ **Cut** chestnuts in half or leave whole if not too large.
♦ **Wrap** with half a strip of bacon and secure with a toothpick.
♦ **Mix** the soy sauce, Worcestershire sauce, lemon juice and spices. Pour over wrapped chestnuts and marinate for 1 to 2 hours.
♦ **Pour** chestnuts and marinade onto a cookie sheet.
♦ **Bake** at 375° until bacon is done, then run under the broiler to crisp bacon.

MARINATED OLIVES

Yield: 1 quart

1 (16 ounce) jar cracked green
 olives with pits, drained
½ cup olive oil
6 cloves garlic, peeled, lightly
 crushed
¼ cup onion, thinly sliced
1 lemon (thin skinned)

♦ **Combine** drained olives, oil
 and garlic in a quart jar with a
 tight fitting lid.
♦ **Peel** lemon in one long thin
 continuous strip, careful not to
 get any of the pulp.
♦ **Add** lemon peel to olives.
♦ **Refrigerate** olives for at least
 one week, shaking
 occasionally.

*This keeps for weeks in the
refrigerator.*

CAN'T GET ENOUGH SNACK CRACKERS •

Yield: 16 to 18 servings

2 (10 ounce) packages oyster
 crackers
1 package Good Seasons
 Italian salad dressing mix
1 teaspoon garlic salt
¼ to ½ cup oil
2 teaspoons dill weed

♦ **Mix** together all ingredients
 except crackers.
♦ **Pour** mixture over crackers.
 Toss well. Cover tightly. Do
 not refrigerate.

INDIAN SUMMER PUMPKIN DIP •

Yield: 24 servings

4 cups powdered sugar
2 (8 ounce) packages cream
 cheese, at room temperature
1 (30 ounce) can pumpkin
2 teaspoons cinnamon
1 teaspoon ginger

♦ **Mix** together powdered sugar
 and cream cheese. Add the rest
 of the ingredients.
♦ **Place** dip in a hollowed out
 pumpkin. Serve with
 gingersnaps or fruit.

CRANBERRY ORANGE COOLER

Yield: 6 servings

1 (6 ounce) can frozen orange
    juice concentrate
6 ounces cranberry juice
6 ounces lemon-lime
    carbonated beverage
Ice to fill the blender

♦ **Put** all ingredients in a blender
and process to a slush.
♦ **Pour** into glasses and garnish
with a fresh orange slice and a
sprig of mint.

*This is excellent for breakfast or
brunch.*

May be adapted for cocktails by
adding 5 ounces of vodka.

ORANGE MINT SPRITZER

Yield: 20 servings

2 cups sugar
2½ cups water
2 oranges, juice and rind
6 lemons, juice and rind
2 bunches fresh mint
    Ginger ale or club soda

♦ **Boil** sugar and water for 10
minutes in large saucepan.
♦ **Add** juices and rinds (careful
not to use bitter white pulp);
add mint leaves.
♦ **Cover** and let stand for 1 hour.
♦ **Strain** into covered jar and
store in refrigerator.
♦ **Serve** in a glass filled with
crushed ice; add ⅓ juice
concentrate and ⅔ ginger ale
or club soda. Garnish with
sprig of fresh mint.

*This is a delicious, not too sweet
summer drink.*

BANANA SLUSH FRAPPÉ

Yield 32 (8 ounce) servings

4 cups sugar
6 cups warm water
1 (46 ounce) can pineapple
    juice
2 (12 ounce) cans orange juice
    concentrate, thawed
12 ounces lemon juice
6 bananas
3 liters Sprite

♦ **Blend** together bananas and
lemon juice in a blender.
♦ **Dissolve** sugar in warm water.
♦ **Mix** together all ingredients
except the Sprite in a very
large container. Freeze.
♦ **Mix** frozen mixture with Sprite
when ready to serve.

*Vodka may be added for an extra
punch.*

APPLE BLOSSOM PUNCH

Yield: 60 to 65 servings

3 quarts apple juice, chilled
3 (12 ounce) cans frozen
  orange juice
3 quarts ginger ale, chilled
2 oranges, sliced
10 red maraschino cherries

♦ **Prepare** ice ring one day in advance by combining orange slices and cherries with water. Freeze.
♦ **Combine** fruit juices and ginger ale in a large punch bowl.
♦ **Add** ice ring just before serving. Add additional orange slices for color if desired.

Easy to prepare on sight. A second ice ring may be needed.

STRAWBERRY CHAMPAGNE PUNCH

Yield: 20 (6 ounce) servings

2 quarts strawberries
½ cup powdered sugar
2 liters chilled Champagne
2 liters sparkling mineral
  water
  Whole berries for ice ring

♦ **Purée** strawberries with sugar. Strain into a pitcher and chill.
♦ **Pour** purée over a molded ice ring in a punch bowl. Gently stir in Champagne and sparkling water.

WHITE SANGRIA

Yield: 6 servings

3½ cups dry white wine, chilled
½ cup Cointreau or any
  orange liqueur
1 (10 ounce) bottle club soda
¼ cup sugar
  Ice cubes
1 orange, thinly sliced
1 lemon, thinly sliced
1 lime, thinly sliced

♦ **Combine** wine, liqueur and sugar and stir in a large clear glass pitcher.
♦ **Add** club soda, ice and fruit just before serving. Pour into white wine glasses and garnish with mint.

MAGNIFICO MARGARITA

Yield: 4 servings

1 (6 ounce) can frozen
   limeade
6 ounces beer
6 ounces tequila

♦ **Put** all ingredients together in a blender. Fill with ice and blend.
♦ **Serve** in salt rimmed glasses. Garnish with lime slices.

GRAND LAKE FEVER

Yield: 4 servings

4 ounces cream of coconut
8 ounces pineapple juice
5 ounces vodka
1 ounce amaretto
1 cup fresh or frozen
   strawberries, sliced

♦ **Add** all ingredients in a blender.
♦ **Fill** blender with ice. Blend.
♦ **Serve** in stemmed glasses and garnish with a fresh strawberry.

SHANGRI-LA SUNRISE

Yield: 4 servings

2 ounces crème de banana
   liqueur
2 ounces light rum
2 ounces Galliano
4 ounces orange juice
4 ounces pineapple juice
Juice of 1 fresh lemon

♦ **Mix** together all ingredients in a blender.
♦ **Serve** over crushed ice. Garnish with fruit.

May fill blender with ice and blend rather than serving over ice.

TUMBLIN' TUMBLEWEED

Yield: 4 servings

1¼ ounces Kahlua
¾ ounce dark crème de cacao
1 quart vanilla ice cream
   Half-and-half

♦ **Mix** all ingredients together in a blender.
♦ **Add** half-and-half as needed for a thinner consistency.

JUST PEACHY FROZEN DRINK

Yield: 2 (8 ounce) servings

½ ounce dark rum
1½ ounces peach brandy
2 ounces grenadine or
  maraschino cherry juice
2 ounces orange juice
2 ounces sweet and sour
  daiquiri mix
Crushed ice
Mint leaf sprigs
Heavy cream, whipped
Fresh peach, skinned and
  sliced

♦ **Blend** together rum, brandy, grenadine, orange juice and daiquiri mix in a blender.
♦ **Add** two peach slices and some of the crushed ice. Continue blending, adding ice as needed until contents thicken to desired consistency.
♦ **Pour** into glasses, top with whipped cream, mint leaf and two fresh peach slices. Serve immediately.

VELVET HAMMER

Yield: 4 servings

2 ounces Grand Marnier
3 ounces brandy
1 ounce Kahlua
  Vanilla ice cream (enough
  to fill a blender)

♦ **Blend** all ingredients together at slow speed.

HEARTHSIDE CHRISTMAS EGG NOG

Yield: 12 to 14 servings

½ gallon eggnog
8 ounces dark rum
4 ounces Irish Whiskey
2 ounces bourbon
4 ounces Kahlua
  Nutmeg

♦ **Pour** eggnog, rum, whiskey, bourbon and Kahlua into a punch bowl and sprinkle with nutmeg.

BREADS & BRUNCH

BUFFALO—a common sight in northeastern
Oklahoma, particularly at Woolaroc
and on the Tallgrass Prairie.

THE HORSE-SHOE BEND

In 1867, Nelson Carr, the first white man to inhabit the future town of Bartlesville, decided the sweeping horse-shoe bend of the Big Caney River was a fine place to establish a grist mill. In those days corn was the major crop of the Territory. It had been grown successfully by Indians for years, and white settlers soon caught on. Carr later sold his mill to an enterprising Kansan named Jake Bartles who expanded it to grind wheat. Bartles established a store alongside the mill, hiring young Canadian William Johnstone and fur trader George Keeler to help run his business.

The two learned quickly from Bartles, and in 1884 the ambitious young men established their own store on the other side of the river. A spirited competition developed, and Bartlesville, Indian Territory, was in business!

A lively melange of inhabitants drifted into the town and the surrounding Territory. Some were in and out quickly, staying only long enough to rob a bank or settle a score. These were the notorious outlaws, Belle Starr, Bill Doolin and the Dalton Brothers, among others.

But the good guys stayed longer, establishing the businesses, ranches and farms that transformed Jake Bartles' town into a place where good folks with enterprise and ambition could flourish. Bartlesville became an incorporated town in 1897.

CRANBERRY SURPRISE LOAF

Yield: 1 (9x5 inch) loaf

2 (3 ounce) packages cream cheese, softened
1 egg
2 cups all-purpose or unbleached flour
1 cup sugar
1½ teaspoons baking powder
¼ teaspoon baking soda
½ teaspoon salt
¾ cup apple juice
¼ cup melted margarine or butter
1 egg, beaten
1½ cups fresh cranberries, coarsely chopped
½ cup chopped nuts

♦ **Grease** and flour bottom only of a 9x5 inch loaf pan.
♦ **Beat** cream cheese till light and fluffy in a small bowl. Add 1 egg; blend well. Set aside.
♦ **Spoon** flour lightly into a measuring cup; level off.
♦ **Mix** flour, sugar, baking powder, baking soda and salt in a large bowl.
♦ **Stir** in apple juice, margarine and beaten egg. Fold in cranberries and nuts.
♦ **Spoon** half of the batter into the loaf pan. Spoon cream cheese mixture evenly over batter. Top with the remaining batter.
♦ **Bake** at 350° for 65 to 75 minutes or until top springs back when touched in center. Cool 15 minutes and remove from pan to wire rack.
♦ **Wrap** lightly; store in the refrigerator.

BANANA CREAM BREAD •

Yield: 2 (9x5 inch) loaves or 6 mini loaves

1⅓ cups oil
3 cups sugar
4 eggs, beaten
6 ripe bananas, mashed √
1 cup sour cream √
4 cups unbleached flour √
1½ teaspoons soda
1½ teaspoons salt
2 teaspoons vanilla
2 cups chopped pecans

TOPPING
Sugar
Chopped pecans

♦ **Combine** oil, sugar, eggs, bananas and sour cream in a large bowl. Blend until smooth.
♦ **Mix** together flour, salt and soda. Stir into the banana mixture and add vanilla and pecans.
♦ **Pour** into 2 large (9x5 inch) greased and floured loaf pans or 6 mini loaf pans.
♦ **Sprinkle** top with sugar and chopped pecans.
♦ **Bake** at 325° for 1 hour for large loaves or 40 minutes for small loaves or until loaves test done.

POPPY SEED BREAD

Yield: 2 (9x5 inch) loaves or 6 mini loaves

BREAD
3 cups flour
2¼ cups sugar
1½ tablespoons poppy seeds
1½ teaspoons salt
1½ teaspoons baking powder
3 eggs
1 cup plus 2 tablespoons oil
1½ cups milk
1½ tablespoons vanilla extract
1½ tablespoons butter extract
1½ tablespoons almond extract

ORANGE GLAZE
¼ cup orange juice concentrate
¾ cup sugar
1 teaspoon vanilla extract
1 teaspoon butter extract
1 teaspoon almond extract

♦ **Mix** dry ingredients together
♦ **Add** liquid ingredients and beat with a mixer for two minutes.
♦ **Pour** into 2 (9x5 inch) loaf pans (or 6 mini pans) which have been well greased.
♦ **Bake** at 350° for 1 hour or until loaves test done.
♦ **Cool** slightly in pans and then remove to wire racks.
♦ **Mix** glaze ingredients together and spread on bread. (Put wax paper under the rack to catch run-off.)

APPLE-DATE LOAF

Yield: 1 loaf

1 cup boiling water
1⅓ cups chopped pitted dates
2¼ cups flour
¾ cup light brown sugar, packed
2 teaspoons baking powder
½ teaspoon baking soda
1 teaspoon cinnamon
2 medium apples
1 egg, beaten
½ cup chopped walnuts
2 tablespoons butter, melted

♦ **Grease** a 9x5x3 inch loaf pan.
♦ **Pour** boiling water over dates and set aside.
♦ **Stir** together flour, brown sugar, baking powder, baking soda and cinnamon in a large bowl then set aside.
♦ **Peel**, core and shred apples. Combine apples, beaten egg, walnuts, melted butter and dates (do not drain). Add apple mixture to flour mixture. Stir until just moistened. Turn into loaf pan.
♦ **Bake** at 350° for 60 to 65 minutes or until tester comes out clean.
♦ **Cool** in pan for 10 minutes and remove from pan. Cool on a wire rack.

WAVIN' WHEAT CHEDDAR BREAD

Yield: l loaf

1¼ cups whole wheat flour
1¼ cups all-purpose flour
⅓ cup brown sugar, firmly packed
1 teaspoon baking powder
1 teaspoon baking soda
½ teaspoon salt
2 cups shredded Cheddar cheese
1 cup chopped pecans
2 teaspoons grated orange peel
1¼ cups milk
¼ cup butter, melted
¼ cup light molasses
1 egg, slightly beaten

♦ **Combine** dry ingredients in a large mixing bowl. Stir in cheese, nuts, and orange peel.
♦ **Combine** milk, butter, molasses, and egg. Stir liquid ingredients into dry ingredient mixture, stirring just until all ingredients are blended.
♦ **Spread** batter evenly in buttered 9½x5½ inch loaf pan.
♦ **Bake** at 350° for 55 to 60 minutes or until a knife inserted in center comes out clean. Let rest in pan 10 minutes. Remove and cool at least 1½ hours on a wire rack. Serve warm with butter.

MINIATURE BROWN BREAD LOAVES

Yield: 20 servings

1½ cups whole wheat flour
½ cup yellow cornmeal
1 teaspoon baking soda
¼ teaspoon salt
½ cup raisins
⅓ cup brown sugar, firmly packed
¼ teaspoon ground ginger
1¼ cups nonfat buttermilk
¼ cup molasses
  Vegetable cooking spray

♦ **Combine** first 7 ingredients in a medium bowl; make a well in center of mixture.

♦ **Combine** buttermilk and molasses; add to dry ingredients, stirring just until dry ingredients are moistened.

♦ **Spoon** batter into two miniature loaf pans coated with cooking spray.

♦ **Bake** at 350° for 35 minutes or until golden. Let cool in pans 10 minutes; remove from pans, and let cool completely on a wire rack.

MEXICAN CORN BREAD

Yield: 15 squares

3 eggs, beaten
⅓ cup vegetable oil
½ cup flour
1 cup yellow cornmeal
1 teaspoon salt
1 tablespoon baking powder
½ teaspoon baking soda
1 cup buttermilk
1 clove garlic, minced
½ green pepper, chopped
1 large onion, chopped
1 - 4 fresh jalapeño peppers, minced
1 (11 ounce) can Mexicorn, drained
1 cup grated sharp Cheddar cheese

♦ **Combine** the first nine ingredients and mix well. Fold in vegetables and cheese.

♦ **Bake** in greased 9x13 inch pan at 450° for 30 to 35 minutes.

SWEDISH RYE BREAD

Yield: 2 loaves

1 package active dry yeast
¼ cup warm water
¼ cup brown sugar
¼ cup light molasses
1 tablespoon salt
2 tablespoons shortening
1½ cups hot water
2½ cups sifted rye flour
1 tablespoon caraway seeds
   or 2 teaspoons grated
   orange peel
3½-4 cups all-purpose flour

♦ **Soften** yeast in warm water (110°).

♦ **Combine** sugar, molasses, salt, and shortening in a large bowl. Add hot water and stir until sugar dissolves. Cool to lukewarm.

♦ **Stir** in rye flour, beat well. Add softened yeast and caraway seed or orange peel; mix well. Stir in enough all-purpose flour to make a moderately stiff dough.

♦ **Knead** on well-floured surface until smooth and satiny (about 10 minutes). Place dough in lightly greased bowl, turning once to grease surface. Cover; let rise until double in bulk (1½ to 2 hours). Punch down.

♦ **Turn** out on lightly floured surface; divide into 2 portions. Shape each into 2 balls (smooth). Cover and let rest 10 minutes. Pat dough in 2 round loaves; place on greased baking sheet. (or shape into 2 loaves; place in greased 9x5 inch loaf pan.) Cover; let rise in warm place until double (1½ to 2 hours).

♦ **Bake** at 375° about 25 to 30 minutes. Place foil loosely over tops last 10 minutes, if necessary. For soft crust brush with melted butter. Cool on rack.

HOME STYLE DILL BREAD

Yield: 8 slices

1 cup cottage cheese, lukewarm
2 tablespoons sugar
1 tablespoon instant minced onion
1 tablespoon butter
2 tablespoons dill seed
1 tablespoon salt
¼ tablespoon soda
1 egg, unbeaten
1 package granulated yeast
2¼-2½ cups all-purpose flour

♦ **Combine** the cottage cheese, sugar, onion, butter, dill seeds, salt, soda, and egg. Beat ingredients well.
♦ **Add** yeast, then add enough flour to make a stiff dough.
♦ **Beat** again and let rise to double in bulk in a warm place.
♦ **Stir** down.
♦ **Place** in a well-greased 8 inch round, 2 quart casserole or other baking pan.
♦ **Let** the dough rise to double in bulk again.
♦ **Bake** at 350° for 30 to 40 minutes. Brush with soft butter and sprinkle with salt.

HAWAIIAN BREAD •

Yield: 2 dozen rolls

1 package yellow cake mix
2 packages yeast
½ teaspoon salt
2½ cups warm water
5 cups flour
4 tablespoons melted butter

♦ **Combine** cake mix and yeast. Combine salt and water and add cake mixture to water and salt mixture. Add flour last. Mix well and knead lightly.
♦ **Let** rise 1 hour and knead lightly again. Pat out and cut for rolls. Place close together on lightly greased cookie sheet.
♦ **Let** rise until double. Bake at 375° until brown; brush with melted butter and bake a little longer.

CARDAMOM BREAD

Yield: 1 (9x5 inch) loaf

2 eggs, well-beaten
1⅓ cups sugar
½ cup oil
2½ cups flour
1 teaspoon cloves
1 teaspoon baking soda
1 teaspoon cardamom
½ teaspoon salt
1 cup milk (sweet, sour or buttermilk)

♦ **Add** sugar to well-beaten eggs and beat in oil.
♦ **Mix** together flour, cloves, soda, cardamom and salt. Add milk and then add the flour mixture to the egg mixture.
♦ **Bake** in a greased and floured 9x5 inch loaf pan at 350° for 1 hour.

JULIA LOOKOUT'S FRY BREAD •

Yield: 2 dozen rolls

1 tin cup of water (2 cups)
4 heaping teaspoons baking powder
1 teaspoon sugar
1 teaspoon salt
Flour to make a soft dough, able to roll out

OSAGE NATION

♦ **Roll** out on a floured board until about ⅓ inch thick.
♦ **Cut** in wedges about 3 inches long, 1 inch wide.
♦ **Fry** in deep fat like doughnuts; drain on a paper towel.

Julia Lookout was the wife of Osage Chief, Fred Lookout. Julia's Fry Bread was always served at the spring Corn Dance and Feast that was held each year in the Indian village on the edge of Pawhuska.

LEMON RASPBERRY MUFFINS
Yield: 12 muffins

2 cups flour
1 cup sugar
3 teaspoons baking powder
½ teaspoon salt
½ cup oil
1 cup half-and-half
1 teaspoon lemon extract
2 eggs
1½ cups fresh or frozen raspberries (without syrup). Do not thaw if frozen

TOPPING
1 teaspoon butter, melted
⅓ cup sugar
1 teaspoon cinnamon

♦ **Combine** flour, sugar, baking powder, and salt. Mix well. Combine half-and-half, oil, lemon extract and eggs. Blend well and add to dry ingredients. Stir just until moistened. Carefully fold in raspberries.
♦ **Fill** muffin cups ¾ full. Sprinkle topping on top of muffins.
♦ **Bake** 18 to 23 minutes at 425°. Cool 5 minutes and remove from pan.

"OH WHAT A BEAUTIFUL MORNING" • MARMALADE MUFFINS
Yield: 12 muffins

2 cups flour
¼ cup sugar
1 tablespoon baking powder
¼ cup shortening
½ cup chopped pecans
1 egg
½ cup orange juice
1 cup orange marmalade

TOPPING
⅓ cup sugar
½ teaspoon cinnamon
½ teaspoon nutmeg
1 teaspoon melted butter

♦ **Sift** flour, sugar and baking powder together in a large bowl. Cut in shortening. Stir in pecans.
♦ **Beat** egg in a smaller bowl. Add orange juice and orange marmalade and blend.
♦ **Stir** egg mixture into flour mixture.
♦ **Spoon** into greased or lined muffin pans, filling three-fourths full.
♦ **Mix** topping ingredients and sprinkle on muffins.
♦ **Bake** at 375° for 20 to 25 minutes.

LITE AND EASY OSAGE ORANGE MUFFINS

Yield: 12 muffins

3 cups reduced-fat biscuit mix (Bisquick)
¾ cup sugar
2 eggs
1¼ cups fresh orange juice
Sliced almonds
Sugar to sprinkle

♦ **Grease** a large muffin tin.
♦ **Combine** biscuit mix, sugar, eggs and orange juice. Beat 30 seconds or until blended.
♦ **Pour** into greased muffin tins, sprinkle with almonds and sugar.
♦ **Bake** for 20 to 25 minutes in a 425° oven.

BLUEBERRY-LEMON MUFFINS

Yield: 12 large muffins

2 cups all-purpose flour
¾ cup sugar
1 teaspoon baking powder
½ teaspoon baking soda
½ teaspoon salt
2 egg whites
½ cup lemon yogurt
½ cup applesauce
2 tablespoons canola oil
1 teaspoon lemon zest, grated
1 cup blueberries

♦ **Combine** flour, sugar, baking powder, baking soda and salt in a large bowl.
♦ **Combine** egg whites, yogurt, applesauce, oil and lemon zest. Stir into dry mixture just until moistened. Fold in blueberries.
♦ **Pour** into 12 large greased muffin cups.
♦ **Bake** at 400° for 25 minutes. Remove muffins to wire rack to cool.

PUMPKIN BRAN MUFFINS

Yield: 12 muffins

No stick cooking spray
1 cup canned solid-pack pumpkin
1 cup natural high-fiber cereal shreds
¾ cup skim milk
⅓ cup Karo light or dark corn syrup
2 egg whites, slightly beaten
1¼ cups flour
⅓ cup sugar
2 teaspoons baking powder
½ teaspoon baking soda
½ teaspoon salt
½ cup raisins

♦ **Spray** 12 (2½ inch) muffin cups with cooking spray. Combine pumpkin, cereal, milk, corn syrup and egg whites in a medium bowl.
♦ **Combine** flour, sugar, baking powder, baking soda and salt in a large bowl. Add pumpkin mixture; stir until well blended. Stir in raisins.
♦ **Spoon** into prepared muffin cups. Bake at 400° for 20 minutes or until toothpick inserted in center comes out clean. Cool in pan 5 minutes. Remove; cool on wire rack.

CINNAMON YOGURT MUFFINS

Yield: 18 muffins

2 cups all-purpose flour
⅔ cup sugar
1 teaspoon baking powder
1 teaspoon baking soda
1 (8 ounce) container low-fat plain or non-fat yogurt
½ cup butter, melted
2 eggs, slightly beaten
1 teaspoon vanilla extract
2 tablespoons sugar
1 teaspoon cinnamon

◆ **Butter** 2½ inch muffin cups or line with paper liners.
◆ **Combine** flour, ⅔ cup sugar, baking powder and baking soda in a large mixing bowl.
◆ **Mix** yogurt, melted butter, eggs and vanilla in small bowl. Stir liquid ingredients into dry ingredients just until combined and moistened, do not over mix.
◆ **Combine** 2 tablespoons sugar and cinnamon.
◆ **Spoon** 1 rounded tablespoonful of batter into each muffin cup. Sprinkle with half of cinnamon and sugar mixture. Repeat using remaining batter and cinnamon sugar.
◆ **Bake** at 400° for 18 to 20 minutes, or until wooden toothpick inserted in center comes out clean. Cool in pan on wire rack 10 minutes.

HONEY LAMB WHOLE WHEAT MUFFINS

Yield: 12 muffins

1¾ cups whole wheat flour
1 tablespoon baking powder
¼ teaspoon baking soda
½ teaspoon salt (optional)
1 large egg
¼ cup honey
1½ cups buttermilk
¼ cup vegetable oil

◆ **Blend** all dry ingredients in a large bowl.
◆ **Beat** egg in a separate bowl. Add honey, buttermilk and oil and stir. Add egg mixture to dry ingredients and quickly stir until moistened.
◆ **Fill** greased or lined muffin cups three-fourths full.
◆ **Bake** at 425° for 20 to 25 minutes. Muffins will be a dark golden brown.

KEY LIME MUFFINS

Yield: 12 muffins

2 cups all-purpose flour
1 cup sugar
1 tablespoon baking powder
2 large eggs
¼ cup milk
¼ cup vegetable oil
⅓ cup Key Lime juice
Sugar for sprinkling
(optional)

♦ **Grease** muffin pans lightly or use paper liners.

♦ **Combine** flour, sugar and baking powder in a large bowl. Make a well in the center of the mixture.

♦ **Whisk** eggs lightly in a small bowl. Add milk, oil and Key Lime juice to eggs and stir with whisk to combine.

♦ **Add** egg mixture to dry ingredients and stir until just moistened. Spoon into muffin pans, filling three-fourths full. Sprinkle with sugar if desired.

♦ **Bake** at 400° for 15 to 18 minutes or until lightly browned and tests done. Remove the muffins from the pan immediately.

ANGEL BISCUITS

Yield: 3½ dozen biscuits

1 package dry yeast
2 tablespoons warm water
2 cups buttermilk
5 cups flour
1 tablespoon baking powder
1 teaspoon baking soda
¼ cup sugar
1 cup shortening

♦ **Dissolve** yeast in warm water, let stand 5 minutes. Stir in buttermilk and set aside.

♦ **Combine** dry ingredients. Cut in shortening until crumbly. Make a well in center and pour in yeast mixture. Stir just until moistened.

♦ **Knead** on lightly floured surface lightly 3 or 4 times. Roll to ¼ inch thickness, cut with a 2 inch biscuit cutter. Place on a greased cookie sheet and let rise, covered, for 30 minutes.

♦ **Bake** at 400° for 10 to 12 minutes or until lightly browned.

CHEESE-CHIVE BISCUITS

Yield: 12 biscuits

2 cups all-purpose flour
2½ teaspoons baking powder
½ teaspoon salt
1 tablespoon diced chives
¾ cup grated sharp Cheddar
cheese
¼ cup shortening
¾ cup buttermilk

♦ **Combine** all dry ingredients. Cut shortening in with dry ingredients in a large mixing bowl. Add chives and cheese. Stir in ¾ cup buttermilk.
♦ **Shape** into medium size balls and place on lightly sprayed cookie sheet. May also be made as drop biscuits using a tablespoon-size spoon.
♦ **Bake** at 350° for 20 to 25 minutes until lightly browned.

BLUE RIBBON BISCUITS

Yield: 4 servings

½ cup butter (do not
substitute)
1½ teaspoons parsley flakes
½ teaspoon dill weed
1 tablespoon onion flakes
2 tablespoons Parmesan
cheese
1 (10 or 11 ounce) can
refrigerator buttermilk
biscuits

♦ **Melt** butter in a 9 inch round cake pan.
♦ **Mix** herbs and cheese together and stir into butter.
♦ **Cut** biscuits into halves or fourths and coat on all sides with herb-butter.
♦ **Bake** at 425° for 12 to 15 minutes.

RUSTLER'S ROLLS

Yield: 25 to 30 rolls

2 cups warm water
2 packages yeast
½ cup sugar
¼ cup margarine, melted
1 egg
2 teaspoons salt
6½-7 cups flour
Beaten egg
Poppy or other seeds
(optional)

♦ **Measure** water into large bowl. Add yeast and stir. Add sugar, margarine, egg, salt and ½ of the flour. Mix well. Add remaining flour.

♦ **Knead** for 10 minutes. Place in greased bowl, turning to grease top. Cover. Punch down occasionally. Refrigerate from 2 hours to several days.

♦ **Pull** off pieces of dough and roll into 7 inch ropes. Cross ends of rope together and knot. If desired, brush with beaten egg and sprinkle with seeds. Place on floured cookie sheet. Allow to rise until double.

♦ **Bake** at 400° for 10 to 12 minutes.

CRESCENT MOON ROLLS

Yield: 2 dozen rolls

⅓ cup oil
8 ounces plain yogurt
½ cup sugar
2 tablespoons yeast
½ cup warm water
1 egg plus 1 egg white
4 cups flour
1 teaspoon salt

♦ **Combine** oil, yogurt and sugar.

♦ **Dissolve** yeast in water and let stand for 5 minutes. Add to yogurt mixture. Add eggs to yogurt mixture and then add flour and salt.

♦ **Refrigerate** dough for 8 hours.

♦ **Form** into crescent rolls by dividing dough in half and rolling each half into a circle. Cut triangles from circle. Roll each piece, beginning with the widest end, point down. Curve roll slightly into a crescent shape.

♦ **Let** rise for 2 hours.

♦ **Bake** at 350° for 12 minutes.

SPINACH AND ZUCCHINI QUICHE •

Yield: 10 servings

PIE CRUST

2⅔ cups all-purpose flour
1 teaspoon salt
1 cup Crisco (do not substitute)
7-8 tablespoons ice water

QUICHE FILLING

1 pound bulk sweet Italian sausage
2 tablespoons butter or margarine
3 cups coarsely chopped zucchini
2 teaspoons seasoned salt
1 package frozen chopped spinach, thawed and squeezed dry
1 (15 ounce) carton ricotta cheese
1 (8 ounce) container cream cheese with herbs and garlic
1 cup shredded mozzarella cheese
2 large eggs
1 tablespoon Tabasco
1 large egg beaten with 1 tablespoon water

♦ **Combine** flour and salt. Cut in Crisco until it resembles coarse crumbs. Sprinkle on water 1 tablespoon at a time and toss with a fork until it is well mixed. Shape in two balls, one larger than the other and refrigerate until ready to make pie crusts.

♦ **Bake** bottom crust in a 10 inch quiche or pie pan for 6 to 8 minutes in a 425° oven. Let cool.

♦ **Brown** sausage in a skillet and drain.

♦ **Cook** zucchini in butter in a skillet and sprinkle with seasonings and cook until tender.

♦ **Combine** next 6 ingredients with sausage and zucchini and put in pastry shell.

♦ **Cover** with top crust. Brush with egg-water glaze.

♦ **Bake** at 375° for 35 to 45 minutes. Cool on a wire rack.

♦ **Serve** warm or hot.

HOME-GROWN TOMATO QUICHE •

Yield: 6 servings

1 (9 inch) pie shell
Unbeaten egg white
2 large ripe tomatoes
¼ cup flour
½ teaspoon salt
⅛ teaspoon coarse ground
pepper
2 tablespoons cooking oil
½ cup sliced ripe olives
1 cup minced scallions (or
less)
3 slices provolone cheese
1 cup heavy cream
1 cup grated aged Cheddar
cheese
2 eggs, slightly beaten

♦ **Brush** pie shell lightly with unbeaten egg white and bake for only 8 minutes at 425°. Cool.

♦ **Cut** tomatoes into 6 slices, ½ inch thick. Mix flour, salt and pepper. Dip each tomato slice into seasoned flour.

♦ **Sauté** quickly in cooking oil. Drain on paper towels. Arrange sliced ripe olives and all but 2 tablespoons of minced scallions in the bottom of pie shell.

♦ **Arrange** provolone cheese and tomato slices over olives and scallions. Combine cream, Cheddar cheese and eggs.

♦ **Pour** into pie shell. Bake at 375° for 40 to 45 minutes, or until filling is set. Sprinkle remaining scallions on top.

♦ **Cool** 5 minutes before cutting.

AUTUMN APPLE QUICHE •

Yield: 6 servings

½-¾ pound mild sausage
1 large apple, cored and
thinly sliced
1 large onion, chopped
1½ cups shredded Cheddar
cheese
3 tablespoons all-purpose
flour
3 eggs, beaten
1 cup half-and-half or canned
milk
2 tablespoons chopped
parsley
⅛ teaspoon dry mustard
⅛ teaspoon celery seed
1 (9 inch) deep dish pie crust

♦ **Brown** sausage in large skillet. Remove from skillet. Drain. Place apples and onion in skillet. Cook for 5 to 6 minutes or until browned.

♦ **Toss** cheese with flour in medium bowl. Combine eggs with half-and-half. Add parsley, mustard and celery seed. Stir in cheese mixture.

♦ **Spoon** sausage in bottom of pie crust. Top with apple-onion mixture. Pour cheese mixture over top.

♦ **Bake** at 375° for 40 minutes or until knife inserted in center comes out clean.

♦ **Cool** for 10 minutes.

Asparagus Brunch Con Queso

Yield: 10 servings

1 pound colby cheese, grated
1 pound Velveeta Cheese, melted
1 (10 ounce) can Rotel
2 (15 ounce) cans asparagus or 1 pound fresh steamed asparagus
12 medium eggs, beaten
Paprika

♦ **Place** the grated colby cheese in a greased 9x13 inch baking dish and cover with beaten eggs.
♦ **Bake** 45 minutes in a 325° oven until eggs are set.
♦ **Remove** from oven and arrange drained asparagus on top.
♦ **Combine** tomatoes and green chilies with melted Velveeta cheese in a saucepan and heat until warm.
♦ **Pour** over top of cooked cheese and egg mixture and return to oven to bake for 5 to 8 minutes.
♦ **Sprinkle** with paprika.

Sunrise Sausage Strata

Yield: 12 to 14 servings

20 slices bread, buttered and crusts removed
2 pounds mild or hot sausage, browned and drained
3 cups grated Cheddar cheese
½ - 1 cup chopped onions
12 eggs
1 quart milk
1½ teaspoons salt
1½ teaspoons dry mustard
Sauce
12 ounces sour cream
2 (10½ ounce) cans cream of mushroom soup
1 (4½ ounce) can chopped green chilies

♦ **Arrange** 10 slices of bread in bottom of a 9x13 inch baking dish buttered side down.
♦ **Layer** browned sausage, grated cheese and chopped onion. Top with last 10 slices of buttered bread, buttered side up.
♦ **Blend** eggs, milk, salt and mustard and pour over casserole.
♦ **Cover** with foil and refrigerate overnight.
♦ **Bake** uncovered at 350° for 1 hour. Then watch closely for 10 to 30 minutes longer until browned.
♦ **Warm** sauce ingredients in sauce pan, being careful not to scorch.
♦ **Cut** strata into squares and top with warmed chili sauce to serve.

"SLEEPIN' IN" OMELETTE

Yield: 8 to 10 servings

1 package onion rolls (6)
10 eggs
¾ cup grated Longhorn
   Cheddar cheese
1 (8 ounce) package cream
   cheese torn into bite-size
   chunks
2 cups milk
1 cup butter
½ teaspoon dry mustard
½ tablespoon chives
½ teaspoon salt
   Dash of cayenne pepper

♦ **Tear** rolls into chunks and place evenly in a well greased 9x13 inch casserole.
♦ **Sprinkle** with cheeses.
♦ **Beat** eggs and remaining ingredients and pour mixture over bread and cheeses.
♦ **Refrigerate** overnight.
♦ **Bake** covered in a 325° oven for 1 hour. Uncover during the last 10 minutes.

COWBOY CASSEROLE

Yield: 8 servings

EGGS
1 loaf white bread, toasted
½ cup butter
6 eggs
3 cups milk
¾ teaspoon dry mustard
¾ teaspoon white pepper
1 pound Cheddar cheese,
   grated

SAUCE
⅓ cup chopped onion
¼ cup chopped green pepper
   (optional)
¾ cup sliced fresh mushrooms
3 tablespoons oil
1 tablespoon cornstarch
1 (16 ounce) can tomatoes,
   with liquid
1 teaspoon salt
   Dash of pepper
2 teaspoons sugar
   Dash of cayenne pepper

♦ **Butter** both sides of bread and cut into cubes. Set aside. Combine eggs, milk, mustard, and pepper.
♦ **Layer** cheese and bread cubes in buttered 9x13 inch casserole. Pour egg mixture over; cover and refrigerate 8 to 12 hours, or overnight.
♦ **Bake**, uncovered, at 350° for 30 to 45 minutes, or until eggs are set.
♦ **Make** sauce by browning onion, green pepper and mushrooms in oil. Combine cornstarch with 2 tablespoons liquid from canned tomatoes and add to vegetable mixture. Add tomatoes and remaining liquid from can, salt, pepper, sugar, and cayenne pepper.
♦ **Cook** over low heat, stirring often, until vegetables are tender and sauce is slightly thickened, 15 to 20 minutes. Serve over egg mixture.

WILD ONIONS AND EGGS

Yield: 8 to 10 servings

2 cups wild onions
6 cups eggs, beaten
Bacon drippings (about ⅓
cup or more)

**CHEROKEE
NATION**

♦ **Dig** wild onions in the spring.
Beat off most of the dirt. Cut
off the root end. Wash well.
Remove any yellowed tops.
♦ **Chop** small bulbs and green
tops into ¼ inch pieces.
♦ **Parboil** onions until they start
to change color. Drain, cool
and store until ready to use.
♦ **Heat** bacon drippings in a
large skillet. Spread onions
evenly in drippings, don't
brown.
♦ **Pour** eggs over onions and stir
continuously. Do not let eggs
brown.
♦ **Remove** to a dish. Serve with
ham, hominy, greens, or any
other vegetables.

*This dish is featured every spring at
the Wild Onion Dinner, hosted by
the Indian Women's Club of
Bartlesville.*

ITALIAN HERB BREAD

Yield: 4 large servings

1 pound frozen bread dough
¼ cup melted butter
1 pound Italian or pork
sausage
¼-½ cup salad olives or black
olives
¼ cup green onion tops
¼ cup grated Romano or
Parmesan cheese
½ cup grated Cheddar cheese
½ cup grated mozzarella
cheese
½ teaspoon Italian seasonings
Salt and pepper to taste

♦ **Let** dough rise. Roll out 6x9
inches, brush with melted
butter, cover and let rise again.
♦ **Cook** sausage and crumble.
Sprinkle sausage over risen
dough.
♦ **Add** onion tops, all cheeses,
olives and seasonings.
♦ **Roll** jelly roll style and pinch
edges to seal. Lay on seam, on
cookie sheet and let rise
another ½ hour.
♦ **Bake** at 350° for 35 to 40
minutes.

May form bread into ring and
bake. While bread is baking,
scramble desired amount of eggs.
Fill center of baked ring with eggs.

CRAZY QUILT ROLL-UPS
Yield: 12 servings

2 (10½ ounce) cans cream of celery soup
1 cup sour cream
3 tablespoons Dijon style mustard
2 (10 ounce) packages frozen spinach, chopped
1½ cups cooked rice
2 cups cottage cheese
3 eggs, slightly beaten
¾ cup finely chopped onion
6 tablespoons flour
24 thin slices broiled ham
Dried bread crumbs
Chopped fresh parsley
Paprika

♦ **Combine** soup, sour cream and mustard in a small bowl. Mix well.
♦ **Thaw** frozen spinach and drain well.
♦ **Combine** spinach, rice, cottage cheese, eggs, onion and flour in a large bowl. Mix well.
♦ **Add** ½ cup of soup mixture to spinach mixture.
♦ **Place** 2 tablespoons of spinach mixture on each slice of ham. Roll ham slices and secure with toothpicks. Arrange in 2 rows of 6 each, seam side down, in two greased 7x11 inch baking dishes. Top ham rolls with remaining soup mixture.
♦ **Sprinkle** bread crumbs, parsley and paprika on top.
♦ **Bake** at 350° for 35 minutes.

"YOU'RE DOIN' FINE" CINNAMON ROLLS •
Yield: 16 to 18 rolls

2 packages dry yeast
2½ cups warm water
1 package yellow cake mix (not pudding mix)
4 cups flour
1 teaspoon salt
FILLING
Melted butter
¾ cup sugar (granulated and brown)
2 tablespoons cinnamon
Nuts (optional)
Raisins (optional)

♦ **Dissolve** yeast in water. Mix cake mix with flour and salt. Add yeast mixture to dry ingredients. Mix and let rise 1½ hours or until double.
♦ **Divide** in half. Roll out on floured surface. Brush with melted butter and sprinkle on cinnamon, sugar, nuts and raisins. Roll up and cut in 1 inch slices. Place in greased 9x13 inch pan. Let rise again.
♦ **Bake** at 350° for 15 to 20 minutes.

APRICOT SQUARES

Yield: 24 squares

1 cup flour
¼ cup sugar
½ cup butter
2 eggs
1 cup light brown sugar
⅔ cup chopped dried apricots, softened in water
1 teaspoon vanilla
½ cup flour
½ teaspoon baking powder
Pinch salt
½ cup chopped nuts

♦ **Mix** flour, sugar and butter and pat into an 8x11 inch pan.
♦ **Bake** at 350° for 20 minutes.
♦ **Beat** eggs with brown sugar. Add apricots, vanilla, flour, baking powder, salt and nuts; mix well.
♦ **Pour** over first layer and bake an additional 25 minutes. Cool and cut in small squares.

SUNNY MORNING BLUEBERRY • COFFEE CAKE

Yield: 10 to 15 servings

1 box yellow butter cake mix
3 eggs
½ cup cooking oil
1 (8 ounce) package cream cheese, softened
2 cups fresh blueberries

♦ **Mix** first four ingredients with an electric mixer and fold in blueberries.
♦ **Grease** and flour a Bundt pan.
♦ **Pour** mixture into pan and bake at 350° for 50 minutes.
♦ **Cool** for 10 to 20 minutes and invert pan to release.

ORANGE CINNAMON COFFEE CAKE

Yield: 6 servings

Pecans (optional)
¾ cup sugar
1 tablespoon cinnamon
1 package ready to bake biscuits
¼ cup orange juice
¼ cup butter or margarine, melted

♦ **Sprinkle** pecans in ring mold.
♦ **Combine** sugar and cinnamon.
♦ **Cut** biscuits in half. Dip in orange juice, then into sugar mixture. Overlap in ring mold, curved side of biscuits down. Pour remaining sugar mixture over top and drizzle with melted butter.
♦ **Bake** at 400° for 20 minutes.

COTTAGE CHEESE ROLLS

Yield: 48 rolls

½ pound unsalted butter
1 pound small curd creamed
   cottage cheese
½ teaspoon salt
2 cups flour

FROSTING
1 tablespoon butter, softened
1½ cups powdered sugar
½ teaspoon vanilla
1½ tablespoons cream or half-
   and-half

♦ **Bring** all ingredients to room temperature. Combine in large bowl and beat until smooth and elastic. Chill for several hours or overnight.

♦ **Divide** into 4 balls and roll in circle ⅛ inch thick. Cut each circle into 12 pie-shaped pieces with a pizza cutter. Roll each piece from the wide end to the point. Place on ungreased baking sheet about 1 inch apart with the point side down.

♦ **Bake** at 350° for 20 minutes. Cool.

♦ **Cream** frosting ingredients and spread on rolls.

FRESH APPLE COFFEE CAKE ♦

Yield: 9 servings

CAKE
1¾ cups flour
1 cup sugar
½ teaspoon baking powder
½ teaspoon baking soda
1 egg
½ cup vegetable oil
¼ cup water
1 teaspoon vanilla
½ cup sour cream
2 medium apples, peeled,
   pared, and shredded (about
   2 cups)

TOPPING
½ cup firmly packed brown
   sugar
½ cup pecan or walnut pieces
2 teaspoons melted butter or
   margarine
1 teaspoon ground cinnamon

♦ **Blend** flour, sugar, baking powder and baking soda into a small bowl and set aside.

♦ **Combine** egg, oil, water and vanilla in a large bowl. Add half of dry ingredients and blend on low speed of mixer. Add half of sour cream and blend. Repeat. Stir in apples when well blended. Spread batter in a 9 inch greased pan.

♦ **Mix** topping ingredients and sprinkle over the top of the batter.

♦ **Bake** at 350° for 45 to 50 minutes or until cake tests done.

CREAMY PEACH-FILLED FRENCH TOAST •   *Yield: 3 to 4 servings*

1 (3 ounce) package cream cheese, softened
½ cup chopped peaches (fresh are best)
2 tablespoons chopped pecans
1 tablespoon honey
6 - 8 slices French bread, cut diagonally 1½ inches thick
2 eggs
½ cup half-and-half
¼ teaspoon vanilla

♦ **Beat** cream cheese in a small bowl until light and fluffy. Add peaches, pecans and honey; blend well.

♦ **Cut** pocket in top rounded edge of each bread slice and carefully fill each with 1½ tablespoons of cheese mixture.

♦ **Heat** large skillet or griddle to 350°.

♦ **Beat** eggs slightly in a shallow bowl. Add half-and-half and vanilla; mix well.

♦ **Grease** heated skillet lightly. Being careful not to squeeze filled slices, dip bread in egg mixture turning to coat both sides.

♦ **Cook** in skillet over medium heat about 3 to 4 minutes on each side or until golden brown.

♦ **Serve** with butter and maple syrup or fruit and Cool Whip.

Strawberries may be used instead of peaches.

BAKED FRENCH TOAST WITH BERRIES AND HOMEMADE BERRY SYRUP

Yield: 10 servings

FRENCH TOAST

1 loaf day old Texas toast
6 large eggs, beaten
2 cups milk
1 can skimmed evaporated milk
⅓ cup sugar
2 tablespoons vanilla extract
2 cups fresh or frozen blueberries, thawed
½ cup flour
½ cup plus 2 tablespoons brown sugar, packed
1 tablespoon cinnamon
½ cup butter or margarine
2 cups fresh or frozen strawberries

HOMEMADE BERRY SYRUP

2 cups sugar
1 cup water
½ lemon, squeezed
2 tablespoons cornstarch
3 cups frozen or fresh berries (blueberries, strawberries, blackberries, cranberries)
1 tablespoon vanilla extract

◆ **Cut** bread diagonally and arrange on greased 9x13 inch baking dish.

◆ **Combine** eggs and next four ingredients; stir well. Pour egg mixture over bread slices. Cover and chill 8 hours.

◆ **Sprinkle** blueberries over bread mixture. Combine flour, brown sugar and cinnamon. Cut in butter until mixture is crumbly; sprinkle over blueberries.

◆ **Bake** uncovered at 375° for 40 to 45 minutes or until set and golden.

◆ **Dissolve** first 4 syrup ingredients in medium sauce pan. Add berries; cook over medium heat until thickened. Add vanilla.

◆ **Serve** French toast with warm syrup and strawberries.

BELGIAN WAFFLES

Yield: 5 waffles

2½ cups flour
½ teaspoon salt
2 tablespoons sugar
1 envelope rapid-rise dry
   yeast
1½ cups very warm water (125°
   to 130°)
¼ cup melted butter
2 eggs, separated
1 teaspoon vanilla
   Oil

♦ **Combine** flour, salt, sugar and yeast in a large bowl. Add water, butter, egg yolks and vanilla all at once, beat well.

♦ **Beat** egg whites until soft peaks form, fold into batter and set aside to rise for 30 minutes.

♦ **Heat** Belgian waffle maker and grease well. Cook waffles according to directions for waffle maker.

♦ **Serve** with strawberry preserves and fresh strawberries.

SWEDISH PANCAKES

Yield: 4 large pancakes (5 to 6 inches diameter)

¾ cup flour
¾ teaspoon baking soda
½ teaspoon salt
½ teaspoon baking powder
1 teaspoon sugar
3 eggs, separated
1½ cups buttermilk
2 tablespoons butter, melted

♦ **Combine** dry ingredients and set aside.

♦ **Beat** egg yolks and whites separately. (Beat yolks well). Add milk to yolks. Mix dry ingredients with yolks and milk. Add melted butter. Fold in stiffly beaten egg whites.

♦ **Heat** pan or skillet until hot, then lower heat. Cook over low heat until golden and done.

♦ **Top** with fresh berries (strawberries, raspberries, blueberries) or peaches and frozen whipped topping or pure maple syrup.

GRAND PANCAKE °

Yield: 6 servings

4 tablespoons butter
1 cup milk
1 cup flour
6 eggs
1 teaspoon salt
1 tablespoon sugar

♦ **Melt** butter in a 9x13 inch Pyrex pan in a 350° oven.
♦ **Blend** next 5 ingredients in a blender for 3 minutes.
♦ **Pour** batter over butter in hot pan.
♦ **Bake** at 350° for 20 minutes and serve immediately. Top with powdered sugar, syrup or jam.

BREAKFAST TO GO

Yield: 12 to 16 servings

12 eggs, hard-boiled
1 pound bacon, cooked and crumbled
1 pound Cheddar cheese, grated
1 cup mayonnaise
1 tablespoon spicy mustard
   Dash soy sauce
   Dash Worcestershire sauce
   Garlic salt
6 English muffins, split

♦ **Mix** all ingredients in a large bowl and spread on English muffins.
♦ **Broil** in oven until brown for approximately 2 to 3 minutes.

Mushroom Turnovers

Yield: 3½ dozen

1 (8 ounce) package cream cheese, softened
1½ cups all-purpose flour
½ cup butter or margarine
3 tablespoons butter or margarine
½ pound mushrooms, minced
1 large onion, minced
¼ cup sour cream
1 teaspoon salt
¼ teaspoon thyme
2 tablespoons flour
1 egg, beaten

♦ **Combine** cream cheese, flour, and ½ cup butter with electric mixer until smooth; shape into ball; wrap; refrigerate 1 hour.

♦ **Melt** 3 tablespoons butter in 10-inch skillet over medium heat. Cook mushrooms and onions until tender. Stir in sour cream, salt, thyme, and 2 tablespoons flour. Set aside.

♦ **Roll** dough ⅛ inch thick on a floured surface with a floured rolling pin. Use 2¾ inch round cookie cutter to cut as many circles as possible.

♦ **Place** one teaspoon of mushroom mixture on half of each dough circle. Brush edges of circles with some egg; fold dough over filling. Using a fork, firmly press edges together to seal; prick tops.

♦ **Place** turnovers on ungreased cookie sheet; brush with remaining egg. Bake at 450° for 12 to 14 minutes until golden. Serve warm.

Unbaked turnovers may be frozen. Add a few minutes to baking time if baking from frozen state.

SALADS

BLACK GOLD!—The Nellie Johnstone
No. 1, Oklahoma's first commercial
oil well, marked the beginning of the
oil industry in Oklahoma.

BLACK GOLD

The Territory was good to settlers and Indians, but withheld its greatest treasure for many years. Black gold buried deep beneath the terrain waited to forever change life in old Indian Territory.

In 1897, the industrious team of Johnstone and Keeler brought in Oklahoma's first commercial oil well—the Nellie Johnstone No. 1, named for Johnstone's daughter.

With the coming of the railroad in 1899, the oil industry flourished. Bartlesville was the closest town of any size to the Burbank Oil Field on the Osage tribal land. This magnetic oil field—then the world's largest and richest— attracted wildcatters, speculators and fieldhands from all over the world, making millionaires of many.

One of the great fortunes was made by H.V. Foster, whose Indian Territory Illuminating Company later became a part of Cities Service Company. J. Paul Getty also made his start in the Burbank Fields, and a barber-turned-banker from Iowa, Frank Phillips by name, seemed to sense opportunity in the Osage Hills of Indian Territory.

MARGARITA CAESAR SALAD

Yield: 6 servings

SALAD

1 large head romaine lettuce, torn
1 cup (4 ounces) shredded Monterey Jack cheese
¼ cup chopped fresh cilantro
1 sweet red pepper cut in thin strips

DRESSING

⅓ cup canola oil
¼ cup lime juice
1½ tablespoons tequila
1½ teaspoons Triple Sec
1 clove garlic, minced
½ - 1 serrano chile, finely chopped
¼ teaspoon salt
¼ teaspoon ground cumin
2 tablespoons egg substitute

◆ **Prepare** dressing by mixing ingredients with a wire whisk. Cover and chill.
◆ **Combine** lettuce, cheese, cilantro and red pepper in a large bowl.
◆ **Toss** dressing and salad gently.

Salt the rims of salad plates by rubbing with lime wedges and rolling rim of plate in Kosher salt. Garnish with lime wedges and tortilla chips.

GOAT CHEESE SALAD

Yield: 6 to 8 servings

SALAD

12 ounces mixed salad greens, rinsed and crisped
1 cup walnut halves or pieces, toasted
8 ounces goat cheese (chèvre)

DRESSING

¼ cup white wine vinegar
1 tablespoon Dijon mustard
¼ cup walnut oil
Salt and freshly ground pepper

◆ **Divide** salad greens and arrange on individual salad plates.
◆ **Slice** cheese into 6 or 8 equal pieces; place on pan and broil about 3 inches below heat until cheese is slightly melted and speckled brown.
◆ **Combine** oil, vinegar, mustard, salt and pepper and whisk to blend.
◆ **Top** salad greens with melted warm cheese, sprinkle with toasted walnuts and drizzle with dressing.

Napa Salad

Yield: 8 servings

Salad

1 stalk Napa cabbage, torn into bite-size pieces
1 large bunch green onions, including tops, chopped
½ cup margarine
3 packages Ramen noodles (do not use seasoning packet), uncooked and crumbled
1 cup slivered almonds
1 cup sunflower seeds

Dressing

1 cup oil
1 cup sugar
1 cup vinegar
½ cup soy sauce

♦ **Mix** dressing ingredients and store in covered container.
♦ **Combine** cabbage and onions and place in separate covered container.
♦ **Brown** almonds and sunflowers in margarine carefully to prevent burning. Remove from heat and add Ramen noodles. Toss to coat and place in separate covered container.
♦ **Mix** contents of three containers right before serving.

Spinach Fruit Salad

Yield: 8 to 10 servings

Salad

1¾ pounds spinach, well washed
1 (11 ounce) can mandarin oranges, drained
1 (8 ounce) can pineapple chunks, drained
2 bananas, cut into chunks

Dressing

¼ cup sugar
2 tablespoons sesame seeds
1 tablespoon poppy seeds
1½ teaspoons grated onion
¼ teaspoon Worcestershire
¼ teaspoon paprika
½ cup vegetable or olive oil
¼ cup wine vinegar
Dash of salt

♦ **Prepare** dressing by combining in a blender the sugar, sesame seeds, poppy seeds, onion, Worcestershire, paprika and oil. Slowly add vinegar until dressing is moderately thick.
♦ **Arrange** fruits over spinach on individual salad plates and pour dressing on top or toss with dressing in large salad bowl.

Strawberries and walnuts are a great addition.

SPINACH SALAD WITH PINE NUT DRESSING   *Yield: 8 servings*

1½ bunches spinach, well
    washed
⅔ cup pine nuts
7 tablespoons olive oil or
    salad oil
2½ tablespoons wine vinegar
⅛ teaspoon cayenne pepper
½ teaspoon grated lemon peel
½ teaspoon tarragon leaves
½ teaspoon salt

♦ **Prepare** dressing by spreading pine nuts in a single layer in a shallow pan. Toast in a 350° oven, stirring occasionally, until golden (5 to 8 minutes). Let cool.

♦ **Blend** pine nuts with oil, vinegar, cayenne, lemon peel, tarragon and salt. Cover and let stand at room temperature for 30 minutes or until next day.

♦ **Select** large spinach leaves to line each of 8 individual salad plates. Sliver remaining spinach and mound onto plates.

♦ **Stir** dressing and spoon over each salad.

PEARS TARRAGON   *Yield: 6 to 8 servings*

1 (29 ounce) can pear halves,
    drained
1 egg
2 rounded tablespoons sugar
3 tablespoons tarragon
    vinegar
½ cup whipping cream
    Salt and pepper
    Paprika

♦ **Beat** egg and add sugar and vinegar. Place bowl of egg mixture in boiling water (or use double boiler) and beat until mixture starts to thicken. Remove from heat but continue to beat until it resembles thick cream. Season and cool.

♦ **Whip** cream and fold into cooled dressing.

♦ **Cover** each pear with dressing and top with paprika.

MINTED ORANGE AND GRAPEFRUIT SALAD   *Yield:3 to 4 servings*

8 fresh mint leaves
4 teaspoons sugar
2 navel oranges, peeled and
  cubed
1 white grapefruit, sectioned
Mint leaves for garnish

♦ **Crush** mint leaves in sugar
  and toss with fruit.
♦ **Chill** for at least one-half hour
  before serving.

DRIZZLED ORANGES   *Yield: 4 servings*

4 thin-skinned and heavy
  juice oranges
⅛ cup olive oil
Fresh ground black pepper

♦ **Peel** oranges and slice one-half
  inch thick. Arrange the slices
  to slightly overlap on platter.
♦ **Drizzle** with olive oil and
  sprinkle generously with
  coarsely ground black pepper.

*This recipe is delicious served as a
salad with spicy Italian food.*

Cinnamon Oranges: Sprinkle
orange slices with cinnamon and
serve with pork roast.

ORANGE AMBROSIA   *Yield: 6 servings*

FRUIT
1 (11 ounce) can mandarin
  oranges, drained
1 (20 ounce) can pineapple
  chunks, drained
  Fresh fruits (white grapes,
  peaches, plums, bananas)
DRESSING
1 cup white grape juice
½ cup orange marmalade
¼ cup Grand Marnier

♦ **Combine** dressing ingredients
  in a jar and shake well.
♦ **Combine** fruits.
♦ **Pour** dressing over fruits and
  chill thoroughly.
♦ **Serve** in wide-rimmed
  champagne glasses garnished
  with sprigs of mint.

*Bananas should be added just before
serving.*

Fantastic Feta Salad •

Yield: 6 to 8 servings

SALAD

- ½ pound feta cheese, drained and crumbled
- ½ stalk celery, trimmed and sliced
- 1 small head cauliflower, cut in bite-size pieces
- 1 small bunch fresh spinach, torn into bite-size pieces
- ½ small red onion, peeled, sliced and separated into rings
- 1 small bunch parsley
- 1 cup Greek olives or black olives
- 1 (5 ounce) can sliced water chestnuts

DRESSING

- ½ cup olive oil
- 2 - 3 tablespoons balsamic or red wine vinegar
- ½ teaspoon dry mustard
- ½ teaspoon salt
- ¼ teaspoon fresh cracked black pepper
- ½ teaspoon minced garlic

♦ **Combine** dressing ingredients.
♦ **Mix** salad ingredients, toss with dressing and serve.

Broccoli Peanut Salad

Yield: 4 to 6 servings

SALAD

- 1 large bunch broccoli
- 12 slices crisp bacon, crumbled
- 1 cup raisins
- 1 small onion, diced
- 1 cup roasted Spanish peanuts

DRESSING

- 1 cup Miracle Whip (not mayonnaise)
- 2 tablespoons sugar
- 2 tablespoons balsamic vinegar

♦ **Combine** dressing ingredients.
♦ **Toss** dressing with salad ingredients. Stir in peanuts just before serving.

ZESTY ZUCCHINI SALAD

Yield: 4 to 6 servings

SALAD

1 zucchini, thinly sliced
1 tomato, diced
1 avocado, peeled and sliced
½ pound mushrooms, sliced
¼ cup chopped green onion

DRESSING

1 tablespoon sugar
1 teaspoon salt
½ teaspoon pepper
½ teaspoon marjoram leaves
4 tablespoons oil
2 tablespoons white wine vinegar

♦ **Mix** dressing ingredients.
♦ **Toss** salad with dressing and refrigerate. Serve within 6 hours.

BLACK-EYED PEA SALAD

Yield: 8 servings

SALAD

2 (15 ounce) cans black-eyed peas, drained
½ cup finely chopped parsley
¼ cup finely chopped green onion
1 cucumber, peeled, seeded and chopped
1 red bell pepper, chopped
½ cup finely chopped celery

DRESSING

1 teaspoon salt
¼ teaspoon pepper
½ teaspoon dry mustard
1 teaspoon celery seeds
2 tablespoons sugar
3 tablespoons olive oil
⅓ cup white wine vinegar

♦ **Mix** all salad ingredients.
♦ **Prepare** dressing by whisking ingredients together.
♦ **Toss** with pea mixture. Cover and refrigerate until well chilled.

Serve in summer with romaine lettuce leaves, fresh garden tomatoes and fresh basil.

Fireside Winter Salad ·

Yield: 6 servings

1 (16 ounce) can red kidney
   beans, drained and rinsed
   well
1 cup frozen black-eyed peas,
   thawed
½ cup pearl barley
1 teaspoon salt
2 cups water
1½ cups frozen corn kernels
⅓ cup finely chopped fresh
   parsley
2 tablespoons finely chopped
   fresh cilantro
2 tablespoons diced red onion
½ teaspoon crushed red
   pepper
3 tablespoons olive oil
½ teaspoon cumin
2 large limes, zest and juice

♦ **Combine** kidney beans and
   thawed peas in a bowl.
♦ **Simmer** barley in water and ½
   teaspoon salt in a saucepan for
   40 minutes. Drain and add to
   beans.
♦ **Cook** corn until tender-crisp,
   about 2 minutes. Drain and
   add to beans and barley.
♦ **Stir** in parsley, cilantro, onion
   and red pepper.
♦ **Whisk** together in a small
   bowl the oil, ½ teaspoon salt,
   lime zest and juice, and cumin.
   Pour over salad and toss
   gently.

 ## Snow Pea Salad

Yield: 6 to 8 servings

SALAD
12 - 16 ounces fresh (not frozen)
   pea pods, cooked until
   tender-crisp and chilled
1 cup cherry tomatoes, halved
1 (5 ounce) can sliced water
   chestnuts, drained
1 bunch scallions, chopped
DRESSING
⅓ cup vegetable oil
1 tablespoon lemon juice
1 tablespoon white wine
   vinegar
½ teaspoon salt
½ teaspoon sugar
1 clove garlic, minced

♦ **Place** pea pods, tomatoes,
   water chestnuts and scallions
   in a salad bowl.
♦ **Prepare** dressing by combining
   ingredients and mix well.
♦ **Toss** with dressing just before
   serving.

Chilled salad plates are a must.

BLEU CHEESE POTATO SALAD •

Yield: 10 to 12 servings

8 medium potatoes
2 tablespoons chopped parsley
3 green onions with tops, chopped
2½ teaspoons salt
1 cup sour cream
½ cup slivered almonds, toasted
¼ teaspoon white pepper
8 ounces bleu cheese (or to taste)
¼ cup wine vinegar
3 eggs, hard-cooked
Bacon, crumbled for garnish

♦ **Boil** and peel potatoes. Cool and dice.
♦ **Combine** remaining ingredients.
♦ **Garnish** with crumbled bacon and refrigerate.

For the bleu cheese lover! Unique and delicious!

TERRITORY TOMATOES •

Yield: 1½ cups marinade

3 - 6 tomatoes, sliced
⅓ cup tarragon vinegar
⅓ cup chopped onion
1 teaspoon chopped cilantro
⅔ cup olive oil
1 teaspoon salt
½ teaspoon pepper
½ teaspoon marjoram
¼ cup chopped parsley
¼ cup chopped chives

♦ **Arrange** tomato slices in a shallow glass dish.
♦ **Combine** remaining ingredients and pour over tomatoes. Cover and marinate in refrigerator for at least 5 hours.

Tomatoes are better the second day; more tomatoes may be added the second day.

MARINATED SPAGHETTI •

Yield: 6 to 8 servings

10 ounces thin spaghetti,
cooked al dente
½ cup sweet pickle juice
1 garlic clove, minced
1½ teaspoons salt
2 tablespoons parsley
2 ribs celery, chopped
8 ounces Italian dressing
⅛ teaspoon red pepper
½ teaspoon caraway seed
1 teaspoon celery seed
1 tablespoon poppy seed
3 green onions, chopped

♦ **Mix** together all ingredients
except spaghetti.
♦ **Pour** over spaghetti and toss.
Marinate overnight.

CURRIED RICE SALAD

Yield: 4 to 6 servings

SALAD
2 cups chilled cooked rice
1 medium green pepper,
shredded or chopped
2 tablespoons pimiento,
drained and chopped
2 tablespoons raisins or
currants
2 tablespoons chopped
parsley
2 green onions, chopped
DRESSING
4 tablespoons olive oil
1½ tablespoons wine vinegar
1½ teaspoons lemon juice
1 clove garlic, crushed
1½ teaspoons sugar
½ teaspoon curry powder
Salt and pepper to taste
Crisp greens
Green pepper rings for
garnish

♦ **Mix** salad ingredients.
♦ **Combine** dressing ingredients.
♦ **Pour** dressing mixture over
salad and mix thoroughly.
♦ **Arrange** in bowl and garnish
with crisp greens and green
pepper rings.

TALLGRASS TABOULI

Yield: 15 to 20 servings

1 pound package tabouli wheat (without ingredients added)
2 large firm, fresh tomatoes, chopped
1 large cucumber, peeled, seeded and chopped
1 large green pepper, chopped
2 bunches of green onions with tops, chopped
2 bunches of parsley, chopped
¼ cup fresh mint leaves, chopped (optional)
2 cloves garlic, minced
2 teaspoons salt
½ teaspoon fresh ground black pepper
½ cup olive oil
⅛ cup red wine vinegar
⅛ cup fresh lemon juice

♦ **Rinse** the wheat in cold water and drain well. Squeeze the wheat as dry as possible.
♦ **Mix** wheat, vegetables, mint and garlic.
♦ **Add** salt and pepper and stir in the vinegar and lemon juice. Add the olive oil. More may be added for moistness.
♦ **Refrigerate** for 24 to 48 hours.

Substitute 1 teaspoon Cajun seasoning, ½ teaspoon salt and ¼ teaspoon pepper for the salt and pepper for a spicy alternative.

GREEN CHILI RICE SALAD

Yield: 8 servings

3 cups cooked rice
½ yellow onion, chopped
4 green onions, chopped
2 ribs celery, chopped
2 hard-boiled eggs, chopped
½ cup sweet relish
1 (4 ounce) can green chilies, chopped
1 cup mayonnaise
½ cup grated longhorn cheese
1 teaspoon paprika
Dash cayenne pepper
Salt and pepper to taste

♦ **Mix** together all ingredients. Chill to allow flavors to blend.

ORIENTAL SALAD WITH SPICY GINGER SAUCE

Yield: 6 to 8 servings

SALAD

2 cups each: shredded lettuce, red cabbage, spinach
1 cucumber, diced
4 - 6 green onions, shredded lengthwise
1 tablespoon chopped cilantro
1 - 2 carrots, shredded
4 chicken breasts, cooked and shredded
1 cup fresh bean sprouts (optional)
1 cup chopped roasted peanuts

DRESSING

3 tablespoons vegetable oil
3 tablespoons rice vinegar
1½ tablespoons low-sodium soy sauce
1 tablespoon sesame oil
1 - 2 teaspoons fresh minced ginger
2 cloves garlic, minced
1 teaspoon sugar
½ teaspoon chili oil or dash cayenne pepper

♦ **Mix** dressing ingredients and let stand for 2 hours to blend flavors.

♦ **Combine** salad ingredients, add dressing and toss.

♦ **Sprinkle** peanuts on top of salad when served.

Russian Chicken Potato Salad

Yield: 8 servings

Salad

- 4 boneless, skinless chicken breasts, approximately 1½ pounds
- 1 large onion, peeled and quartered
- 2 teaspoons salt
- 1 pound small new potatoes
- 3 hard-boiled eggs, peeled and chopped
- ½ cup dill pickle, chopped

Dressing

- ¾ cup mayonnaise
- ¾ cup sour cream
- 2 tablespoons fresh snipped dill
- ½ teaspoon black pepper
  Capers
  Lettuce leaves
  Tomato wedges or halved cherry tomatoes

♦ **Prepare** dressing by mixing sour cream, mayonnaise, black pepper and 1 tablespoon dill together.

♦ **Place** chicken, onion and salt in a pot with 1½ quarts water. Bring to a boil. Partially cover, reduce heat and simmer gently for 20 minutes. Remove chicken, cool slightly and shred meat.

♦ **Boil** potatoes until tender in same liquid as above (add water if necessary). Cool, skin and slice.

♦ **Combine** half of dressing with chicken, potatoes, eggs and pickles.

♦ **Line** a serving platter with lettuce leaves. Mound salad on lettuce and "frost" with the rest of the dressing. Sprinkle with remaining dill and decorate with drained capers and tomato wedges or halves.

CHICKEN AND ASPARAGUS PASTA SALAD   *Yield: 4 to 6 servings*

SALAD

12 ounces dry rotelle or fusilli pasta

2 boneless, skinless chicken breasts

1 pound asparagus

6 water chestnuts, sliced

½ cup coarsely chopped walnuts

DRESSING

½ cup olive oil

½ cup lemon juice

2 cloves garlic, pressed

1 teaspoon dried tarragon

Salt and white pepper to taste

♦ **Cook** the pasta al dente, drain and rinse. Toss pasta with a little olive oil and set aside.

♦ **Bake** chicken breasts at 350° for about 45 minutes or until done. Allow the chicken to cool and slice into one-inch strips.

♦ **Steam** asparagus until tender. Cool and cut into one-inch pieces.

♦ **Combine** pasta, chicken, asparagus, water chestnuts and walnuts in a large bowl.

♦ **Mix** all of dressing ingredients and pour half over the salad and toss well. Add more dressing if desired.

♦ **Refrigerate** salad until ready to serve.

SOUTHWESTERN PASTA SALAD •   *Yield: 6 servings*

1 (16 ounce) package penne or bowtie pasta, uncooked

Lettuce leaves

1 (15 ounce) can black beans, rinsed and drained

1 (8¾ ounce) can whole kernel corn, rinsed and drained

1 sweet red pepper, chopped

3 green onions, sliced

¼ cup chopped fresh cilantro

DRESSING

1 (8 ounce) carton nonfat sour cream

1 (16 ounce) jar mild thick-and-chunky salsa

½ teaspoon ground cumin

2 cloves garlic, minced

♦ **Combine** all dressing ingredients; chill.

♦ **Cook** pasta according to package directions; drain. Rinse with cold water and drain.

♦ **Combine** pasta and 1¾ cups dressing; toss gently. Chill.

♦ **Spoon** pasta mixture onto a lettuce-lined serving platter. Top with black beans and next 4 ingredients. Garnish with fresh cilantro sprigs, if desired. Serve with remaining dressing.

BLACK BEAN SALAD WITH GRILLED CHICKEN BREASTS

Yield: 6 servings

SALAD

6 boneless, skinless chicken breasts, marinated and grilled

2 (15 ounce) cans black beans, drained

1 (11 ounce) can sweet corn, drained

1 small green pepper, diced

1 medium tomato, chopped

1 bunch green onions, chopped

1 teaspoon fresh cilantro, chopped

2 tablespoons canned chopped green chilies

DRESSING

¼ cup extra-virgin olive oil

¼ cup lime juice

2 cloves garlic, minced

¼ teaspoon chili powder

¼ teaspoon salt

MARINADE

½ cup lime juice

½ cup olive oil

♦ **Marinate** chicken breasts for at least 2 hours. Grill on outdoor or indoor grill.

♦ **Combine** black beans with all other ingredients.

♦ **Mix** dressing ingredients and pour over salad. Allow to sit several hours or overnight.

Serve on lettuce leaf, placing sliced, grilled chicken on top of bean salad. Top with salsa or specialty salsa such as raspberry. Serve with corn chips.

AMARETTO CHICKEN SALAD

Yield: 6 servings

SALAD

4 cups diced cooked chicken

1 (15 ounce) can crushed pineapple

¾ cup chopped celery

½ cup slivered almonds, toasted

½ cup mayonnaise

Pineapple rings

DRESSING

1 cup mayonnaise

¼ cup amaretto

♦ **Stir** dressing ingredients together.

♦ **Combine** chicken, crushed pineapple, celery, half of the almonds (save half for garnish) and mayonnaise. Chill for several hours.

♦ **Serve** on lettuce leaves with pineapple rings. Top with dressing and sprinkle with almonds.

PASTA FRUIT SALAD

Yield: 4 to 6 servings

1⅓ cups rotini, uncooked
2 cups chopped cooked
   chicken (2 large breasts)
1½ cups sliced celery
1 cup seedless green grapes,
   halved
¼ cup chopped green pepper
¼ cup chopped purple onion
1 (11 ounce) can mandarin
   oranges, drained
1 (8 ounce) can sliced water
   chestnuts, drained
¼ cup prepared buttermilk
   ranch dressing
¼ cup mayonnaise
Salt and pepper to taste
1 cup slivered almonds,
   toasted

♦ **Cook** pasta and drain. Rinse with cold water; drain.
♦ **Combine** all ingredients except dressing and mayonnaise. Toss.
♦ **Combine** dressing, mayonnaise and seasonings. Pour over pasta mixture, tossing gently. Cover and chill.
♦ **Sprinkle** with toasted almonds before serving.

CHICKEN SALAD ROYALE

Yield: 8 to 10 servings

SALAD
4 cups cooked cubed white
   chicken (6 breasts)
1 (8 ounce) can sliced water
   chestnuts
1 (15 ounce) can pineapple
   chunks
3 ribs celery, diced
1 bunch green onions, sliced
½ cup golden raisins
   (optional)
1 (3 ounce) can chow mein
   noodles
DRESSING
1 cup mayonnaise
1 cup sour cream
1 teaspoon curry powder
¼ cup Major Grey's chutney

♦ **Mix** all ingredients, except noodles, with dressing and chill several hours or overnight.
♦ **Mix** in chow mein noodles right before serving. Serve over lettuce.

GRILLED CHICKEN AND SPINACH SALAD • WITH RASPBERRY DRESSING

Yield: 4 servings

SALAD

8 cups torn spinach

4 boneless, skinless chicken breast halves (1¼ pounds), grilled and sliced

1 (8 ounce) can sliced water chestnuts, drained
Toasted almonds (optional)

DRESSING

1 pint raspberries, or individually frozen raspberries

1 (8 ounce) package reduced-fat cream cheese

3 tablespoons raspberry vinegar or white wine vinegar

3 tablespoons sugar

♦ **Prepare** dressing in blender by combining ½ cup raspberries, cream cheese, vinegar and sugar until well combined.

♦ **Arrange** spinach on individual serving plates and top with sliced chicken. Sprinkle remaining raspberries and water chestnuts over chicken. Drizzle dressing on top and sprinkle with toasted almonds.

HEARTS OF PALM AND SHRIMP SALAD •

Yield: 6 servings

SALAD

1 (14 ounce) can hearts of palm, drained
Romaine lettuce leaves

DRESSING

2 tablespoons white wine vinegar

4 tablespoons olive oil or salad oil

3 tablespoons minced green onion

⅓ pound small shrimp, cooked
Salt

♦ **Prepare** dressing by combining vinegar, oil, green onion, shrimp and salt to taste.

♦ **Cut** each heart of palm stalk crosswise into ½ inch thick slices; place in deep bowl.

♦ **Mix** dressing gently with hearts of palm; cover and chill for 2 to 6 hours.

♦ **Arrange** several romaine leaves on each of 6 salad plates. Spoon equal portions of hearts of palm mixture onto lettuce.

AVOCADO SHRIMP SALAD •
Yield: 6 to 8 servings

SALAD
2 pounds medium-size
shrimp
1 large avocado, cubed
Leaf, romaine or Boston
lettuce, shredded

DRESSING
½ cup olive oil
¼ cup white wine vinegar
2 tablespoons lemon juice
½ teaspoon garlic salt
⅛ teaspoon seasoned pepper
½ cup minced green onion

♦ **Place** shrimp in a pan, cover
with boiling water and simmer
5 to 8 minutes or until shrimp
turn pink. Shell and devein
shrimp.
♦ **Place** shrimp and avocado in
bowl.
♦ **Mix** dressing ingredients and
pour over shrimp and avocado
to coat well. Cover and chill 1
to 2 hours.
♦ **Lift** shrimp and avocado from
dressing and serve on platter
with shredded lettuce. Use
remaining dressing as needed.

TUNA TO SHARE
Yield: 8 individual molds or 1 (8 inch) square Pyrex baking dish.

2 packages Knox gelatin
1 can mushroom soup
1 (8 ounce) package cream
cheese, softened
¾ cup mayonnaise
2 tablespoons lemon juice
½ teaspoon Mister Mustard
2 (6 ounce) cans solid water-
packed tuna
1 cup chopped celery
Green olives, sliced
(optional)

♦ **Dissolve** gelatin in ½ cup cold
water. Heat in pan of warm
water until completely
dissolved.
♦ **Heat** mushroom soup in a
medium saucepan.
♦ **Add** cream cheese, gelatin
mixture, mayonnaise, lemon
juice, mustard, tuna and
celery. Mix well.
♦ **Pour** into mold that may be
lined with stuffed green olive
slices.
♦ **Refrigerate** until firm.

SALMON WITH CUCUMBERS

Yield: 10 to 12 servings

CUCUMBER SALAD

2 medium cucumbers, thinly sliced
1 small onion, thinly sliced
1 tablespoon coarse salt
1 tablespoon minced fresh dill
6 tablespoons white wine vinegar
2 tablespoons sugar

SALMON MOLD

1 envelope unflavored gelatin
¼ cup cold water
½ cup boiling water
¼ cup mayonnaise
¼ cup sour cream
1 tablespoon grated onion
1 teaspoon paprika
1 tablespoon capers
2 cups cooked salmon
½ cup heavy cream

♦ **Combine** cucumber, onion slices and salt. Set aside for 2 hours. Rinse under cold water and drain well. Toss with dill.

♦ **Heat** vinegar and sugar until sugar dissolves. Pour over cucumbers and toss well. Refrigerate until well chilled.

♦ **Soften** gelatin in cold water. Add boiling water and stir to dissolve. Cool. Add mayonnaise, sour cream, minced onion and paprika. Whisk well and stir in capers.

♦ **Mash** salmon finely with fork or process briefly in food processor. Do not over process.

♦ **Stir** salmon into gelatin mixture. Whip cream and fold into salmon mixture. Spoon into heavily buttered, five-cup ring mold. Chill at least 4 hours or until set.

♦ **Unmold** salmon onto a platter and place a bowl of the cucumber salad in the center of the ring.

DENIM & DIAMOND STEAK SALAD •

Yield: 6 to 8 servings

SALAD

2 pounds leftover (rare to medium) steak or roast beef, cut diagonally in strips
1 sweet red onion, sliced thinly
2 large avocados, sliced and cut into large chunks
1 small red bell pepper, sliced
6 - 8 fresh mushrooms, sliced
2 - 3 fresh Italian tomatoes, cut in wedges
4 tablespoons chopped fresh parsley
2 cups uncooked pasta

DRESSING

¾ cup red wine vinegar
3 teaspoons Dijon mustard
2 teaspoons salt
1½ tablespoons chopped parsley
¾ cup canola oil
6 tablespoons olive oil

♦ **Mix** in blender the vinegar, mustard, salt and parsley; slowly add oils.
♦ **Marinate** beef and onions in a portion of the dressing (overnight if desired).
♦ **Cook** pasta 3 to 4 hours before serving. Cool.
♦ **Add** avocados, pepper, mushrooms, tomatoes, parsley, cooked pasta, beef and onions, and more dressing as desired; toss and chill.
♦ **Serve** on a bed of lettuce.

AVOCADO DRESSING •

Yield: 6 servings

1 ripe avocado
1 tablespoon chopped green onion
1 clove garlic, crushed
½ cup chopped celery
¼ teaspoon Tabasco
¼ teaspoon salt
1 tablespoon Dijon mustard
3 tablespoons wine vinegar
½ cup olive oil

♦ Prepare dressing by mashing the avocado with fork. Add green onion, celery and garlic. Whisk together Tabasco, salt, mustard and vinegar. Slowly whisk in olive oil. Stir into avocado mixture and refrigerate at least two hours.
♦ Pour over greens.

Great with Mexican or spicy food.

EASY VINAIGRETTE

Yield: 10 to 12 ounces

Salt
Pepper
¼ - ½ teaspoon garlic powder
½ teaspoon mustard powder
or 1 teaspoon Dijon
mustard
Red wine vinegar
Oil

♦ **Cover** the bottom of a 10-12 ounce glass jar with salt and add 10 pinches of pepper. Add garlic powder and mustard.

♦ **Fill** bottom quarter of glass jar with red wine vinegar. Fill the rest of the jar with oil. Cover jar tightly and shake vigorously.

This is good on salad or as a vinaigrette sauce for artichokes or asparagus.

GREEN GODDESS DRESSING

Yield: 8 servings

1 clove garlic, minced
2 tablespoons chopped fresh chives
1 tablespoon anchovy paste
2 tablespoons chopped fresh tarragon
1 tablespoon lemon juice
2 tablespoons white wine vinegar
½ cup chopped fresh parsley
½ teaspoon minced capers (optional)
½ cup sour cream
1 cup mayonnaise
Salt and pepper to taste

♦ **Combine** ingredients in an electric blender and blend until smooth. Season to taste with salt and pepper. Cover and refrigerate.

GERMAN-STYLE DRESSING

Yield: 1½ cups

1 tablespoon flour
¾ cup sugar
½ teaspoon salt
¼ teaspoon black pepper
1 egg
1 cup cider vinegar
1 tablespoon bacon drippings
2 tablespoons mayonnaise

♦ **Mix** dry ingredients in a small saucepan. Stir in egg. Add vinegar a little at a time to mix well.
♦ **Cook** over medium-low heat until it thickens and cooks about 3 minutes, stirring often to prevent sticking.
♦ **Remove** from heat, stir in bacon drippings and mayonnaise.
♦ **Pour** over salad and mix well.

Bacon drippings may be substituted with salad oil and 1 teaspoon real bacon bits.

This dressing has an authentic German flavor and is good on potato salad, three-bean salad or cabbage slaw.

ROQUEFORT SALAD DRESSING ·

Yield: 2 cups

1 cup mayonnaise
½ cup buttermilk
¼ cup sour cream
¼ cup cottage cheese
2 cloves garlic, minced
3 ounce wedge Roquefort cheese
Juice of ½ lemon
Salt and cracked pepper to taste

♦ **Mix** all ingredients thoroughly in blender.

HONEY PLUM DRESSING

Yield: 2 cups

2 fresh California plums, cut
  into chunks
¼ cup honey
¼ cup plain no-fat yogurt
¼ cup lite mayonnaise
½ cup sliced almonds, toasted

♦ **Purée** honey and plums in blender or food processor.
♦ **Blend** in yogurt and mayonnaise. Chill.
♦ **Spoon** over individual fruit salad servings and garnish with almonds.

MUSTARD VINAIGRETTE SALAD DRESSING

Yield: 1 cup

2 tablespoons Dijon mustard
½ - ¾ cup olive oil
1 tablespoon fresh lemon
  juice
5 teaspoons white vinegar
¼ teaspoon minced garlic
½ teaspoon fresh basil (or ¼
  teaspoon dried)
½ teaspoon fresh thyme (or ¼
  teaspoon dried)
¼ teaspoon salt
¼ teaspoon fresh tarragon (or
  ⅛ teaspoon dried)
  Freshly ground black
  pepper to taste
  Pinch of sugar

♦ **Combine** all ingredients in blender and blend well.

SOUPS & SANDWICHES

FRANK PHILLIPS MANSION—Built in
1908, this 26-room Greek Revival home
of Frank and Jane Phillips was deeded to
the Oklahoma Historical Society
in November of 1973, marking Frank
Phillips' 100th birthday.

UNCLE FRANK

Of the many sizable oil companies born of the Osage Fields, only one, Phillips Petroleum Company, continues to operate in Bartlesville. Founded by Frank Phillips in 1917, the now-global corporation has interests in all areas of the petroleum industry, from pumping and drilling to the discovery of new uses for plastics and petrochemicals. Since the pioneer days of the oil industry, Phillips has remained the lifeblood of Jake Bartles' settlement at the bend in the Caney River.

Frank Phillips divided his business operations between New York City and Bartlesville and loved to entertain eastern financiers and businessmen at his Woolaroc Ranch. At his famous "Cow Thieves and Outlaws Reunions" he would treat them to all the delights of Indian Territory and Old West hospitality. Guests would be "held up" at the entrance by Phillips' friend Henry Wells, an authentic outlaw who had realized the error of his ways. Phillips always invited his many Indian friends, business associates and employees as well as reformed outlaws and cattle thieves. The spread was plentiful—buffalo steaks with all the trimmings and plenty of liquid refreshment.

"Uncle Frank," as he is still affectionately known, was an honest businessman and a fair employer. He and his wife "Aunt Jane" were extremely generous to the town in which they made their fortune. They funded many worthwhile philanthropies which continue to benefit the residents of Bartlesville and Oklahoma.

COLD PEACH SOUP

Yield: 4 servings

½ cup white Rhine wine
1 package frozen peaches or 2
    cups fresh peaches
Sugar, honey or granulated
    sugar substitute, to taste

♦ **Process** peaches, wine and
    sugar in a food processor using
    a steel blade.
♦ **Add** water to get desired
    consistency.
♦ **Serve** cold. Garnish with fresh
    mint sprigs.

SUMMERTIME STRAWBERRY SOUP

Yield: 8 servings

1 quart strawberries
½ cup plus 2 tablespoons
    powdered sugar
⅓ cup Grand Marnier
3 cups yogurt
1 cup whipping cream
1 tablespoon chopped mint
    leaves

♦ **Sprinkle** strawberries with
    two tablespoons sugar and
    Grand Marnier and chill one
    hour.
♦ **Blend** 10 strawberries in
    blender. Add remaining
    ingredients. Blend again and
    chill.
♦ **Slice** remaining berries and
    add when serving. Garnish
    with mint sprigs and serve
    very, very cold.

GARDEN GAZPACHO SOUP ❖

Yield: 8 servings

4 tomatoes, peeled, seeded
    and chopped
1 large cucumber, chopped
1 small to medium onion,
    chopped
1 green pepper, chopped
2 ribs celery, chopped
¼ - ½ cup chopped cilantro
    (optional)
1 quart tomato or V-8 juice
3 tablespoons wine vinegar
    (red or white)
2 tablespoons olive oil
¼ teaspoon garlic powder
1 teaspoon Worcestershire
    sauce
¼ cup lemon juice
Salt and pepper to taste
Dash of Tabasco

♦ **Combine** all ingredients.
♦ **Chill** several hours or
    overnight.
♦ **Serve** chilled. Garnish with a
    lemon slice or small celery
    stick with leaves on.

SHRIMP GAZPACHO

Yield: 6 servings

1 quart bottle clamato juice
¼ cup seeded, finely chopped cucumber
⅓ cup thinly sliced green onions
2 tablespoons olive oil
2 tablespoons red wine vinegar
1 tablespoon sugar
1 cup tomato juice
1 clove garlic, crushed
½ teaspoon Tabasco
2 tablespoons lemon juice
½ - ¾ pound tiny cooked shrimp
Salt and pepper to taste
1 avocado, finely chopped
4 ounces cream cheese, well chilled and finely chopped
Fresh chives, finely chopped

♦ **Place** all ingredients, except shrimp, avocado, cream cheese and chives in a bowl and mix well.
♦ **Add** the shrimp. Add salt and pepper to taste. Chill well (at least 8 hours).
♦ **Ladle** the soup into bowls and top with the avocado and cream cheese pieces. Garnish with fresh chives.

CREAM OF ASPARAGUS • SOUP WITH CRABMEAT

Yield: 8 to 10 servings

1 onion, chopped
2 tablespoons margarine
3 cans cream of potato soup √ (with 3 cans water)
1 can tender asparagus
1 tablespoon white wine Worcestershire sauce
1 teaspoon white pepper
1 pint heavy cream
2 cans crabmeat

♦ **Sauté** onions in margarine in a soup pot.
♦ **Add** cream of potato soup with water. Add asparagus. Heat thoroughly.
♦ **Purée** soup in a blender.
♦ **Pour** soup back into the soup pot and add Worcestershire sauce and white pepper. Add heavy cream. Season to taste.
♦ **Add** crabmeat 10 minutes before serving.

SHRIMP AND SCALLOP SOUP •

Yield: 8 cups

½ pound fresh shrimp
4 cups chicken broth
1 rib celery, diced
1 medium onion, chopped
1 medium red or green
  pepper, seeded and
  chopped
1 (16 ounce) can chopped
  stewed tomatoes
2 medium potatoes, peeled
  and diced
½ pound fresh scallops
½ cup skim milk
½ teaspoon paprika
¾ teaspoon salt
½ teaspoon ground red
  pepper
1 tablespoon lemon juice

♦ **Peel** and devein shrimp, reserving shells. Chop shrimp and set aside.

♦ **Combine** shrimp shells and chicken stock in a large saucepan; bring to a boil and cook until mixture is reduced to 3 cups (about ½ hour); set aside.

♦ **Coat** a Dutch oven with non-stick vegetable spray. Place over low heat until hot. Add celery, onion, and red or green pepper and sauté lightly, about 5 minutes. Add stewed tomatoes and potatoes. Cover and cook 10 minutes, stirring occasionally.

♦ **Strain** the shrimp stock through a fine sieve into the Dutch oven; bring to a boil, cover, reduce heat, and simmer 15 minutes. Stir in scallops and shrimp and simmer 2 minutes or until seafood is done, stirring occasionally.

♦ **Place** 1 cup stock mixture in electric blender; add milk, salt and paprika and process until puréed. Stir purée into soup and season with red pepper and lemon juice.

poff - Tom
creamy - W.Wine

Lobster Bisque •

Yield: 6 servings

5 cups of stock, either shrimp or fish
½ cup butter
½ cup flour
1 cup whipping cream (do not substitute)
⅔ cup sherry
¼ teaspoon cayenne or to taste
¼ teaspoon white pepper
1 teaspoon salt
¾ pound lump lobster meat

♦ **Cook** butter and flour (roux) in a saucepan for 5 to 7 minutes on low to medium heat, stirring constantly. Do not allow roux to brown.
♦ **Whisk** roux into stock and cook until bisque thickens, about 3 or 4 minutes.
♦ **Add** cream, sherry, cayenne, white pepper and salt. Simmer and then cook for a few minutes.
♦ **Fold** in lobster and sprinkle with a light touch of white pepper, parsley or cayenne.

Stock may be made by boiling 1 pound of shrimp shells, heads and tails in 5 cups of water for 45 minutes.

Crab is a delicious substitute for the lobster.

Chicken Cheese Soup

Yield: 8 servings

4 chicken breast halves
2 cups water
4 potatoes, cubed
1 rib celery, sliced
1 carrot, grated
¼ cup chopped onion
3 tablespoons butter
2 cans cream of chicken soup
1 chicken bouillon cube
16 ounces Velveeta cheese
Dash salt and pepper

♦ **Cook** chicken with water in a stock pot until done. Remove chicken, cool, cube and set aside.
♦ **Boil** potatoes, celery, carrot and onion in the chicken broth until tender.
♦ **Add** butter, soup and chicken bouillon cube; heat thoroughly.
♦ **Add** the cheese and stir until completely melted.
♦ **Stir** in chicken, salt and pepper.

CHANGE IN THE WEATHER • SEAFOOD CHOWDER

Yield: 14 to 16 servings

2 (19 ounce) cans Chunky New England Clam Chowder
1 pound cooked shrimp
1 pound fresh or frozen scallops
1 pound fresh or frozen crabmeat
2 (6½ ounce) cans chopped clams
1 pound frozen haddock or cod
1 pint skim milk
½ bunch celery, finely chopped
1 green pepper, finely chopped
1 red pepper, finely chopped
1 bunch green onions, finely chopped
1 (5 ounce) can water chestnuts
Pinch of dill weed
¼ - ½ pound margarine
1 cup chicken bouillon

♦ **Pour** cans of chowder in large kettle. Add shrimp, scallops, crab and clams.
♦ **Boil** haddock or cod for 6 minutes with dill weed. Cut in chunks and add to chowder.
♦ **Add** remaining ingredients and heat very slowly.

Lemon Chicken Soup

Yield: 8 servings

3 - 4 pound stewing chicken
2½ quarts cold water
1 tablespoon salt
2 tablespoons butter
4 ribs celery
1 onion
2 carrots
2½ cups cooked rice
3 eggs
¼ - ½ cup fresh lemon juice
2 tablespoons dried parsley

♦ **Stew** chicken in cold water with coarsely chopped fresh vegetables for about 1½ hours or until chicken is tender. Remove chicken and cut meat into serving size pieces.
♦ **Strain** broth, discarding vegetables, and return to pot, setting chicken aside.
♦ **Heat** broth to boiling.
♦ **Beat** eggs well and stir in lemon juice.
♦ **Add** 2 cups of hot broth gradually to the egg mixture to temper. Incorporate this mixture gradually into the soup.
♦ **Add** chicken, rice, salt and pepper to taste.

For a thicker soup, add a mixture of ⅓ cup of flour and ⅓ cup of broth, or use a can of cream of chicken soup.

Garnish with a slice of lemon sprinkled with parsley.

Wild Rice Soup With Chicken

Yield: 6 to 8 servings

½ cup wild rice, rinsed
4 cups defatted chicken broth
½ cup diced celery
½ cup diced carrots
1 small onion, chopped
¼ cup sliced almonds
¼ teaspoon lemon pepper
1 cup cubed chicken
WHITE SAUCE
1 cup 1% milk
1 tablespoon cornstarch

♦ **Simmer** rice, broth, and vegetables for 30 to 40 minutes.
♦ **Heat** together white sauce ingredients. Stir slowly to thicken. Add to vegetables.
♦ **Add** remaining ingredients. Heat through and serve immediately.

Yogurt may be substituted for white sauce.

AUNT JANE'S JAMBALAYA °

Yield: 10 to 12 servings

1 tablespoon butter
1 pound boneless chicken breasts, cut into 1½ inch chunks
½ pound andouille or chorizo sausage, cut into ¼ inch rounds
½ pound smoked ham, cut into ½ inch chunks
12 (or more) medium shrimp, shelled, deveined and halved
1 medium onion, chopped
1 medium green pepper, chopped
2 medium celery ribs, chopped
5 cloves garlic, finely chopped
1 tablespoon Creole meat seasoning
1 (28 ounce) can Italian peeled tomatoes, with juices
1 cup chicken stock or canned broth
5 bay leaves
2 tablespoons Worcestershire sauce
1 tablespoon Tabasco
½ teaspoon paprika
½ teaspoon salt
2 cups long-grain rice
2 scallions, thinly sliced

♦ **Melt** the butter in a large flameproof casserole or heavy kettle over moderately high heat. Add the chicken and sauté, stirring occasionally for 2 minutes. Add sausage and ham and cook 2 minutes longer.

♦ **Add** the onion, bell pepper, celery and garlic. Stir in the Creole meat seasoning and the tomatoes with juices and cook for 1 minute.

♦ **Add** the chicken stock, bay leaves, Worcestershire sauce, Tabasco, paprika, salt and shrimp. Bring to a boil, reduce the heat and simmer for 5 minutes.

♦ **Add** the rice and bring to a boil. Reduce the heat to moderately low. Stir in the scallions. Cook uncovered for 12 minutes. Cover, remove from the heat and let stand until the rice is tender (about 10 minutes).

This may be prepared a day ahead and reheated, covered for one hour in a low oven. If more liquid is needed, add a small amount of V-8 or tomato juice.

DUCK SEASON GUMBO

Yield: 6 to 8 servings

2 ducks
4 ribs of celery, chopped
1 medium onion, chopped
1 cup white rice
1 - 1½ cups frozen sliced okra
    Salt and pepper to taste
    Filé Gumbo Spice to taste

♦ **Clean** ducks and place in a large soup kettle. Cover with water and add half of the onion and celery, salt and pepper. Cook uncovered for 2 to 3 hours until the meat is loose from the bone.

♦ **Remove** duck from the broth, debone and cut into bite size pieces.

♦ **Save** the broth and add water if necessary to make 2½ cups of broth.

♦ **Return** duck to broth and add rice and remaining celery and onion.

♦ **Cook** over low heat for 10 minutes; add frozen okra and continue to cook until rice is done.

♦ **Season** to taste.

CREAM OF ZUCCHINI SOUP

Yield: 4 servings

1 pound peeled zucchini, sliced (about 4 cups)
½ cup water
1 teaspoon salt
½ teaspoon sugar
2 tablespoons chopped onion
2 tablespoons butter
2 tablespoons flour
2 cups milk
    Black pepper to taste

♦ **Place** zucchini, water and a ½ teaspoon salt and sugar in a pan and bring to a boil. Simmer 15 minutes until zucchini is tender. Purée in blender.

♦ **Cook** onion in butter until tender; blend in flour, remaining ½ teaspoon salt and pepper.

♦ **Add** the milk and zucchini, cook and stir until the soup thickens.

HUNGRY HUNTER'S PHEASANT SOUP

Yield: 6 to 8 servings

1 tablespoon olive oil
1 tablespoon unsalted butter
3 carrots, diced
2 medium-size yellow onions, diced
3 ribs celery, diced
1 medium-size parsnip, peeled and diced
3 cloves garlic, minced
4 cups canned or fresh chicken broth, defatted
3 cups canned plum tomatoes, drained and crushed
1 cup dried lentils, rinsed
1 (1½ to 2 pound) pheasant, quartered, with backbone removed and reserved
6 tablespoons parsley
1 tablespoon fresh rosemary, chopped; or 1 teaspoon dried
¼ teaspoon ground allspice
Freshly ground black pepper to taste
Salt to taste
½ - ¾ cup dry sherry

♦ **Heat** oil and butter in a soup pot. Add carrots, onions, celery, parsnip and garlic. Cook covered over medium heat to wilt vegetables. Stir once.

♦ **Add** broth, tomatoes, lentils, pheasant legs and backbone. Simmer partially covered for 15 minutes.

♦ **Add** pheasant breasts and simmer another 15 minutes. Remove legs and breasts and reserve. Leave backbone in pot.

♦ **Add** 4 tablespoons of parsley, rosemary, allspice, pepper and salt. Stir, cover and simmer another 20 minutes.

♦ **Remove** skin from pheasant and shred meat while soup simmers.

♦ **Remove** cover from soup, add shredded pheasant, sherry and remaining parsley. Serve immediately.

This recipe may be made with any poultry.

Crème de Tomate Duberry

Yield: 10 to 12 servings

3 pounds ripe tomatoes, peeled
3 tablespoons butter or margarine
3 large onions, chopped
3 large carrots, sliced
   Bay leaf
   Salt and pepper
3 tablespoons powdered sugar
2 strips lemon peel
   Zest of 3 oranges, saving a little for garnish
6 cups chicken broth, defatted
2 cups half-and-half
4 tablespoons butter
4 tablespoons flour

♦ **Sauté** onions in butter. Do not brown. Add all the remaining ingredients except the half-and-half, 4 tablespoons of butter and flour. Cook for 20 minutes.
♦ **Purée** mixture in processor and strain. Return to pan.
♦ **Mix** flour and butter together and form small balls for thickener. Add half-and-half gradually to soup, then thicken by stirring in one ball at a time until the desired thickness is attained.
♦ **Garnish** with basil and orange zest.

This soup may be served hot or cold.

Ten Carrot Soup

Yield: 6 to 8 servings

1 pound bacon, cooked crisp and drained
4 tablespoons butter or margarine
1 cup chopped onion
1 clove garlic, minced
10 carrots, peeled and chopped
5 potatoes, peeled and chopped
6 cups chicken broth
½ teaspoon salt
½ teaspoon sugar (optional)
½ teaspoon white pepper
1 cup half-and-half
   Sour cream
   Parsley

♦ **Sauté** onion and garlic in butter until tender.
♦ **Add** broth, carrots, potatoes, and seasonings and simmer until vegetables are cooked.
♦ **Blend** (in a blender) soup and bacon.
♦ **Reheat** soup in a soup pot. Add half-and-half; stir for one minute and serve.
♦ **Garnish** with a teaspoon of sour cream and a sprig of parsley.

TOMATO BASIL SOUP

Yield: 8 servings

4 cups tomatoes, peeled, cored and chopped (or 4 cups canned whole tomatoes, crushed)
4 cups tomato juice (or mixture of tomato juice and vegetable or chicken stock)
12 - 14 fresh basil leaves
1 cup heavy cream
¼ cup unsalted butter
¼ teaspoon cracked pepper
Salt to taste

♦ **Combine** tomatoes, juice and stock in a large sauce pan. Simmer over medium-low heat for 30 minutes.
♦ **Cool** slightly. In batches, purée with basil leaves in food processor.
♦ **Return** to saucepan. Add cream and butter and stir over low heat until butter melts.

RED PEPPER SOUP WITH FRESH DILL

Yield: 4 to 6 servings

4 large red bell peppers, chopped
2 medium onions, chopped
6 tablespoons butter
½ large potato, peeled and grated
2½ cups chicken stock
½ cup heavy cream
2 tablespoons fresh lemon juice
2 tablespoons chopped fresh dill
Ground black pepper
Salt (optional)

♦ **Melt** butter in a large saucepan. Add peppers and onions. Cover and cook for 35 to 45 minutes over medium heat.
♦ **Add** potato and chicken stock and bring to a boil. Simmer over low heat for 15 minutes.
♦ **Purée** the mixture in a food processor.
♦ **Return** to the pan and add cream, lemon juice, salt, pepper and fresh dill. Simmer briefly.

More cream may be added to make soup less thick, or whole milk may be used instead of cream.

May top with a spoonful of sour cream and garnish with dill sprigs.

OLD-FASHIONED MUSHROOM SOUP

Yield: 8 servings

1 pound fresh mushrooms
6 tablespoons butter or
   margarine, divided
2 cups finely chopped carrots
2 cups finely chopped celery
1 cup finely chopped onions
1 clove garlic, minced
2 (10½ ounce) cans condensed
   beef broth
3 (10½ ounce) soup cans
   water
3 tablespoons tomato paste
¼ teaspoon salt
   Pinch ground black pepper
4 sprigs parsley
   Celery leaves
1 bay leaf
3 tablespoons dry sherry
   Sour cream

♦ **Rinse**, pat dry and finely chop ½ pound of the mushrooms and slice remaining ½ pound. Set aside.

♦ **Melt** 4 tablespoons butter in a large saucepan. Add the chopped mushrooms; sauté 5 minutes. Add carrots, celery, onions and garlic; sauté 5 minutes. Stir in broth, water, tomato paste, salt and pepper.

♦ **Tie** together parsley, celery leaves and bay leaf; add to saucepan. Bring to the boiling point. Cover, reduce heat and simmer 1 hour. Remove and discard parsley, celery leaves, and bay leaf.

♦ **Purée** soup in a blender or food mill. Return to the saucepan.

♦ **Melt** remaining 2 tablespoons butter in a medium skillet. Add reserved sliced mushrooms; sauté 5 minutes. Add to soup along with sherry; reheat.

♦ **Serve** with a dollop of sour cream.

SOONER SOUP

Yield: 10 to 12 servings

1 - 2 pounds ground beef,
   browned
2 (10¾ ounce) cans
   minestrone soup
2 (15 ounce) cans ranch style
   beans
1 (10 ounce) can Rotel
1 (8 ounce) can tomato sauce
   Salt and pepper to taste

♦ **Brown** ground beef in a Dutch oven; drain. Add remaining ingredients. Heat for 20 minutes.

FRENCH ONION SOUP

Yield: 6 to 8 servings

24 small white onions, peeled and thinly sliced
½ cup butter
Sugar
6 cups heavy beef stock
¼ cup cognac
Salt and cracked pepper
6 - 8 slices French bread, toasted
Gruyère cheese, grated

♦ **Heat** butter in a large saucepan with a little sugar, add onion rings and cook gently over low heat, stirring constantly with a wooden spoon until golden brown.

♦ **Add** beef stock gradually and stir until soup begins to boil. Lower heat, cover pan, and simmer gently for about one hour.

♦ **Add** cognac, salt and pepper just before serving.

♦ **Serve** French bread heaped with Gruyère in each of the soup bowls.

CAJUN CORN SOUP

Yield: 12 servings

1 cup chopped onion
1 cup chopped green pepper
6 green onions, sliced
¼ cup cooking oil
½ cup flour
3 cups water
1 (14½ ounce) can Cajun-style stewed tomatoes
2 cups tomatoes, peeled and chopped
1 (6 ounce) can tomato paste
2 (16 ounce) packages frozen corn
3 cups cooked ham, cubed
1½ pounds fully cooked smoked sausage, sliced
Cayenne pepper to taste
Salt and pepper to taste

♦ **Sauté** onion, green pepper and green onion in oil until tender. Add flour and cook until bubbly.

♦ **Add** water and all tomatoes. Stir in corn, ham and sausage. Add seasonings.

♦ **Bring** to boil, reduce heat and simmer 1 hour.

GOOD NEIGHBOR CORN SOUP

Yield: 6 to 8 servings

4 cups fresh corn kernels or 1
  pound frozen sweet corn,
  thawed
¼ cup chopped onion
2 tablespoons butter
4 tablespoons flour
2 cups chicken broth
2 cups milk (2% or skim)
2 cups shredded Cheddar or
  Monterey Jack cheese
1 (4 ounce) can chopped
  green chilies
  Tortilla chips
½ cup bacon, cooked and
  crumbled
  Dash salt and pepper

♦ **Sauté** corn and onion in butter
  in a large stock pot, until
  tender.
♦ **Add** flour, salt and pepper.
  Cook 1 minute.
♦ **Add** broth gradually,
  alternating with milk, until
  thickened. Add cheese and
  green chilies; do not overheat.
♦ **Top** with crumbled bacon and
  tortilla chips.

MAINSTREET MINESTRONE •

Yield: 8 to 10 servings

8 - 10 tablespoons extra virgin
  olive oil
3 onions, thinly sliced
4 carrots, diced
2 ribs celery, diced
2 - 3 medium potatoes, peeled
  and diced
1 (16 ounce) can cannellini or
  other Italian white beans
2 medium zucchini, sliced
6 ounces fresh green beans
5 - 8 ounces savoy cabbage,
  shredded
6 cups beef broth (3 cans or 3
  beef stock cubes)
1 (16 ounce) can Italian
  tomatoes
1 serving spaghetti noodles,
  broken and uncooked
4 - 6 ounces shredded ham
  (optional)
  Parmesan cheese, grated

♦ **Cook** each vegetable with the
  olive oil in the order listed 2 to
  3 minutes before adding the
  next vegetable.
♦ **Add** beef broth, canned beans,
  tomatoes, and pasta. Simmer
  covered for at least 3 hours.
♦ **Top** with freshly grated
  Parmesan cheese. Serve with
  hot crusty bread.

*The secret to the rich flavor of this
soup is the long slow simmering of
the vegetables in the olive oil before
any liquid is added.*

BLACK BEAN SOUP WITH HAM •

Yield: 8 servings

1 cup chopped onion
⅓ cup chopped celery
½ cup chopped carrot
2 tablespoons butter
1 medium clove garlic, minced
¼ cup diced ham
2 quarts chicken stock
1¼ cups dried black beans, rinsed
1 bay leaf
1 sprig fresh thyme or ¼ teaspoon dried thyme
Salt and freshly ground pepper to taste
½ cup sour cream
1 small red bell pepper (¾ cup), cored, seeded and finely diced
1 tablespoon chopped fresh parsley

♦ **Cook** the onion, celery and carrot in butter over medium heat until soft but not brown. Add the garlic and ham and cook for 2 more minutes.

♦ **Add** the beans, chicken stock, bay leaf and thyme. Bring to a boil, reduce heat, cover and cook until the beans are very tender, about 2 hours. Season to taste with salt and pepper.

♦ **Remove** the bay leaf and thyme sprig, then purée the cooked beans and their liquid until very smooth. May do this in batches if necessary. Taste and correct seasonings.

♦ **Ladle** hot soup into warmed bowls. Top with a spoonful of sour cream, then sprinkle with diced peppers and parsley.

More garlic and ham may be added.

OIL BARON BEAN SOUP •

Yield: 8 to 10 servings

2½ - 3 cups mixed dried beans
1 (14½ ounce) can tomatoes
2 (10 ounce) cans Rotel
2 cups chopped celery
2 cups chopped onion
2 cloves garlic, minced
1 pound smoked sausage, sliced
2 chicken bouillon cubes
2 - 3 teaspoons Tabasco

♦ **Presoak** beans overnight in 2 to 3 quarts of water.

♦ **Drain** beans and place in a large soup pot. Add 2 quarts of water and all the other ingredients. Simmer until beans are tender (about 4 hours).

May be served over rice.

NORTH OF THE BORDER WHITE CHILI

Yield: 8 to 10 servings

1 pound large white beans or 4 (16 ounce) cans
6 cups chicken broth
2 cloves garlic, minced
2 medium onions, chopped and divided
1 tablespoon oil
2 (4½ ounce) cans chopped green chilies
2 teaspoons ground cumin
1½ teaspoons dried oregano
¼ teaspoon ground cloves
¼ teaspoon cayenne pepper
4 cups diced cooked chicken breasts
3 cups grated Monterey Jack cheese

♦ **Combine** beans, chicken broth, garlic and half of the onions in a large soup pot and bring to a boil. Reduce heat and simmer until beans are very soft, 3 hours or more. Add more chicken broth if necessary.
♦ **Sauté** remaining onions in oil until tender. Add chilies and seasonings and mix thoroughly. Add to bean mixture with chicken and simmer for 1 hour.
♦ **Serve** topped with grated cheese.

Serve with condiments such as chopped tomatoes, chopped parsley, chopped ripe olives, guacamole, chopped scallions, sour cream or tortilla chips.

NO-ALARM CHILI °

Yield: 10 to 12 servings

1 large onion, chopped
6 cloves garlic, crushed
3 ribs celery, chopped
1 cup chopped fresh parsley
6 large mushrooms, quartered
2 tablespoons olive oil
1½ pounds ground turkey
1 teaspoon each: dried thyme, rosemary, chili powder, and cumin
2 teaspoons dried oregano
¼ cup dry white wine
2 (28 ounce) cans crushed Italian tomatoes, with juice
1 (15½ ounce) can kidney beans
1 tablespoon cornstarch
¼ cup tomato paste

♦ **Sauté** chopped vegetables and garlic in oil until tender.
♦ **Add** turkey and all seasonings. Stir constantly for 5 minutes.
♦ **Add** wine and tomatoes. Heat thoroughly. Add beans.
♦ **Mix** together cornstarch and tomato paste then add to chili.
♦ **Cover** and simmer up to one hour.

If desired, thin with tomato juice or chicken broth.

BLACK BART'S VEGETARIAN CHILI

Yield: 6 to 8 servings

1 pound dry black beans
1 pound fresh whole
  mushrooms, sliced
4 cloves garlic, chopped
8 small zucchini and/or
  yellow crookneck squash
8 fresh Roma tomatoes
5 ribs celery
2 bell peppers (green, red or
  yellow), seeded and
  chopped
2 large yellow onions
½ cup olive oil
1 (6 ounce) can tomato paste
2 teaspoons salt
1 teaspoon sugar
1 tablespoon ground cumin
2 tablespoons chili powder
1 tablespoon Italian herbs
1 - 4 small pickled jalapeño
  peppers, seeded and
  chopped

◆ **Cook** black beans in plain water for 2 hours or until soft. Set aside.

◆ **Wash,** trim and coarsely chop all the vegetables.

◆ **Heat** olive oil in a stock pot. Sauté garlic and mushrooms. Remove the mushrooms and set aside.

◆ **Sauté** the vegetables in batches in the stock pot, stirring carefully to keep pieces whole. Put sautéed mushrooms back in the pot.

◆ **Add** seasonings and tomato paste. Add drained beans and enough "bean water" to make the consistency right for chili.

◆ **Simmer** gently until vegetables are done. Check seasonings and add jalapeños until "heat" is to your taste.

◆ **Serve** with sour cream and/or grated cheese and cornbread.

CHICKEN TORTILLA SOUP

Yield: 8 servings

1 medium onion, chopped
1½ teaspoons minced garlic
4 cups Healthy Request fat-free chicken broth
1 (10½ ounce) can Rotel (do not drain)
1 (16 ounce) can stewed tomatoes (do not drain)
1 teaspoon chili powder
4 boneless, skinless cooked chicken breasts, diced
5 flour tortillas, cut into ¼-½ inch strips
1 can fat-free refried beans
1 (8 ounce) package grated nonfat Cheddar
8 tablespoons fat-free sour cream
1 teaspoon Mexican seasoning

♦ **Sauté** onion and garlic in ¼ cup chicken broth in a large nonstick skillet.
♦ **Add** cans of tomatoes, Rotel, chicken broth, chili powder, Mexican seasoning and chicken.
♦ **Heat** to boiling, reduce heat and simmer 20 to 30 minutes partially covered.
♦ **Add** the tortilla strips and simmer 15 minutes longer.
♦ **Garnish** each serving with grated cheese and 1 tablespoon of sour cream.

SUMMERTIME SANDWICHES

Yield: 1 sandwich

Crusty French bread, sliced
Butter
Cucumbers, sliced
Sweet red onion, sliced
New York sharp Cheddar cheese, sliced
Red or green bell peppers, sliced
Radishes, thinly sliced
Black pepper, freshly ground

♦ **Layer** vegetables and cheese between two slices of buttered French bread. Sprinkle with lots of pepper.

SOPA DEL SOL

Yield: 8 to 10 servings

6 cups chicken broth or 3 (16 ounce) cans
½ cup tequila (optional)
3 cups chopped cooked chicken (4 breasts)
1 cup chopped onion
1 cup diced celery
1 green pepper, diced
1 (15 ounce) can red beans
½ cup uncooked rice
½ cup sweet corn
1 (1 pound, 12 ounce) can tomatoes, diced
1 (4½ ounce) can green chilies
1 (2½ ounce) can black olives, sliced or diced
2 - 3 cloves garlic, minced
1 teaspoon chili powder
1 teaspoon cumin
½ teaspoon oregano
½ teaspoon salt
16 ounces Velveeta cheese
Juice of 1 lime

- ♦ **Combine** all ingredients except cheese and lime juice. Simmer for 45 minutes to 1 hour.
- ♦ **Cube** the cheese and melt into the mixture. Add lime juice just before serving.
- ♦ **Serve** with crumbled tortilla chips as a topper.

Freezes and re-heats well.

CREAMY-NUTTY TUNA SANDWICH •

Yield: 8 servings

1 (8 ounce) package cream cheese, at room temperature
2 tablespoons lemon juice
½ cup mayonnaise
½ cup chopped ripe olives
1 can tuna, flaked
½ cup chopped toasted pecans
¼ teaspoon MSG (optional)
Butter or margarine

- ♦ **Blend** cheese, lemon juice and mayonnaise.
- ♦ **Stir** in olives, nuts, tuna and MSG.
- ♦ **Spread** bread with butter, then tuna mixture.
- ♦ **Cover** and refrigerate overnight.

For tea sandwiches: cut bread in any shape or use alternating slices of very thin white and wheat bread.

SWISS TUNA GRILL

Yield: 4 servings

1 (7 ounce) can solid white
  tuna, drained and flaked
½ cup shredded Swiss cheese
½ cup chopped celery
¼ cup mayonnaise
¼ cup sour cream
  Dash pepper
  English muffin or bagel

♦ **Blend** together all ingredients.
♦ **Spread** on an English muffin or bagel and put on a baking sheet.
♦ **Broil** until hot and lightly browned.
♦ **Serve** hot or cold.

Use only natural Swiss or Jarlsberg cheese.

Add fresh lemon juice and a dash of Tabasco for extra zest. Top with sliced green onion.

CRAB CROISSANTS

Yield: 8 servings

½ cup mayonnaise
¼ teaspoon dried dill weed
  (optional)
½ - 1 teaspoon garlic powder
¼ cup minced fresh parsley
⅛ teaspoon cayenne pepper
⅔ pound crabmeat (2 small cans)
1 cup shredded Cheddar cheese
1 cup shredded Monterey Jack cheese
1 (2¼ ounce) can black olives, sliced (optional)
1 (10 ounce) can artichoke hearts, finely chopped
4 large croissants or English muffins

♦ **Combine** all ingredients in a medium bowl. Cover and refrigerate overnight.
♦ **Split** croissants or English muffins horizontally before serving. Spread each with crab mixture and place on baking sheets.
♦ **Broil** 5 inches from heat for 3 to 4 minutes or until heated through.

COMPANY'S COMIN' CHICKEN SANDWICHES

Yield: 9 servings

SANDWICH

18 slices of bread, with a large round cut from each slice
1 small onion, minced
2 cups finely chopped cooked chicken
4 hard-boiled eggs, finely chopped
½ cup finely chopped green stuffed olives
⅔ cup real mayonnaise
   Tabasco
   Curry
   Salt and pepper

FROSTING

2 (5 ounce) jars Kraft Old English cheese
1 egg
½ cup soft butter

♦ **Combine** onion, chicken, hard-boiled eggs, olives, mayonnaise and seasonings to taste.

♦ **Spread** chicken mixture between two slices of bread.

♦ **Combine** jars of cheese, egg and soft butter for frosting mixture.

♦ **Frost** only the tops and sides of sandwiches and place on a cookie sheet. Refrigerate overnight.

♦ **Bake** sandwiches at 375° for 15 minutes. The frosting will run onto the cookie sheet. Just scoop it around the sandwich to serve.

CHICKEN SALAD CROISSANTS

Yield: 12 sandwiches

8 chicken breast halves, cooked and cubed
1¼ cups diced celery
4 hard-boiled eggs, chopped
   Juice of 1 lemon
   Salt to taste
   Paprika to taste
½ teaspoon white pepper
1½ cups mayonnaise
¾ cup chopped pecans
12 bakery croissants

♦ **Combine** chicken, celery, eggs, lemon juice, seasonings and mayonnaise. Refrigerate overnight.

♦ **Stir** in chopped pecans and adjust seasonings just before serving.

♦ **Slice** croissants and warm uncovered in a 350° oven for 5 to 8 minutes.

♦ **Fill** warm croissants with a generous portion of chilled chicken salad.

SAVORY CRESCENT CHICKEN SQUARES

Yield: 4 servings

3 ounces cream cheese, softened
2 tablespoons butter or margarine, melted
2 cups diced cooked chicken
¼ teaspoon salt
⅛ teaspoon pepper
2 tablespoons milk
1 tablespoon chopped chives or onion
1 tablespoon pimiento
1 can crescent rolls
Crushed, seasoned bread crumbs

♦ **Blend** cream cheese and butter.
♦ **Add** chicken, salt, pepper, milk, chives and pimiento and mix well.
♦ **Separate** crescent rolls into 4 rectangles; seal perforations.
♦ **Spoon** ½ cup of chicken mixture onto center of rectangle, fold over and seal. Brush tops with butter and sprinkle with bread crumbs.
♦ **Bake** on ungreased cookie sheet at 350° for 20 to 30 minutes.

HAM AND CHEESE BREADWICH

Yield: 10 to 12 servings

1 (16 ounce) package frozen chopped broccoli
2 (1 pound) loaves frozen bread dough, thawed
3 cups shredded cheese (Cheddar, Swiss and/or Monterey Jack)
2 cups finely chopped fully-cooked ham
2 tablespoons butter or margarine, melted
1 teaspoon poppy seeds

♦ **Cook** broccoli according to package directions. Drain and cool.
♦ **Roll** each loaf of dough into a 15x10 inch rectangle.
♦ **Place** one dough rectangle into a greased, 15x10x1 inch baking pan. Sprinkle with broccoli, cheese and ham to within ½ inch of edges. Place second dough rectangle on top, sealing edges.
♦ **Brush** the top of dough with butter and sprinkle with poppy seeds.
♦ **Bake** at 350° for 35 to 45 minutes or until golden brown.
♦ **Slice** and serve warm.

FRENCH BREAD SAUSAGE ROLLS

Yield: 8 to 10 servings

4 ounces sliced garlic sausage, chopped
½ cup chopped salted cashews
4 green onions, chopped
1 green pepper, seeded and chopped
2 ribs celery, chopped
1 (8 ounce) package cream cheese with chives, softened
1 tablespoon plus 1 teaspoon tomato paste
1 clove garlic, crushed
Salt and pepper to taste
1 thin loaf French bread

♦ **Combine** first eight ingredients in a bowl, season with salt and pepper and mix well.
♦ **Cut** bread in half crosswise, then cut off crusty ends. Cut soft bread away from the inside of each half, leaving a shell.
♦ **Stuff** shells with the cream cheese mixture, pushing in well from both ends to prevent any gaps.
♦ **Wrap** each half in foil and refrigerate at least 2 hours.
♦ **Slice** into 1 inch slices after cheese has set. Serve open faced. Garnish as desired.

Garnish ideas: stuffed olives, tomato roses or green onions.

FRENCH DIP SANDWICHES

Yield: 8 to 12 sandwiches

4 pounds eye of round roast, trimmed
1 tablespoon olive oil
4 fresh cloves garlic, crushed
Coarse kosher salt
Fresh ground pepper
BMT beef broth
Wheat or sour dough hoagie buns, split and toasted

♦ **Line** bottom of heavy shallow pan with aluminum foil.
♦ **Rub** roast with olive oil, garlic, salt and pepper. Place roast in pan.
♦ **Roast** in preheated 450° oven for 30 minutes. Reduce heat to 325° and bake 12 minutes per pound.
♦ **Allow** to stand 10 to 15 minutes before carving.
♦ **Prepare** beef broth according to package directions and add pan drippings for extra flavor.
♦ **Stack** thin slices of hot beef on split and toasted buns. Cut buns in half diagonally so as to have tip end for dipping.

CHEESE AND ROAST BEEF CROISSANTS

2 tablespoons butter
½ pound fresh mushrooms, sliced
⅛ teaspoon pepper
4 bakery croissants
4 teaspoons prepared mustard
½ pound thin sliced roast beef
1 large tomato, thinly sliced
½ pound Brie or Port au Salut cheese

♦ **Cook** mushrooms in butter and pepper in a 2 quart saucepan for 5 minutes. Stir.
♦ **Slice** Croissants. Spread bottom halves with mustard. Top with roast beef slices, sautéed mushrooms, tomato slices and cheese (cutting cheese to fit.) Replace top halves.
♦ **Place** sandwiches on cookie sheet. Cover loosely with foil. Bake at 375° for 15 minutes or until cheese is melted.

Yield: 4 sandwiches

STEAK SANDWICH WITH • ROQUEFORT BUTTER

4 thinly sliced steaks (sirloin or rib eye)
Rye bread, toasted
1 tablespoon butter
1 tablespoon Roquefort cheese
Salt and pepper
Chives, minced

♦ **Grill** steaks.
♦ **Mash** together butter and Roquefort and spread on rye toast.
♦ **Sprinkle** steak with salt, pepper and chives.

MULLENDORE CROSS BELL SANDWICH

Yield: 1 sandwich

1 New York strip steak
Seasoned salt to taste
1 pear

**MULLENDORE
CROSS BELL RANCH**

♦ **Cook** inside in skillet sprayed with non-stick vegetable spray or outside on grill.
♦ **Serve** on Texas toast accompanied by tomato wedges, kosher dill pickles and green onions on a large lettuce leaf.
♦ **Garnish** each plate with its own brand. Make the bell by using the top half of a pear and make the cross by using two slices from the bottom half.

No steak sauce of any kind is offered. The true flavor of a good steak should never be covered.

SIDE DISHES

DEPOT—The coming of the railroad in 1899 opened Bartlesville to oil production and sped up the development of the town. Today, the fully-restored depot is the home of the Bartlesville Area Chamber of Commerce.

BOOM TOWN

They came from everywhere when the news broke. The Osage Fields were spewing liquid gold! It was the Oklahoma version of the California gold rush.

Many came to Bartlesville by train—roustabouts, fieldhands and wildcatters. If they did not actually drill in the field, they went to work supplying the growing boom town. Fortunes were made overnight, and soon there was a demand for luxuries and finery. Merchants followed to fill these needs.

Sizable immigrant populations of Germans, Poles, Russians and other Europeans grew up around the town. Many made outstanding contributions, such as Armais Artunoff, whose submergible electric pump transformed the fledging oil industry. Reda Pump Company, which still operates in Bartlesville, is Artunoff's legacy.

Today, the descendants of these early immigrants continue to live in Bartlesville, contributing to the Territory of their fathers and mothers.

RICE PILAF •

Yield: 4 to 6 servings

4 tablespoons margarine
3 handfuls thin egg noodles
1 cup rice (not instant)
1 envelope dry onion soup mix
1 (4 ounce) can mushrooms and juice
2½ cups water

♦ **Melt** margarine in a saucepan. Add noodles and brown over low heat.
♦ **Remove** from heat and add remaining ingredients.
♦ **Bring** to a boil. Cover and simmer for 45 minutes.

PECAN WILD RICE

Yield: 6 servings

1 cup raw wild rice (approximately ½ pound)
5½ cups defatted chicken stock, or canned chicken broth
1 cup shelled pecan halves
1 cup yellow raisins
Grated rind of 1 large orange
¼ cup chopped fresh mint
4 green onions, thinly sliced
¼ cup olive oil
⅓ cup fresh orange juice
1½ teaspoons salt
Freshly ground pepper to taste

♦ **Put** rice in a strainer and run under cold water to rinse.
♦ **Place** rice and stock in a medium pan. Bring to rapid boil, then simmer uncovered for 45 minutes. Check after 30 minutes as rice should not get too soft. Place a thin towel inside colander and turn rice into colander to drain. Transfer drained rice to a bowl.
♦ **Add** remaining ingredients to rice and toss gently. Taste for seasonings, adjust if desired.
♦ **Let** stand for 2 hours to allow flavors to blend. Serve at room temperature.

This is delicious served over a bed of shredded lettuce with grilled cubed chicken breast on top. Excellent with a lemon pepper dressing.

ALMOND PILAF

Yield: 4 servings

2 tablespoons toasted slivered almonds
2 teaspoons vegetable oil
1 onion, finely chopped
2 tablespoons pine nuts
1 cup uncooked rice
2½ cups low salt chicken stock
½ cup golden raisins
1 teaspoon saffron (optional)
½ teaspoon ground cinnamon
½ teaspoon salt
¼ teaspoon red pepper flakes (optional)
⅛ teaspoon ground cardamom

♦ **Heat** oil in a heavy saucepan over medium heat. Sauté onions and pine nuts until onions are soft. Stir in rice. Add chicken stock, raisins, saffron, cinnamon, salt, pepper flakes and cardamom.

♦ **Reduce** heat to low, cover and simmer 18 minutes. Do not uncover during cooking.

♦ **Remove** from heat and fluff with a fork.

♦ **Sprinkle** with almonds and serve.

Turmeric may be substituted for saffron. English walnuts may be substituted for pine nuts.

Excellent with chicken or lamb.

RICE PILAF WITH SAFFRON AND GRUYÈRE CHEESE

Yield: 6 to 8 servings

2 tablespoons butter or margarine
1 large onion, thinly sliced
1 cup uncooked long grain rice
Good pinch saffron soaked in ½ cup hot water (may substitute turmeric)
2 cups chicken stock (fresh, canned or cubed)
1 tablespoon butter or margarine
1½ ounces Gruyère cheese, grated (Jarlsberg or Swiss may be substituted)

♦ **Melt** 2 tablespoons butter in 3-6 quart pot. Add onion; cook slowly until clear.

♦ **Add** rice and fry for a few minutes until rice looks clear. Add saffron and stock and bring to boil. Cover and put in a 350° oven for 20 to 30 minutes.

♦ **Stir** in 1 tablespoon butter and cheese with fork just before serving.

May be cooked on top of stove.

OKLAHOMA RICE

Yield: 12 servings

4 cups cooked rice, salted to taste
2 (4½ ounce) cans chopped green chili peppers
2 (16 ounce) cartons sour cream
¾ pound Monterey Jack cheese, sliced
Grated Cheddar cheese

♦ **Cool** the rice. Add salt, chilies, and sour cream.
♦ **Layer** rice mixture and sliced cheese in a 9x13 inch casserole dish, starting and ending with rice.
♦ **Sprinkle** with cheese.
♦ **Bake** at 350° for 25 to 30 minutes, until bubbly.

MUSHROOMS AND RICE

Yield: 6 to 8 servings

2⅔ cups cooked rice
6 tablespoons salad oil
1 (4 ounce) can sliced mushrooms, drained
1 bunch green onions, chopped
2 cans beef consommé, undiluted
2 tablespoons soy sauce
½ teaspoon salt

♦ **Mix** in a 2 quart casserole dish.
♦ **Bake** covered at 350° until water is absorbed, no more than 30 to 45 minutes. Do not stir.

To prepare in advance, place dry ingredients in casserole. Add liquids just before baking.

MASHED POTATO CASSEROLE

Yield: 10 servings

8 - 10 large potatoes, cooked and mashed
1 (8 ounce) package cream cheese, softened
1 cup sour cream
1½ teaspoons garlic salt
3 tablespoons dried chives
Salt and pepper to taste
2 tablespoons melted butter
Paprika

♦ **Beat** all ingredients together until fluffy.
♦ **Place** in a greased three quart casserole dish. Drizzle with melted butter and sprinkle with paprika.
♦ **Bake** at 350° for 30 minutes.

May be prepared the day before and reheated for 1 hour before mealtime. May be prepared in a Crock-pot on high for 4 hours.

New Potatoes in White Wine

Yield: 4 servings

1½ pounds new potatoes, red or white
4 tablespoons butter
⅔ cup dry white wine
3 tablespoons chopped parsley
1 tablespoon chopped dill
Salt and pepper, to taste

◆ **Cook** unpeeled potatoes in salted water until barely tender, 8 to 10 minutes.

◆ **Melt** 2 tablespoons butter in a large skillet over medium heat. Roll potatoes in skillet until light brown crust forms. Add wine and remaining butter. Raise the temperature and cook, stirring constantly, until wine is reduced and the sauce is fairly thick (5 minutes).

◆ **Sprinkle** with salt, pepper, parsley and dill. Stir gently to coat potatoes.

One clove of minced garlic may be substituted for dill.

Heartland Potato Casserole

Yield: 12 servings

8 large baking potatoes, with skins
1 pint sour cream
8 ounces Cheddar cheese
8 ounces Velveeta cheese
½ bunch green onions, chopped
½ cup milk
1½ cups coarse French bread crumbs
½ cup butter (do not substitute)

◆ **Boil** potatoes, cool thoroughly, and grate on hand grater.

◆ **Mix** sour cream, grated cheese, green onions and milk in a bowl.

◆ **Fold** gently into potatoes. Spread in a greased 9x13 inch pan.

◆ **Melt** butter and mix with bread crumbs. Sprinkle over potato mixture.

◆ **Bake** at 350° for 30 minutes, until bubbly.

Great accompaniment to prime rib, tenderloin, brisket, or burgers.

Rum Sweet Potatoes *

Yield: 4 to 6 servings

4 large sweet potatoes
salt
½ cup butter
1 egg, beaten
1 cup brown sugar
½ cup rum
Large marshmallows

♦ **Cook** potatoes with skins in salted water. Cool and peel. Beat in mixer until smooth. Set aside.

♦ **Mix** butter, egg, brown sugar and rum in a double boiler and cook until thickened. Do not boil.

♦ **Place** potatoes in a 3 quart casserole dish. Make a well in the center of the potatoes. Pour rum mixture in the well.

♦ **Bake** at 350° for 10 minutes. Dot with large marshmallows and bake 10 minutes more until bubbly.

Potato Gratin °

Yield: 6 to 8 servings

2 large garlic cloves, cut in half lengthwise
3 pounds new potatoes, unpeeled, scrubbed and thinly sliced
3½ cups 1% milk
2 eggs, lightly beaten
Black pepper, freshly ground
6 - 8 tablespoons Parmesan cheese, freshly grated

♦ **Rub** the inside of a large oval gratin dish with cut side of garlic.

♦ **Slice** garlic into thin slivers and toss with potatoes. Layer potatoes and garlic.

♦ **Mix** together milk, eggs and salt and pour over potatoes. Add a generous amount of pepper.

♦ **Bake** uncovered 1 to 1¼ hours at 400°. Every 20 minutes break up the top layer of potatoes and fold into the rest of the dish.

♦ **Sprinkle** with Parmesan cheese after 1 hour of baking. Bake 15 to 20 minutes more until golden brown on top.

MEXICAN CORN CASSEROLE

Yield: 8 servings

2 (10 ounce) packages frozen corn, thawed
½ cup butter, melted
2 eggs
1 cup sour cream
10 ounces Monterey Jack cheese, grated
½ cup yellow cornmeal
1 (4½ ounce) can diced green chilies, drained
1½ teaspoons salt

♦ **Purée** butter, eggs and half the corn in a food processor.
♦ **Mix** remaining ingredients in a large bowl. Add puréed mixture and mix well.
♦ **Pour** into a greased 7x11 inch pan.
♦ **Bake,** uncovered, at 350° for 50 to 60 minutes.

GOURMET GREEN BEANS

Yield: 4 servings

¼ cup butter
1 (9 ounce) package frozen French or Italian style green beans, thawed and drained
¾ teaspoon oregano
½ cup chopped pecans
¼ teaspoon garlic salt
1 (2 ounce) jar pimiento, undrained
1 (7 ounce) can artichoke hearts, quartered

♦ **Melt** butter in a 2 quart saucepan over medium heat. Stir in all ingredients except artichokes and pecans. Cover and cook, stirring occasionally, until beans are crisp tender, 5 to 7 minutes.
♦ **Stir** in artichokes and pecans. Cover and cook until artichokes are heated through, about 2 to 3 minutes.

HOMESTEAD HOMINY

Yield: 8 to 10 servings

3 tablespoons margarine
1 small onion, minced
½ cup chopped green pepper
3 tablespoons flour
1 teaspoon salt
½ teaspoon dry mustard
Dash of cayenne
1½ cups milk
1 cup grated Cheddar cheese
½ cup chopped pitted ripe olives
1 (1 pound, 13 ounce) can hominy, drained
½ cup buttered bread crumbs

♦ **Melt** butter in saucepan. Add onion and green pepper and sauté 5 minutes. Blend in flour and seasonings. Add milk and cook and stir until mixture thickens and comes to a boil.
♦ **Add** grated cheese and stir until melted. Remove from heat. Add olives and hominy.
♦ **Pour** into a 1½ quart casserole. Sprinkle with buttered bread crumbs.
♦ **Bake** at 375° for 30 minutes, or until browned.

HOT OR COLD ASPARAGUS

Yield: 6 to 8 servings

1 pound fresh asparagus
3 hard-cooked eggs, sliced
¼ cup light olive oil
3 green onions (with tops), finely chopped
2 - 3 tablespoons garlic red wine vinegar
1½ teaspoons honey Dijon mustard
2 tablespoons chopped fresh parsley (1 teaspoon dried)
Salt and fresh ground pepper, to taste

♦ **Cook** asparagus uncovered in small amount of water until crisp tender, about 5 minutes. Drain.
♦ **Mix** oil, onions, wine vinegar, mustard, parsley, salt and pepper in a container with a lid and shake until blended.
♦ **Place** asparagus in a serving dish and spoon dressing over it. Garnish with hard-cooked egg slices. Serve warm.

May serve over mixed torn fresh greens and top the eggs with sliced black olives and fresh red pepper rings or pimiento strips.

ROASTED ASPARAGUS

Yield: 4 servings

1 pound fresh asparagus
¼ cup extra virgin olive oil
2 - 3 teaspoons fresh lemon juice or balsamic vinegar
¼ cup fresh ground Parmesan cheese
Salt and pepper to taste

♦ **Place** asparagus in a shallow baking dish. Coat with olive oil. Season with salt and pepper.
♦ **Spread** in single layer and roast at 400° until tender, about 10 minutes. Watch carefully.
♦ **Toss** asparagus with lemon juice or vinegar and Parmesan cheese. Serve warm or at room temperature.

SHOE PEG CORN CASSEROLE

Yield: 6 to 8 servings

2 (3 ounce) packages cream cheese
2 tablespoons margarine
¼ cup milk
1 (4½ ounce) can chopped green chilies
2 (11 ounce) cans white Shoe Peg corn

♦ **Melt** cream cheese with margarine. Add milk, chilies and corn. Mix thoroughly.
♦ **Bake** uncovered in an 8 inch square casserole at 350° for 30 minutes.

115

GREEN BEAN BUNDLES

Yield: 4 servings

1 pound fresh green beans
2 strips bacon, cut in half
¼ cup margarine
Dash of garlic powder
½ cup brown sugar
2 dashes Worcestershire
sauce

♦ **Wash** and snap beans. Divide into four portions. Wrap a strip of bacon around each bundle. Secure with a toothpick.
♦ **Melt** margarine, garlic powder, brown sugar and Worcestershire sauce in a saucepan.
♦ **Place** bundles in an 8x8 inch casserole dish. Pour sauce over beans.
♦ **Bake** at 350° for 35 minutes.

May use up to 1½ pounds of beans and 3 strips of bacon without increasing the sauce.

ROASTED GREEN BEANS WITH GARLIC

Yield: 4 servings

1 pound fresh green beans, washed and ends cut off
3 cloves garlic, crushed
3 sprigs fresh thyme, ground, or ½ teaspoon dried thyme
¼ cup extra virgin olive oil
2-3 teaspoons fresh lemon juice
Salt and fresh ground pepper, to taste

♦ **Toss** beans, garlic, thyme and olive oil in a shallow baking dish. Season with salt and pepper.
♦ **Spread** beans in a single layer and roast at 450° until tender, about 15 minutes.
♦ **Toss** with lemon juice. Serve warm or at room temperature.

HONEY BABY CARROTS

Yield: 6 servings

2 tablespoons lightly salted butter
2 tablespoons honey
Baby carrots, peeled and trimmed (10 per person)
2½ tablespoons ginger ale
Kosher salt and freshly ground pepper, to taste

♦ **Heat** butter in a 12 inch sauté pan. Add carrots and sauté one minute. Add honey, salt and pepper and toss.
♦ **Pour** in ginger ale and bring to boil. Cover and cook for 3 minutes. Remove lid and cook until liquid turns to a glaze (5 to 8 minutes).

MARINATED CARROTS WITH WALNUTS

Yield: 6 to 8 servings

1 bunch carrots (about 1 pound)
1 cup white wine
1 cup chicken broth
2½ tablespoons olive oil
3 tablespoons white-wine vinegar
2 shallots, finely chopped
1 clove garlic, finely chopped
1 teaspoon sugar
1 teaspoon salt
Pepper, to taste
Bouquet garni of: 1 bay leaf, ¼ teaspoon thyme, and 3 sprigs parsley
12 walnut halves
Lemon zest strips
Chopped parsley
Lemon juice

♦ **Peel** carrots. Cut into strips about 2 inches long and ¼ inch wide.

♦ **Combine** wine, broth, olive oil, wine-vinegar, shallots, garlic, sugar, salt, pepper and bouquet garni in a saucepan. Bring mixture to a boil and simmer, uncovered, for 5 minutes.

♦ **Add** carrots and cook for 5 to 8 minutes, until tender. Let mixture cool, and refrigerate for at least 24 hours.

♦ **Brown** walnut pieces lightly in 1 tablespoon olive oil and set aside. Transfer the carrots and some of the marinade to a glass bowl and add lemon juice to taste.

♦ **Garnish** with walnut halves and lemon zest. Sprinkle with chopped parsley. Serve warm or cold.

EGGPLANT SOUFFLÉ

Yield: 6 servings

1 medium eggplant, peeled and chopped
2 tablespoons butter
2 tablespoons flour
1 cup milk
½ cup grated Cheddar cheese
¾ cup bread crumbs
2 tablespoons grated onion
1 tablespoon catsup
1 teaspoon salt
2 egg yolks
2 egg whites, stiffly beaten

♦ **Cook** eggplant in boiling water for 5 to 10 minutes. Drain and mash.

♦ **Melt** butter. Add flour and slowly add milk, stirring until thick.

♦ **Add** cheese, bread crumbs, onion, catsup, salt, egg yolks and eggplant, in order.

♦ **Fold** egg whites in gently. Place in a buttered two quart casserole.

♦ **Bake** at 350° for 45 minutes.

AUBERGINES DE KIEVIET ◦

Yield: 4 servings

EGGPLANT

2 medium eggplants
⅓ cup finely chopped onion
⅓ cup sliced mushrooms
½ cup peeled, seeded and
    finely chopped tomatoes
1 package frozen King
    crabmeat
2 cloves garlic
1 teaspoon paprika
1 teaspoon freshly ground
    pepper
1 teaspoon salt
1 tablespoon cream
1 cup fresh bread crumbs
    Butter
    Dry vermouth

CHEESE SAUCE

2 cups milk
3 tablespoons flour
3 tablespoons butter
½ cup white wine
2 tablespoons Kirsch
½ cup Parmesan cheese
3 egg yolks, beaten

♦ **Cut** off tops and bottoms of eggplants and cut in half lengthwise. Remove and discard seeds. Scoop out pulp and chop finely.

♦ **Make** a sauce of butter, flour and milk. Stir in white wine and Kirsch. Heat thoroughly, but do not boil. Remove mixture from heat and add egg yolks stirring constantly. Stir in cheese and set aside.

♦ **Sauté** onions in butter. Add mushrooms, tomatoes, crabmeat, garlic and eggplant. Flambe with a small amount of dry vermouth. Add spices and cream and thicken with the bread crumbs. Fill eggplant cases with mixture. Place in greased casserole and cover each eggplant with cheese sauce.

♦ **Bake** for 20 minutes at 350° until cheese is lightly brown.

This recipe is from the restaurant of the de Kieviet Hotel in the Hague, Netherlands. This may be served as a main course with cold soup, a large salad and garlic bread.

CALABACITAS

Yield: 6 servings

3 - 4 yellow squash, sliced
1 onion, chopped
2 tablespoons oil (non-stick
    cooking spray may be
    substituted)
1 (4½ ounce) can chopped
    green chilies
1 cup frozen corn kernels
1 cup fat-free cheese, grated

♦ **Sauté** squash and onion in oil until barely done. Add chilies and corn. Cook until thoroughly heated. Add cheese and heat until cheese is melted.

CHEESE STUFFED ZUCCHINI

Yield: 12 servings

6 large zucchini
2 eggs, well-beaten
1½ cups grated Cheddar cheese
½ cup small curd cottage
  cheese
2 tablespoons parsley flakes
2 tablespoons chopped onion
½ teaspoon salt
⅛ teaspoon pepper
½ cup cracker crumbs
2 tablespoons butter, melted

♦ **Cut** off ends of zucchini and scrub. Cook zucchini in boiling, salted water until tender (about 12 minutes). Cut into halves lengthwise. Scoop out center pulp. Invert on paper towels and drain.

♦ **Combine** eggs, Cheddar cheese, cottage cheese, onions, salt and pepper. Fill zucchini shells.

♦ **Toss** crumbs with butter. Sprinkle over zucchini. Arrange on greased jelly roll pan. Bake at 350° for 25 minutes.

SENSATIONAL SUMMER SQUASH ◦

Yield: 6 to 8 servings

4 small zucchini squash,
  trimmed and sliced
4 small yellow crook-neck
  squash, trimmed and sliced
2 tablespoons olive oil
1 teaspoon sugar
½ teaspoon minced garlic
½ teaspoon salt
¼ teaspoon freshly ground
  black pepper
⅓ cup chopped fresh basil
¼ cup grated Parmesan cheese
¼ teaspoon grated nutmeg

♦ **Place** squash in a 1½ to 2 quart casserole. Add oil, sugar, garlic, salt and pepper. Stir to mix well.

♦ **Cover** casserole with lid or plastic wrap and microwave on high for 7 to 10 minutes. Uncover carefully and stir in fresh basil.

♦ **Cover** again and microwave for 1 to 3 more minutes. Squash should be tender, crisp and flavorful.

♦ **Stir** in Parmesan and nutmeg before serving.

This is loaded with flavor, but still tastes delicate and garden fresh. It makes a great side dish for fish or chicken entrees.

Italian seasoning

ZUCCHINI STUFFED WITH RED PEPPER PURÉE

Yield: 6 servings

4 red bell peppers
4 - 5 tablespoons olive oil
Pinch of fresh or dried thyme
Salt and pepper, to taste
6 small zucchini, ends trimmed

♦ **Cut** peppers in half. Remove seeds and ribs. Flatten out (skin side up) and broil 3 inches from heat until skin blisters and turns black, about 10 to 12 minutes. Put peppers in a paper bag and leave to sweat for 10 minutes. Rub charred skin off with a small knife. Cut each pepper into 3 or 4 slices.

♦ **Heat** 2 tablespoons oil in a skillet. Add peppers, thyme, salt and pepper. Sauté 1 minute on each side.

♦ **Remove** mixture and purée peppers.

♦ **Cook** zucchini in a pan of boiling salted water for about 2 minutes. Drain and refresh in cold water. Cut in half lengthwise. Carefully scoop seeds leaving a boat-shaped shell (be careful not to pierce the sides).

♦ **Place** zucchini in a shallow, oiled baking dish. Bake at 400° for 5 minutes.

♦ **Spoon** pepper purée evenly into shells, and bake 10 minutes, until tender.

SHADY LADY SPINACH CASSEROLE

Yield: 8 to 10 servings

2 (10 ounce) packages chopped, frozen spinach
1 stick butter, melted
1 (8 ounce) package cream cheese, softened
1 (13½ ounce) can artichokes, drained and quartered
1 (6 ounce) can water chestnuts, drained and sliced
1 teaspoon onion powder
½ teaspoon garlic salt
½ cup fresh bread crumbs (toasted in 2 tablespoons melted butter)
⅓ cup grated Parmesan cheese

♦ **Thaw** spinach in microwave and strain, squeezing out all moisture.
♦ **Place** spinach in a mixing bowl. Add butter, cream cheese, artichokes, water chestnuts, onion powder, garlic salt and mix well.
♦ **Place** in greased 2 quart casserole dish. Cover with bread crumbs and Parmesan cheese.
♦ **Bake** in preheated 400° oven for 20 to 25 minutes.

SPINACH MADELEINE

Yield: 5 to 6 servings

2 (10 ounce) packages frozen, chopped spinach
4 tablespoons butter or margarine
2 tablespoons flour
2 tablespoons chopped onion
½ cup evaporated milk
½ cup spinach liquid
½ teaspoon black pepper
¾ teaspoon celery salt
¾ teaspoon garlic salt
1 (6 ounce) roll jalapeño cheese, cut into small pieces
1 teaspoon Worcestershire sauce

♦ **Cook** spinach according to package directions. Drain and reserve liquid.
♦ **Melt** butter in saucepan over low heat. Add flour, stirring until blended and smooth. Add onion and cook until soft. Add liquid slowly. Cook, stirring constantly, until smooth and thick. Add seasonings and cheese. Stir until melted.
♦ **Combine** with cooked spinach. Serve immediately, or put into a casserole and top with bread crumbs. Bake at 350° for 30 minutes.

ROTKRAUT (RED CABBAGE)

Yield: 8 servings

2 pounds red cabbage, thinly cut
2 tablespoons butter
3-4 tablespoons vinegar
1 whole onion studded with 3-4 whole cloves
1 apple, peeled, cored and cut into quarters
1 cup water or chicken broth
Sugar to taste
Salt to taste

♦ **Place** cabbage in large saucepan. Add remaining ingredients. Simmer until done, approximately 30 to 40 minutes. Remove onion and serve.

Best when reheated the next day. Great side dish for pork.

TOMATO AND BASIL SORBET

Yield: 4 to 6 servings

4-6 medium, fresh tomatoes
1 (8 ounce) can ready-cut tomatoes with green chilies
2 teaspoons tomato paste
1 teaspoon sugar
2 teaspoons red wine vinegar
½ teaspoon onion salt
1 teaspoon Worcestershire sauce
2 teaspoons chopped fresh basil
1 tablespoon plus 1 teaspoon vodka

♦ **Remove** tops from fresh tomatoes. Scoop out the seeds and flesh. Place tomato shells and tops in freezer.
♦ **Purée** canned tomatoes in blender. Add remaining ingredients and blend for 2 to 3 minutes.
♦ **Place** in a plastic container and freeze to a slush.
♦ **Blend** again until slightly softened and pale.
♦ **Spoon** loosely into frozen shells. Return to freezer until firm.

This is a wonderful accompaniment to any brunch menu, supper salad plate or served with cheese and toast points as a first course.

ROASTED BELL PEPPERS AND ONIONS

Yield: 8 to 10 servings

1 medium clove garlic
2 pounds red, green and/or yellow bell peppers
3 medium yellow onions
3-4 tablespoons extra virgin olive oil
½ teaspoon salt
⅛ teaspoon coarsely ground black pepper
2 tablespoons finely chopped parsley
1 teaspoon finely chopped fresh mint (or ½ teaspoon chopped dried mint flakes)
1 tablespoon fresh lemon juice

♦ **Peel** and halve garlic. Rub inside surface of shallow 9x13 inch baking dish with cut sides of garlic. Leave garlic in dish.

♦ **Wash,** dry and quarter peppers, discarding core and seeds. Peel onions and quarter through the stem end. Combine peppers and onions in prepared dish; drizzle with olive oil and sprinkle with salt and pepper.

♦ **Roast** vegetables on top rack of 400° oven, turning occasionally with spatula, about 45 minutes or until browned and tender.

♦ **Turn** peppers and onions into serving bowl. Sprinkle chopped parsley and mint over roasted vegetables. Drizzle with lemon juice and toss gently.

♦ **Cover** and let stand until ready to serve at room temperature.

This dish is good with meats, such as roast pork. Great for parties because it can be made ahead and doesn't have to be refrigerated and reheated.

More Peas, Please ◦

Yield: 10 to 12 servings

2 pounds freshly shelled peas, plus a few pods (may use frozen)
1 clove garlic
1 small onion, whole
1 tablespoon minced parsley
1 tablespoon olive oil
3 thin slices boiled ham, chopped
1 tablespoon butter
½ teaspoon salt

♦ **Sauté** parsley, whole onion, and garlic lightly in oil for 2 minutes. Add ham to oil and stir until ham shrinks, about 5 minutes.

♦ **Remove** garlic and add peas. Mix ingredients to soak up sauce. Add 2 tablespoons water, salt and butter. Add a few pods for flavor.

♦ **Simmer,** covered, until tender, about 15 minutes. Remove whole onion before serving.

Kahahpon (Dried Corn-in-the-milk Bread) ◦

Yield: 4 to 6 servings

4 cups water
1 (10 ounce) package corn chips, unsalted
Salt or sugar to taste

Delaware Nation

♦ **Boil** water in large saucepan. Gradually add the corn chips. Reduce heat when water begins to boil again. Continue cooking for about 5 minutes. Stir frequently until it has the consistency of cooked oatmeal with very little water left on top.

♦ **Turn** off heat. Stir a few more times. Add either salt or sugar to taste and serve.

This is a modern day variation of an old Delaware Indian recipe. The original recipe called for finely grating field corn and baking until the consistency of cornbread. It was then broken apart and dried for 7 days in the sun and 7 nights inside which imparted a unique flavor. The dried corn was cooked in boiling water, usually seasoned with pork or beef, for 1½ to 2 hours over medium heat.

GNOCCHI PARISIENNE

Yield: 6 to 8 servings

GNOCCHI
- 1 cup water
- ½ cup butter or margarine
- 1 teaspoon salt
- 1 cup flour
- 4 eggs
- ¼ cup grated Swiss cheese
- 1 teaspoon dry mustard

SAUCE
- 2 tablespoons butter
- 2 tablespoons flour
- ½ teaspoon salt
- 1⅓ cups light cream
- 4 tablespoons grated Swiss cheese
- Dash cayenne pepper

TOPPING
- 1½ tablespoons butter
- 3 tablespoons grated Swiss cheese

♦ **Combine** water, butter and salt in 2 quart saucepan. Bring to boil and remove from heat. Beat in flour with a wooden spoon. Beat mixture over low heat until it leaves the side of the pan and forms a ball, 1 to 2 minutes.

♦ **Remove** from heat and add eggs, one at a time, beating with electric mixer or wooden spoon after each addition. Continue beating until dough is shiny and satiny. Stir in cheese and mustard.

♦ **Boil** 2 quarts salted water in a 4 quart pan. Reduce heat so water is below boiling point. remove 1 teaspoon dough with a heated spoon (dip in simmering water). Use another heated spoon to slide dough into simmering water.

♦ **Cook** about ¼ of dough (10) at a time. Simmer, uncovered, 10 to 12 minutes or until Gnocchi are firm and rise to surface.

♦ **Remove** with slotted spoon. Drain well on paper towels. Arrange in single layer in shallow 9x13 inch baking dish.

♦ **Prepare** sauce by combining butter, flour, salt, cream, cheese and cayenne in a small saucepan over medium heat. Pour over Gnocchi and sprinkle with Swiss cheese. Dot with 1½ tablespoons butter.

♦ **Broil** about 4 inches from heat for about 5 minutes.

These may be made a day ahead, ready to broil. Do not freeze.

SZECHUAN COLLARD GREENS

Yield: 4 servings

COLLARD GREENS

2 tablespoons oil (peanut, sunflower, or canola)

3-4 scallions, minced

1 fresh hot pepper, minced (cayenne or jalapeño)

3 tablespoons unsalted peanuts (or pine nuts)

1 clove garlic, minced

1 bunch fresh collard greens, including stems, washed and chopped (about 1½ pounds)

COOKING SAUCE

2 tablespoons Chinese Dark Soy (substitute 1 tablespoon molasses and 1½ tablespoons soy sauce)

1 clove garlic, minced

1 tablespoon dark sesame oil

1 tablespoon Chinese cooking wine (or Japanese sake)

2 tablespoons rice wine vinegar (or white wine vinegar)

1 teaspoon Chinese red pepper paste (optional)

1 teaspoon Arrowroot powder or cornstarch (optional)

♦ **Prepare** cooking sauce by combining all ingredients. Set aside.

♦ **Heat** oil in wok. Stir-fry scallions for 30 seconds. Add peanuts and hot pepper. Continue to stir-fry for 1 more minute, then add garlic. Add collard greens. Stir-fry about 1½ minutes.

♦ **Add** cooking sauce. Cook for 1 more minute. Serve immediately.

A delicious variation for this versatile vegetable.

SHEWAHSAPAN (GRAPE DUMPLINGS) *Yield: 4 servings*

COOKING LIQUID
1 (48 ounce) can grape juice
   Dab of shortening
1 cup sugar

DUMPLINGS
½ cup butter
1½ cups grape juice
3 cups flour

DELAWARE
NATION

♦ **Heat** all but 1½ cups grape juice in a large cooking pot.
♦ **Mix** dumpling ingredients until a bit thicker than biscuit dough.
♦ **Roll** dough into four 12 inch circles. Each circle should be ¼ inch thick. Cut circles into ¾ inch wide strips. Cut strips into 3 inch lengths.
♦ **Drop** individual dumplings into boiling juice. Boil slowly for about 15 minutes.

NOSEY FOLKS' ARTICHOKES *Yield: 4 servings*

4 artichokes
2 lemons
6 cloves garlic, peeled and crushed
1 tablespoon whole peppercorns
2 bay leaves
4 whole cloves
1 tablespoon salt
1 teaspoon thyme
1 teaspoon marjoram
1 teaspoon basil
1 star anise

♦ **Trim** off sharp points of leaves and stem end of artichoke. Remove outer round of bottom leaves.
♦ **Cover** artichokes with water in large saucepan. Bring water to a boil. Squeeze juice from lemons and throw in lemon rinds. Add remaining ingredients. Simmer until the bottom of the artichoke is easily pierced with a fork (about 30 minutes). Cool slightly.
♦ **Remove** inner leaves with a grapefruit spoon. Scoop out the thistle and discard.

These are delicious warm or cold. They are very flavorful and do not need to be dipped in lemon butter.

BROCCOLI SOUFFLÉ

Yield: 6 to 8 servings

1 (10 ounce) package chopped frozen broccoli
3 tablespoons butter
3 tablespoons flour
1 teaspoon salt
1 cup milk
⅛ teaspoon nutmeg
1 teaspoon lemon juice
4 egg yolks
4 egg whites

♦ **Cook** broccoli and drain.
♦ **Melt** butter. Add flour and salt and cook over medium heat until bubbly. Stir in milk. Cook until thick, stirring frequently. Add nutmeg, lemon juice and broccoli. Cool slightly.
♦ **Beat** egg yolks and add to mixture. Allow mixture to cool.
♦ **Beat** egg whites until stiff. Fold into broccoli mixture.
♦ **Pour** into buttered 1½ quart casserole. Place in hot water bath and bake, uncovered, at 325° until firm.

RANCHO BAKED BEANS ⋅

Yield: 8 to 10 servings

2 pounds lean ground beef
1 onion, chopped
1 cup ketchup
1 teaspoon salt
2 teaspoons vinegar
2 tablespoons mustard
¼ cup brown sugar
¼ cup molasses
1 (3 pound) can pork and beans

♦ **Brown** ground beef in a skillet. Add onion and cook until done.
♦ **Combine** all ingredients in a 9x13 inch glass baking dish.
♦ **Bake** at 400° for 30 to 40 minutes.

FREDERICK
DRUMMOND RANCH

ENTREES

COWPUNCHING—With thousands of acres of bountiful prairie surrounding the city, the round-up is still a way of life on the many ranches around Bartlesville.

BLUESTEM BOUNTY

Texas ranchers introduced longhorn cattle to Indian Territory during the great cattle drives after the Civil War.

At first, the drovers only intended to pass through Oklahoma on their way to the Kansas City railheads. But they quickly discovered that Indian Territory offered ideal ranching conditions—abundant grass, water and mild winters which allowed cattle to feed on dry grass on the open range.

Soon other breeds of cattle were introduced and the predominance of the longhorn, whose meat was tough and stringy, faded. The cross-bred cattle raised on today's ranches still graze on native Bluestem grass and provide some of the best beef available to America's tables.

SIRLOIN TIPS OVER • ALMOND RICE

Yield: 8 servings

1 pound mushrooms, sliced
¼ cup butter
2 tablespoons vegetable oil
3 pounds sirloin steak, cut in
  1 inch cubes
¾ cup beef bouillon
¾ cup red wine
2 tablespoons soy sauce
2 cloves garlic, crushed
½ onion, grated
2 tablespoons cornstarch
½ cup beef bouillon
½ can cream of mushroom
  soup

ALMOND RICE
½ cup slivered almonds
3 tablespoons butter
1½ cups rice
3½ cups water

FOSTER
RANCH

♦ **Sauté** mushrooms in 2 tablespoons butter in a skillet until brown. Spoon into 3 quart casserole.
♦ **Add** remaining butter and oil to skillet. Brown meat. Spoon over mushrooms.
♦ **Combine** ¾ cup bouillon, wine, soy sauce, garlic and onion in skillet.
♦ **Blend** cornstarch with ½ cup bouillon. Stir into skillet. Cook, stirring, until thick. Spoon over meat. ♦
♦ **Bake** covered at 275° for at least 1 hour. Add mushroom soup and a dash of salt. Bake 15 minutes longer.
♦ **Prepare** almond rice by sautéing almonds in butter. Add rice and water. Stir briefly, cover and cook for 20 minutes.
♦ **Serve** sirloin tips over almond rice.

The Foster Ranch is still a working cattle ranch operated by H. V. Foster's grandson and great grandson under the name of Crossed J Cattle Co. Sadako Fujioshi, the Japanese cook at the Foster ranch from 1931 until the early 70's, worked for H. V. and Marie Foster. Foster named the ranch "El Rancho de la Codorniz" or "Ranch of the Quail".

BEEF ROULADES ⦾

Yield: 6 servings

1½ pounds round steak, thinly
   sliced
1 clove garlic, halved
1 teaspoon salt
⅛ teaspoon pepper
¾ pound pork sausage
2 tablespoons chopped fresh
   parsley
2 tablespoons chopped onion
1½ cups California Burgundy
1½ tablespoons tomato paste
½ cup ripe olives
8 ounces fresh mushrooms,
   sliced
Flour

♦ **Cut** steak into 6 equal pieces and flatten with a mallet into 4x6 inch pieces. Rub each piece with garlic. Season with salt and pepper.
♦ **Spread** a thin layer of sausage over each piece of meat. Sprinkle with parsley and onion.
♦ **Roll** each piece and tie with a string at both ends.
♦ **Dredge** each roulade in flour and brown well in a heavy skillet. Pour off excess fat.
♦ **Mix** tomato paste and wine and stir into skillet.
♦ **Cover** and cook on low for 1 hour.
♦ **Add** olives and mushrooms and cook uncovered for 15 minutes.

STEAK TOURNEDOS

Yield: 6 servings

1½ pounds flank steak
½ pound bacon, cooked, but
   not crisp
1 teaspoon garlic salt
½ teaspoon fresh ground
   pepper
2 tablespoons parsley

♦ **Pound** steak to even thickness (about ½ inch). Sprinkle with garlic salt and pepper.
♦ **Score** steak in a diamond pattern. Place bacon lengthwise on steak. Sprinkle with parsley.
♦ **Roll** up jelly-roll style starting at the small end. Skewer at 1 inch intervals. Cut into 1 to 1½ inch slices.
♦ **Grill**, turning once.

Serve with tarragon Hollandaise sauce and garnish with fresh parsley.

Boeuf Au Fromage

Yield: 4 servings

1½ pounds filet mignon, sliced in ¼ inch strips 3 inches long
½ cup flour seasoned with ¼ teaspoon pepper
2 tablespoons peanut oil (may need more)
2 tablespoons butter
1 cup beef stock
1 tablespoon sour cream
4 tablespoons Roquefort or blue cheese dressing
4 tablespoons grated Parmesan cheese

♦ **Coat** beef strips lightly with seasoned flour.
♦ **Heat** oil and butter in a large heavy skillet. Sauté beef on both sides, a few strips at a time. Remove beef from the skillet.
♦ **Pour** beef stock and sour cream into skillet and mix well over low heat. Add beef and stir carefully. Remove from heat.
♦ **Place** beef and sauce into a greased 2 quart casserole. Top with dressing and Parmesan cheese.
♦ **Place** under a preheated broiler until slightly brown. Serve immediately.

Beef Parmigiana •

Yield: 6 servings

1½ pounds round steak
1 egg, beaten
⅓ cup grated Parmesan cheese
⅓ cup fine bread crumbs
⅓ cup oil
1 medium onion, minced
1 teaspoon salt
¼ teaspoon pepper
½ teaspoon sugar
½ teaspoon marjoram
1 (6 ounce) can tomato paste
2 cups hot water
½ pound mozzarella cheese, sliced

♦ **Pound** flour into round steak. Trim off fat and cut into pieces. Dip meat into beaten egg. Roll meat in bread crumbs and Parmesan cheese.
♦ **Heat** oil in a large skillet. Brown steak on both sides. Lay in shallow baking dish.
♦ **Cook** onions until soft in the same skillet used to brown steaks. Stir in seasoning and tomato paste. Add hot water and stir.
♦ **Pour** most of sauce over meat. Top with cheese slices and remaining sauce.
♦ **Bake** at 350° for 1 hour.

Sauce recipe may be doubled and served with spaghetti.

COW THIEVES AND OUTLAWS HORSERADISH BEEF

Yield: 6 to 8 servings

1½ pounds top round of beef
1 tablespoon oil
1 medium onion, chopped
Salt and pepper
½ cup beef broth or red wine
¼ cup prepared horseradish

♦ **Brown** beef over moderate heat in a skillet.
♦ **Add** the onion, salt, pepper, broth and wine.
♦ **Spread** horseradish on beef.
♦ **Cook** covered for 1½ hours.

CAMPFIRE FLANK STEAK

Yield: 6 to 8 servings

½ cup tomato sauce
½ cup ketchup
½ cup chili sauce
3 tablespoons brown sugar
3 teaspoons Worcestershire sauce
2 tablespoons wine vinegar
2 tablespoons vegetable oil
2 cloves garlic, sliced
1 teaspoon salt
½ teaspoon pepper
½ teaspoon dry mustard
2 flank steaks

♦ **Mix** together all ingredients and marinate steak overnight or longer covered in the refrigerator.
♦ **Grill** steaks to desired doneness.
♦ **Slice** diagonally in thin slices.

CHUCK ROAST ON THE GRILL

Yield: 8 servings

2½ pounds boneless chuck roast, 2 inches thick
¼ cup brown sugar
5 ounces soy sauce
1 tablespoon lemon juice
¼ cup bourbon
1 teaspoon Worcestershire sauce
1½ cups water

♦ **Combine** marinade ingredients and pour over roast in a shallow dish. Refrigerate at least 8 hours.
♦ **Grill** meat 5 inches from coals for 30 minutes per side or to desired doneness. Baste often with marinade.
♦ **Divide** roast with fork (never slice).

CLASSIC CHICKEN FRIED STEAK

Yield: 4 to 6 servings

2 pounds round steak, ½ inch thick
2 teaspoons salt
2 teaspoons cider vinegar
2 cups water
Salt and pepper
Flour
Cooking oil

CREAM GRAVY
2 tablespoons oil from the frying pan
2 tablespoons flour
2 cups whole milk

♦ **Tenderize** the steak by pounding it thin. Cut into serving size pieces.

♦ **Soak** the meat in salt, vinegar and water solution. Cover and refrigerate for 2 hours. Blot dry when ready for frying.

♦ **Heat** a large skillet filled with ¼ inch deep cooking oil.

♦ **Dredge** meat in salt, pepper and flour mixture and brown in hot oil until tender (about 3 minutes per side). Set aside, keeping warm.

♦ **Pour** off all but 2 tablespoons of oil from frying pan. Sprinkle flour over the oil and stir to brown flour and loosen bits of meat.

♦ **Add** a small amount of the milk to make a paste. Continue adding milk and stirring over low heat while gravy bubbles gently and cooks to the right consistency.

Serve with home-made mashed potatoes and fresh vegetables from the garden - a meal fit to please natives of any territory!

MARINATED BEEF TENDERLOIN ⚬

Yield: 12 to 16 servings

6 - 8 pounds beef tenderloin
¼ cup olive oil
1 cup soy sauce
3 fresh cloves garlic, chopped
1 tablespoon chopped ginger
½ cup sherry

♦ **Rub** beef with olive oil.

♦ **Combine** remaining ingredients and marinate beef several hours.

♦ **Bake** at 350° for 45 to 50 minutes or until internal temperature reaches 130° for rare or 140° for medium. Baste with marinade.

TERIYAKI BEEF ROAST •

Yield: 6 servings

1 (4-5 pound) U.S. choice arm roast, cut 2½ inches thick
½ cup orange juice
¼ cup soy sauce
¼ cup sherry
¼ cup vegetable oil (optional)
1 clove garlic, minced
1 teaspoon sugar
½ teaspoon ground ginger

GALLERY
RANCH

♦ **Trim** fat from beef and pierce deeply on both sides with a fork. Place in 9x13 inch glass dish.

♦ **Mix** remaining ingredients and pour over meat.

♦ **Cover** and place in refrigerator at least 3 hours (or overnight). Turn occasionally.

♦ **Remove** meat from marinade and place on a rack in broiler pan. Broil meat 4 inches from heat for 6 minutes per side.

♦ **Place** meat on rack in roasting pan and bake at 350° for 25 minutes for rare or 30 minutes for medium rare.

♦ **Slice** diagonally across the grain and serve.

BURGUNDY-ROASTED VENISON

Yield: 8 to 10 servings

6 - 7 pounds of venison-roast, leg (bone removed) or back strap
6 slices salt pork or bacon
MARINADE
2 cups burgundy
1 cup beef bouillon
1 medium onion, sliced
1 clove garlic, crushed
1 bay leaf
3 juniper berries (optional)
1 teaspoon salt

♦ **Place** meat in large bowl. Cover with marinade. Cover and refrigerate for 24 hours.

♦ **Remove** meat; either tie or skewer into compact shape. Strain and reserve marinade.

♦ **Arrange** meat on rack in shallow pan. Place slices of salt pork over top.

♦ **Roast,** uncovered in 450° oven for 10 minutes. Reduce heat to 325° and roast 15 to 18 minutes per pound. Roast until well done. Baste meat occasionally with marinade. Strain drippings, discard fat, and serve drippings over sliced roast.

TRADITIONAL BUFFALO ROAST ❦

Yield: 6 to 8 servings

1 (3-4 pound) buffalo roast
2 tablespoons flour
½ cup red wine vinegar
½ cup water
Salt
1 bay leaf
8 whole cloves
1 medium onion, diced
1 teaspoon dried thyme

KEN-ADA
RANCH

♦ **Place** flour in a small (10x16 inch) plastic roasting bag and shake until bag is well coated. Place bag in a 2 inch deep roasting pan. Pour vinegar and water into bag and stir until well mixed with flour.
♦ **Rub** roast with salt and put into bag.
♦ **Add** bay leaf, cloves, onion and thyme around meat. Close bag with twist tie.
♦ **Make** six ½ inch slits in top of bag near the twist tie. A meat thermometer may be inserted through slits into center of meat.
♦ **Cook** at 325° for 2 to 2½ hours or until internal temperature reaches 170°.
♦ **Serve** liquid in bag as au jus or thicken with flour.

STUFFED TENDERLOIN ❦

Yield: Allow 4 to 6 ounces beef per serving

1 whole beef tenderloin
2 tablespoons butter
4 green onions, chopped
8 ounces fresh mushrooms, sliced
1 clove garlic, minced
4 - 5 sprigs fresh parsley, chopped
3 tablespoons blue cheese
Butter, melted

MONTGOMERY
RANCH

♦ **Slit** tenderloin with a sharp knife and set aside.
♦ **Sauté** onions, mushrooms, garlic and parsley in butter.
♦ **Fill** tenderloin with vegetables and then blue cheese. Close slit with toothpicks or sew together with heavy string. Brush surface with melted butter.
♦ **Grill** over charcoal until degree of doneness is obtained using a meat thermometer.
♦ **Slice** tenderloin after removing toothpicks.

Fillet of Beef with Brown Sugar and Poached Pears

Yield: 8 servings

3 - 4 pounds beef tenderloin, cut
    into 1½ inch serving pieces
4 pears, peeled
1 quart red wine
1 cinnamon stick
    Brown sugar
⅔ cup beef stock
2 tablespoons butter
1 lemon zest
1 orange zest
    Salt and pepper

♦ **Simmer** pears in a non-metallic pan with the red wine, cinnamon, orange zest and lemon zest until fork tender. Store in liquid in a cool place until ready to use.

♦ **Salt** and pepper the beef slices and thinly coat them with brown sugar, pressing the sugar into the meat.

♦ **Cook** the beef in hot oil until desired doneness, (approximately 5 minutes for medium rare). Remove from oil.

♦ **Deglaze** pan with some of the pear cooking liquid. Stir in the beef stock and reduce by cooking until liquid is ⅓ of original volume and is almost creamy. Add butter and shake pan in circles to thicken. Do not stir or use a whisk.

♦ **Halve** pears, remove core and slice lengthwise ½ inch from stem end through the bottom. Spread in a fan shape and heat in a very hot oven for 3 minutes.

♦ **Place** pear halves on each plate along with hot tournedo of beef. Pour sauce over just before serving. Serve remainder of sauce in a warmed gravy boat.

STEAK IN A BAG •

Yield: 8 servings

1 cup bread crumbs
2 - 3 pounds top sirloin, cut 2½ inches thick
4 tablespoons butter
4 tablespoons vegetable oil
1 teaspoon crushed garlic
2 teaspoons seasoned salt
2½ teaspoons seasoned pepper
1 cup shredded sharp cheese

HUGHES
RANCH

♦ **Trim** fat from steak.
♦ **Combine** butter, oil, garlic, salt and pepper in a bowl. Spread on all sides of steak.
♦ **Mix** bread crumbs and cheese. Press into butter mixture, coating steak well.
♦ **Place** steak in a clean brown paper bag. Fold end over and staple. Refrigerate several hours.
♦ **Bring** steak to room temperature (30 minutes) and set in a pan before cooking.
♦ **Bake** in a 375° preheated oven for 30 minutes. Raise the temperature to 425° for 15 minutes longer for medium rare.
♦ **Remove** from oven and let rest for 5 minutes. Carve thinly.

FIVE HOUR BEEF STEW •

Yield: 8 to 10 servings

3 pounds stew meat
3 tablespoons olive oil
2 cups diced carrots
1 cup diced celery
1 green pepper, diced
2 medium onions, quartered
4 medium potatoes, diced
2 tablespoons tapioca
1 tablespoon sugar
1 tablespoon salt
1 tablespoon Worcestershire sauce
Pepper to taste
2 (14 ounce) cans tomatoes
½ cup red wine

♦ **Brown** meat in oil in a 6 quart Dutch oven. Add and sauté carrot, celery, onion and green pepper.
♦ **Add** seasonings, tomatoes and wine and stir well.
♦ **Bake** covered at 250° for 5 hours. Do not raise lid until done.

GIN STEW

Yield: 6 servings

6 slices thick bacon
3 pounds chuck roast, cut into
 2½ inch chunks, 1 inch thick
 Flour
 Salt and pepper
1½ cups chopped onion
1½ cups sliced carrots
1½ cups sliced mushrooms
1½ cups tomatoes, peeled,
 seeded and diced
1 teaspoon Italian seasoning
2 cloves garlic, minced
1 cup dry vermouth
¼ cup gin
 Beef broth

FINAL FLAVORING
1 clove garlic, minced
 Pinch saffron
1 tablespoon capers
2 tablespoons Dijon mustard
2 tablespoons olive oil
2 tablespoons finely minced
 parsley

♦ **Blanch** bacon and place in the bottom of a Dutch oven.

♦ **Toss** meat in flour, salt and pepper and shake off excess. Divide in thirds.

♦ **Combine** vegetables with Italian seasoning. Divide in half.

♦ **Layer** meat and vegetables on top of bacon ending with meat.

♦ **Pour** in vermouth and gin. Heat on top of stove for 10 to 15 minutes. Add beef broth, if needed, so that liquid comes halfway up casserole.

♦ **Cover** and bake at 325° for 2 hours.

♦ **Mash** garlic with saffron and capers. Add mustard and oil and mash. Stir in parsley. Stir into stew and serve.

ROBUST RIB TICKLIN' BARBECUE SAUCE ⚬

Yield: 1½ cups

1 cup chili sauce
½ cup wine vinegar
1 teaspoon dry mustard
1 small onion, grated
4 tablespoons brown sugar ✓
1 tablespoon paprika
1 teaspoon chili powder
1 teaspoon salt
1 teaspoon Worcestershire
 sauce
½ lemon, grated rind and juice
½ cup red wine

♦ **Combine** ingredients in a saucepan. Simmer 15 minutes, but do not boil.

Excellent on ribs, chicken or any meat. This can be prepared ahead and kept in the refrigerator for days.

CHILI CON CARNE (OKLAHOMA STYLE)

Yield: 4 to 6 servings

3 pounds chili-grind choice
  arm roast
10 cloves garlic
2 teaspoons salt
½ teaspoon pepper
1 teaspoon cumin
½ tablespoon sugar
½ teaspoon oregano leaves
4 tablespoons chili powder
2 tablespoons ground
  crackers (optional)

♦ **Brown** the meat lightly in a greased skillet. Remove meat and juices to a heavy Dutch oven.

♦ **Dice** the garlic cloves in a food processor. Add to meat. Add enough water to cover meat.

♦ **Simmer** slowly until tender, about 2 to 3 hours.

♦ **Add** salt, pepper, cumin, sugar and oregano leaves.

♦ **Dissolve** chili powder in some of the meat liquid before adding to the mixture.

♦ **Simmer** 20 to 30 minutes longer. Turn off burner.

♦ **Add** ground crackers. Stir thoroughly.

INDIAN TACOS (CONTEMPORARY DISH)

Yield: 1 serving

Chili with beans
Lettuce, chopped
Tomatoes, chopped
Onions, chopped
Cheese, grated
Picante sauce
Fry bread, cut into round
4-5 inch pieces

♦ **Make** your favorite chili recipe with beans.

♦ **Place** fry bread (page 43) on a plate. Top with chili, then with chopped vegetables and sprinkle with grated cheese. Picante sauce may be poured over the top.

One Indian taco is a meal.

DELAWARE NATION

ROLLED BEEF ENCHILADAS

Yield: 5 to 8 servings

16 corn tortillas
  Salad oil or shortening
2½ cups canned Mexican red
  enchilada sauce, heated
1 pound ground beef,
  browned and seasoned with
  garlic powder, salt, pepper
  and oregano
¾ cup chopped onion
1½ cups shredded sharp
  Cheddar cheese
  Sour cream (optional)

♦ **Dip** each tortilla into medium hot shallow oil for just a few seconds, until it begins to blister and becomes limp. Do not fry until firm or crisp. Remove with tongs or a pancake turner.

♦ **Dip** hot tortillas into the heated sauce in a pan just bigger than the tortillas.

♦ **Spoon** 3 tablespoons ground beef down the center of each tortilla and sprinkle with 2 teaspoons onion. Roll tortilla around filling and place, flap side down, in an ungreased shallow casserole. Place filled enchiladas side by side.

♦ **Pour** enough sauce over the enchiladas to moisten entire surface of the casserole. Sprinkle with cheese. Top with onion.

♦ **Bake** uncovered at 350° for 15 to 20 minutes or just until hot throughout.

♦ **Top** with chilled sour cream.

Serve with refried beans and plain, hot tortillas.

For convenience you may fill and sauce the enchiladas up to 8 hours ahead. Be sure to pour a little more sauce over them just before baking to prevent drying out, then bake 15 to 20 minutes before serving.

Mushrooms Bourguignon Sauce •

⅓ cup butter
2 green onions, chopped
1 clove garlic, crushed
1 pound fresh mushrooms,
  sliced
1 cup Burgundy or other red
  wine
½ teaspoon salt
⅛ teaspoon freshly ground
  pepper
2 tablespoons chopped fresh
  parsley

♦ **Sauté** onion, garlic, and
  mushrooms in butter until
  tender.
♦ **Add** wine, salt, pepper and
  parsley. Simmer until wine is
  reduced by one half.
  Mushrooms will be quite dark.

Serve over beef.

Flank Steak Marinade
Yield: 2 cups

½ cup honey
½ cup lemon juice (2 large
  lemons)
⅓ cup soy sauce
½ teaspoon oregano
⅛ teaspoon garlic powder

♦ **Punch** holes in the meat with a
  fork.
♦ **Mix** all ingredients together
  and marinate steak for 2 to 3
  hours.
♦ **Grill** meat to desired
  doneness.

Veal Scallopine Piquante
Yield: 2 servings

4 (¼ pound) veal scallopine,
  pounded thin
Flour
Salt and pepper
2 tablespoons olive oil
4 tablespoons butter
½ large lemon
1 tablespoon capers
1 teaspoon anchovy paste
  (optional)
1 tablespoon minced parsley

♦ **Salt** and pepper veal. Dredge
  in flour.
♦ **Heat** olive oil and butter in hot
  skillet until frothy. Sauté veal
  for 3 minutes per side and
  remove to a heated platter.
  Pour fat from pan.
♦ **Return** pan to heat and
  squeeze in juice of lemon half
  to deglaze. Add 2 tablespoons
  butter, stirring rapidly. Toss in
  capers, parsley and anchovy
  paste. Stir a few seconds and
  pour over veal.

VEAL WITH MUSTARD CRABMEAT SAUCE

Yield: 4 servings

SAUCE

2 cups whipping cream
3 tablespoons country style Dijon mustard
1 tablespoon prepared horseradish
6 ounces frozen crabmeat, thawed and drained
Salt and pepper to taste

VEAL

1 pound boneless veal cutlets
½ cup flour
4 tablespoons butter

♦ **Pour** cream in medium heavy-bottomed saucepan. Boil gently over medium heat until cream has reduced to 1 cup (about 10 minutes). Stir in mustard and horseradish. Add crab, salt and pepper. Remove from heat. Cover and reserve. (This sauce can be made several hours ahead and refrigerated.)

♦ **Pound** veal to ⅛ inch thick between sheets of heavy plastic.

♦ **Dredge** veal in flour and shake off excess.

♦ **Melt** butter in a heavy skillet over medium heat. Add veal and sauté 15 seconds on each side.

♦ **Remove** to a serving plate. Spoon sauce over the top.

Garnish with finely chopped chives and a lemon slice.

VEAL WITH QUEEN ANNE CHERRIES

Yield: 4 to 6 servings

4 - 6 slices veal scaloppine
1 clove garlic, halved
½ cup fine dry bread crumbs
1 egg, beaten with 2 tablespoons water
¼ cup butter
½ cup chicken stock
1 cup cream
1 (14½ ounce) can Queen Anne or light, sweet cherries, drained and pitted

♦ **Rub** meat with garlic clove. Cut each slice into 2 or 3 smaller pieces.

♦ **Dip** pieces in egg then lightly in bread crumbs.

♦ **Heat** butter and lightly brown meat over medium heat.

♦ **Pour** stock and cream over meat. Cover. Reduce heat to very low. Cook until sauce has thickened.

♦ **Pour** cherries over meat and cook 5 minutes longer.

LEMON VEAL SCALLOPS WITH AVOCADO

Yield: 6 servings

1 pound veal scallopine (5 - 6 slices about ⅛ inch thick)
1 egg, well-beaten
2 tablespoons flour
3 tablespoons butter
1 tablespoon oil
¼ cup vermouth
½ cup chicken broth
3 tablespoons lemon juice
¾ teaspoon salt
¼ teaspoon white pepper
¼ cup chopped fresh parsley
1 large or 2 small avocados

♦ **Soak** veal in the beaten egg and refrigerate for at least 1 hour. Remove to a plate and sprinkle evenly with the flour, patting gently into both sides of the meat. Discard any excess flour.

♦ **Melt** butter and oil in a 10-12 inch skillet over moderate heat. Sauté half the veal at a time for about 3 minutes per side and remove to a plate. After all pieces are browned, return to skillet.

♦ **Add** vermouth to veal and stir gently. Add broth, 2 tablespoons lemon juice and salt and pepper. Stir well. The sauce will become creamy. Cover and simmer 10 to 15 minutes. During the last 5 minutes gently stir in chopped parsley.

♦ **Peel** and slice avocado while veal is cooking. Sprinkle with 1 tablespoon lemon juice. Place slices in an oven proof dish and bake at 300° for 5 minutes.

♦ **Place** veal on heated platter and surround with warm avocado slices.

♦ **Pour** sauce from sauté pan over all and serve at once.

SCANDINAVIAN ROAST PORK WITH SALAD

Yield: 6 servings

2 pounds pork tenderloin
¼ pound dried prunes, seeds removed
Port wine or Madeira
2 - 4 tablespoons butter
SALAD
2 large crisp apples, chopped
1 bunch green onions, chopped
2 ribs celery hearts, chopped
Lemon juice to taste
Mayonnaise to taste
Blanched almonds to taste
2 sprigs parsley, finely chopped

♦ **Cover** prunes with wine and soak overnight.
♦ **Slice** roast and place drained prunes in between slices. Salt and pepper to taste. Tie roast and place in a small roasting pan so juices can collect around it.
♦ **Bake** uncovered at 400° for 45 minutes or until roast is done.
♦ **Add** butter to the pan after cooking begins and baste roast occasionally with juices.
♦ **Combine** all salad ingredients and serve with roast.

ROAST TENDERLOIN OF PORK WITH PLUM SAUCE

Yield: 6 to 8 servings

1 - 2 pork tenderloins
Kikkoman's teriyaki marinade
PLUM SAUCE
1 cup plum preserves
2 tablespoon ketchup
1 tablespoon vinegar
2 tablespoons brown sugar
Pinch of ginger

♦ **Sprinkle** tenderloin with teriyaki marinade.
♦ **Roast** in a 350° oven for 30 minutes. Baste with marinade.
♦ **Combine** all plum sauce ingredients and heat until hot and well-blended.
♦ **Baste** with plum sauce during the last 30 minutes of baking or until the internal temperature reaches 175°.
♦ **Slice** tenderloin and serve with remaining plum sauce.

BAKED STUFFED PORK TENDERLOIN WITH MUSTARD SAUCE

Yield: 4 servings

1 (2-3 pound) pork tenderloin
½ cup soy sauce
½ cup bourbon
4 tablespoons brown sugar
4 cups cubed stale white bread
¼ cup chopped onion
2 tablespoons chopped parsley
¼ cup chopped celery
⅓ cup butter, melted
1 teaspoon salt
1 teaspoon sage
¼ teaspoon pepper

MUSTARD SAUCE

⅓ cup sour cream
⅓ cup mayonnaise
1 tablespoon dry mustard
2 tablespoons finely chopped green onions
1½ teaspoons vinegar
Salt to taste

♦ **Marinate** pork in soy sauce, bourbon and brown sugar for several hours or overnight, turning occasionally. Remove meat from marinade.
♦ **Sauté** onions, parsley and celery in butter. Mix cubed bread, vegetables and seasonings in a bowl.
♦ **Slice** pork down the middle lengthwise, being careful to slice only half way through. Stuff tenderloin with bread mixture. Tie together loosely with twine.
♦ **Place** marinade and tenderloin in a roasting pan.
♦ **Bake** at 325° for about 1 hour, basting frequently with marinade.
♦ **Mix** all mustard sauce ingredients together.
♦ **Slice** tenderloin into thin diagonal slices and serve with mustard sauce on the side.

CINNAMON PORK CHOPS •

Yield: 4 servings

4 bone-in pork chops, cut 1¼ - 1½ inches thick
Vegetable oil
Cinnamon
Salt

LIQUID

½ cup ketchup
2 tablespoons white wine vinegar
½ cup water
1 teaspoon Worcestershire sauce

♦ **Brown** chops in a lightly oiled pan.
♦ **Place** chops in a casserole. Salt and generously sprinkle with cinnamon.
♦ **Combine** liquid ingredients and spoon over chops, being careful not to wash off the cinnamon.
♦ **Cover** tightly with a lid or foil and bake at 325° for 3½ to 4 hours, depending on the thickness of the chops.

STUFFED PORK FILLET

Yield: 12 servings

2 (1½ pound) pork tenderloin fillets
2 tablespoons butter or margarine, divided
1 shallot, finely chopped
1 apple, finely chopped
½ cup finely chopped raisins
⅓ cup finely chopped walnuts
1 tablespoon finely chopped parsley
½ cup bread crumbs
1 egg, slightly beaten
Dried basil
Oregano
Marjoram
1 cup cider
CRÈME FRAICHE
¼ cup sour cream
½ cup whipping cream

♦ **Combine** sour cream and whipping cream and heat to 110°. Let stand at room temperature until thickened, about 8 hours.
♦ **Split** tenderloin open and flatten with a meat mallet. Trim the fillets to an even size.
♦ **Prepare** stuffing by sautéing the shallot in 1 tablespoon butter for 1 to 2 minutes. Add next 6 ingredients.
♦ **Season** the inside of the fillets with salt and pepper and layer with the stuffing. Tie together. Brush outside of fillets with 1 tablespoon melted butter and sprinkle with herbs.
♦ **Roast** at 350° for 50 minutes.
♦ **Deglaze** pan with cider. Add 2 to 3 tablespoons crème fraiche and pour over tenderloin just before serving.

CHUTNEY GLAZED HAM

Yield: 10 to 12 servings

1 precooked bone-in ham (approximately 8 pounds)
Cloves
GLAZE
¼ cup chutney
¼ cup plum jam
1 teaspoon rice wine vinegar
⅛ teaspoon Tabasco
1 tablespoon Dijon mustard
1 clove garlic, minced
½ cup brown sugar

♦ **Remove** rind and excess fat from ham with a sharp knife. Score ham in a diamond pattern and stud with cloves at each intersection.
♦ **Bake** at 325° until internal temperature reaches 130°.
♦ **Combine** all glaze ingredients in a saucepan and heat until syrupy.
♦ **Spread** glaze over ham one hour before ham is done.

GRILLED MARINATED PORK CHOPS •

Yield: 8 servings

16 center cut pork chops
MARINADE
1 cup pineapple juice
¼ cup rice wine vinegar
1 cup soy sauce
⅛ cup finely minced fresh
  ginger
¼ cup chopped fresh cilantro
½ cup chopped pineapple
½ cup water
APPLE SAUCE
10 green apples, sliced
1 ounce butter
½ cup white wine
½ cup maple syrup
¼ cup brandy
  Cinnamon, nutmeg and
  mace to taste

♦ **Combine** all marinade ingredients. Marinate pork chops for at least 3 hours or up to 2 days.

♦ **Grill** lightly oiled chops over hot mesquite charcoal until medium done (approximately 4 to 5 minutes on each side.)

♦ **Sauté** apples lightly in butter. Add white wine and bring to a rapid boil, stirring constantly for 5 minutes. Mix in all other ingredients. Serve hot with pork chops.

HONEY BASTING MARINADE •

Yield: 5 ounces

2 tablespoons olive oil
1 onion, finely chopped
1 clove garlic, crushed
4 tablespoons orange juice
2 tablespoons clear honey
3 tablespoons wine vinegar
1 tablespoon Worcestershire
  sauce
1 teaspoon horseradish sauce
  or creamed horseradish
1 teaspoon dry mustard
  Salt and pepper
  Large pinch rosemary
  Large pinch thyme

♦ **Heat** oil in a small saucepan. Add onion and garlic and cook uncovered over low heat until soft, not brown.

♦ **Stir** in remaining ingredients and simmer uncovered 5 minutes. Allow to cool. Use as marinade for chicken or pork.

POLENTA WITH ITALIAN SAUSAGE

Yield: 4 servings

1 pound Italian sausage
1 small onion, chopped
1 tablespoon olive oil
1 (14½ ounce) can diced
   tomatoes
Salt and pepper
1½ quarts water salted with 1
   teaspoon salt
2 cups polenta or yellow
   cornmeal
1 cup grated Parmesan cheese

♦ **Slice** sausage in 2 inch pieces. Place in a heavy skillet with ½ inch water. Cook over medium high heat until water evaporates.

♦ **Brown** sausage and onion in oil over medium heat. Drain. Add tomatoes, salt and pepper. Simmer 1 hour, stirring occasionally. While sauce is cooking prepare polenta.

♦ **Boil** 1½ quarts salted water. Pour polenta slowly into water while stirring vigorously. Cook over low heat until polenta leaves sides of pan, stirring constantly, about 20 to 30 minutes. Remove from heat and add ½ cup Parmesan cheese.

♦ **Pour** half the polenta onto a large deep platter. Pour ½ the sausage and sauce on top of polenta. Layer the remaining polenta and sausage. Top with remaining cheese. Serve at once.

GRILLED CHICKEN MARGARITA

Yield: 4 servings

4 chicken breasts, cut into 1½
   inch cubes
1 cup Margarita Mix (or 1 cup
   lime juice, 6 teaspoons
   sugar and ½ teaspoon salt)
1 teaspoon ground coriander
1 clove garlic, minced
2 tablespoons butter, melted

♦ **Combine** all ingredients and pour over chicken breasts. Marinate for 1 hour or longer.

♦ **Thread** on skewers and grill until done.

♦ **Serve** with grilled zucchini, onions, and tomatoes.

GRILLED HOISIN LEG OF LAMB

Yield: 6 to 8 servings

⅓ cup hoisin sauce
3 tablespoons rice vinegar
2 tablespoons soy sauce
2 tablespoons minced garlic
¼ cup minced scallions
1 tablespoon honey
½ teaspoon salt
1 (6½-7½ pound) whole leg of lamb, trimmed, boned and butterflied

♦ **Mix** together first 7 ingredients in a bowl.

♦ **Place** lamb in a large shallow dish and spread marinade on both sides. Cover and chill for 24 to 48 hours, turning occasionally.

♦ **Bring** lamb to room temperature.

♦ **Grill** 12 to 15 minutes per side for medium rare. (Lamb may be broiled instead.)

♦ **Transfer** lamb to a cutting board and let stand 20 minutes.

♦ **Hold** knife at a 45° angle and cut lamb across grain into thin slices.

ORANGE GINGER CHICKEN BREASTS

Yield: 4 servings

4 frozen (or thawed) boneless, skinless, chicken breasts
2 tablespoons olive oil
1 thumb-sized piece of ginger root
Cavender's Greek seasoning
⅓ cup fresh orange juice
⅓ cup white wine

♦ **Heat** the oil in a non-stick skillet on medium high. Add the chicken and lightly brown.

♦ **Arrange** the browned breasts in a baking dish. Sprinkle generously with Cavender's seasoning. Place a big slice of peeled ginger root on each. Pour orange juice and wine around the breasts. Cover with foil.

♦ **Bake** at 350° for 25 minutes. Remove the ginger slice and garnish with a half slice of fresh orange, sprinkled with chopped parsley.

LEG OF LAMB WITH ORZO

Yield: 8 servings

3 pounds leg of American lamb
4 - 5 cloves garlic, halved
  Greek oregano
  Salt and pepper
1 pound orzo
1 (6 ounce) can tomato paste

♦ **Wash** leg of lamb. Remove excess fat. Rub with olive oil.

♦ **Slit** meaty part of the leg 8 to 10 times with a sharp knife. Rub in salt, pepper and oregano. Put a garlic slice inside each slit.

♦ **Salt** and pepper lamb and rub with oregano. Place in a large metal roasting pan and add an inch of water.

♦ **Bake** at 375° for 1½ hours or until juices are clear when pricked with a fork. While baking, turn meat over when brown.

♦ **Remove** lamb from pan and cover with foil. Reserve juice.

♦ **Turn** oven to 500°.

♦ Add 2 cups boiling water to reserved juices in roasting pan. Mix in ½ can tomato paste. Set pan in hot oven and heat at least 10 minutes.

♦ **Pour** orzo into boiling juices and stir. Add enough boiling water to completely cover orzo. Add salt and pepper to taste. Stir frequently to prevent sticking. Continue to add boiling water as needed, careful of the steam from the very hot oven.

♦ **Cook** about 10 minutes or until orzo is tender. It will thicken as it stands.

♦ **Serve** immediately along with lamb slices.

LAMB MARRAKECH

Yield: 6 to 8 servings

3 pounds lean lamb (from leg or shoulder) cut into 1 inch pieces
½ cup peanut or olive oil
2 large onions, finely chopped
3 cloves garlic, chopped
2 teaspoons salt
1 teaspoon crushed red chili pepper
¼ teaspoon cinnamon
¼ teaspoon clove
¼ teaspoon cumin
1 teaspoon turmeric or ½ teaspoon saffron threads
1 cup chicken stock
3 large ripe tomatoes, peeled, seeded and chopped or 3 cups canned peeled Italian tomatoes
1 cup white raisins, soaked in sherry
1 cup almond slivers, toasted
Crisp French fried onion rings

♦ **Brown** lamb in oil in a Dutch oven. Remove lamb and set aside.

♦ **Add** onions and garlic to pot and brown lightly until onions are wilted.

♦ **Return** meat to the pot and add the seasonings, tomatoes and raisins. Bring to a boil.

♦ **Add** enough chicken stock to cover lamb. Cover and simmer for 1½ hours.

♦ **Garnish** with onion rings, almonds and parsley.

May be made ahead and reheated just before serving.

CRISPY CHICKEN ♦

Yield: 8 servings

8 chicken breast fillets
½ cup butter or margarine
2 cups crushed Ritz crackers
¾ cup Parmesan cheese
¼ cup chopped parsley
1 - 2 cloves garlic, crushed
2 teaspoons salt
⅛ teaspoon pepper

♦ **Melt** butter or margarine.

♦ **Blend** cracker crumbs, Parmesan cheese, parsley, garlic, salt and pepper.

♦ **Dip** chicken pieces first in melted butter then in crumb mixture.

♦ **Place** in an 8x11 inch Pyrex pan and bake at 350° for 45 minutes. Do not turn.

CHICKEN WITH PEACH SALSA

Yield: 6 servings

½ cup chopped onion
1 (14½ ounce) can whole
tomatoes, drained, chopped
⅔ cup diced peaches
½ cup peach preserves
1 cinnamon stick
1 tablespoon chopped fresh
cilantro
1 teaspoon chopped fresh
ginger root or ¼ teaspoon
dried ginger
¼ teaspoon salt
⅛ teaspoon pepper
3 whole chicken breasts,
skinned, boned, halved
3 cups cooked rice

♦ **Spray** a medium non-stick saucepan with cooking spray. Heat over medium heat until hot. Add onion; cook and stir 3 minutes.

♦ **Add** next 8 ingredients. Bring to a boil, reduce heat. Simmer uncovered 20 to 30 minutes or until sauce thickens, stirring occasionally.

♦ **Keep** salsa warm. When ready to serve, remove and discard cinnamon stick.

♦ **Broil** chicken 4 to 6 inches from heat for 18 to 20 minutes or until chicken is fork-tender, turning once halfway through broiling. Or, charcoal the chicken on a grill for approximately 20 minutes.

♦ **Serve** chicken breast on top of rice; spoon salsa over chicken.

CHICKEN SPECTACULAR

Yield: 10 to 12 servings

3-4 cups chicken, cooked,
boned, and chopped
1 package Uncle Ben's wild
rice (cooked according to
package directions)
1 can cream of celery soup
1 (2 ounce) jar pimientos
1 medium onion, chopped
2 (15½ ounce) cans French
style green beans, drained
1 cup mayonnaise
1 (4 ounce) can sliced water
chestnuts, drained
Salt and pepper

♦ **Mix** all ingredients. Pour into a 9x13 inch casserole dish sprayed with cooking spray. Bake 45 minutes to 1 hour at 350°.

Can be frozen but do not cook before freezing.

CHICKEN LOMBARDY •

Yield: 6 servings

6 chicken breasts, skinned, boned, pounded thin
½ cup flour
4 tablespoons butter
Salt and pepper
1½ cups sliced mushrooms
¾ cup dry white wine
½ cup chicken stock
½ cup grated mozzarella cheese
½ cup grated Parmesan cheese

♦ **Dredge** chicken in flour. Sauté in 2 tablespoons butter until brown. Remove from skillet and place in greased casserole dish. Sprinkle with salt and pepper.
♦ **Sauté** mushrooms in 2 tablespoons butter and drippings. Sprinkle over chicken.
♦ **Boil** down wine and stock in the skillet and pour over chicken. Sprinkle with cheeses.
♦ **Bake** covered 20 to 30 minutes at 350°. Uncover for the last 10 minutes.

BAKED PINEAPPLE CHICKEN

Yield: 6 servings

1 (30 ounce) can pineapple slices
1 clove garlic, crushed
2 teaspoons cornstarch
2 teaspoons Worcestershire sauce
2 teaspoons Dijon mustard
1 teaspoon rosemary, crushed
6 chicken breasts, boned and skinned
1 lemon, thinly sliced

♦ **Drain** pineapple, reserving juice. Combine reserved juice with garlic, cornstarch, Worcestershire sauce, mustard and rosemary.
♦ **Place** chicken in a 9x13 inch baking pan or broiler-proof dish. Broil until browned.
♦ **Stir** sauce and pour over chicken. Bake at 400° for 30 minutes.
♦ **Arrange** lemon and pineapple slices around chicken and garnish with fresh rosemary or parsley.

Hawaiian Chicken

Yield: 6 to 8 servings

2 (3 pound) chickens cut in pieces or 8 individual boneless, skinless chicken breasts
1 cup cornstarch
½ cup salad oil
2 large white onions, sliced in half rings
1 cup chopped celery
1 large green bell pepper, sliced in rings
1 (30 ounce) can chunk pineapple, drained, reserving juice
¼ cup brown sugar
¼ cup soy sauce

♦ **Put** chicken in a bag with cornstarch and shake. Fry chicken in oil until golden brown (less time for boneless, skinless breasts). Remove chicken. Transfer to ovenproof casserole.
♦ **Sauté** onions, celery and pepper in the oil. Do not brown. Put vegetables and pineapple around chicken. Arrange pepper rings on top.
♦ **Mix** brown sugar, soy sauce and pineapple juice. Pour over chicken. Bake covered at 350° for 1 hour (less for boneless, skinless breasts). Serve with rice.

Swiss Enchiladas

Yield: 6 to 8 servings

1 onion, chopped
2 tablespoons oil
1 clove garlic, crushed
2 cups tomato purée
2 (4½ ounce) cans chopped green chilies
2 cups chopped cooked chicken
1 dozen tortillas, with additional oil for frying
6 chicken bouillon cubes
3 cups hot cream
½ pound Monterey Jack or Swiss cheese, grated

♦ **Sauté** onion until soft in 2 tablespoons oil. Add garlic, tomato purée, green chilies, and chicken. Season with salt and simmer for 10 minutes.
♦ **Fry** tortillas in about 1 inch hot oil. Do not let them crisp, as they are to be rolled.
♦ **Dissolve** chicken bouillon cubes in hot cream. Dip each tortilla in this, cover generously with chicken filling and roll up.
♦ **Arrange** rolls in 9x13 inch baking dish and cover with remaining cream mixture. Top with grated cheese.
♦ **Bake** in a 350° oven for 30 minutes.

CAJUN CHICKEN

Yield: 4 to 6 servings

2 whole boneless chicken breasts, cut into thin strips
¾ teaspoon dried tarragon
¼ cup butter or margarine
3 tablespoons flour
1½ cups milk

CAJUN SPICE BLEND
¼ teaspoon ground black pepper
¼ teaspoon ground cayenne pepper
¼ teaspoon ground white pepper
¼ teaspoon ground garlic powder
¼ teaspoon ground onion powder
¼ teaspoon ground paprika
¼ teaspoon ground salt
¼ teaspoon ground thyme
Tabasco

♦ **Combine** Cajun spice blend ingredients and set aside.
♦ **Sauté** chicken in 2 tablespoons butter. Sprinkle chicken with tarragon and ½ of Cajun spice blend. Cook chicken until done then spoon onto a plate and set aside.
♦ **Melt** remaining butter in same skillet. Stir in flour and cook for 2 minutes. Add milk and remaining Cajun spice blend. Cook, stirring constantly until thickened.
♦ **Return** chicken to sauce and serve over rice along with Tabasco.

May substitute shrimp for chicken.

ZESTY CHICKEN, RICE AND GREENS •

Yield: 4 servings

2 tablespoons olive oil
2 cloves garlic, chopped
1 large yellow onion, peeled and chopped
4 boneless, skinless, chicken breasts
1 cup raw rice
1 bunch collard greens or mustard greens, washed well and rough-chopped
1 (10 ounce) can Rotel
½ cup canned chicken broth
Cajun seasoning

♦ **Heat** olive oil in a Dutch oven on medium heat. Sauté garlic and onion. Remove and set aside.
♦ **Sauté** chicken breasts until lightly browned.
♦ **Put** garlic and onion on top of chicken and sprinkle raw rice on top of and around chicken.
♦ **Heap** chopped greens on top.
♦ **Add** Rotel and chicken broth and a healthy sprinkle of Cajun seasoning. Cover tightly, reduce heat to low and cook 15 minutes. Check to see if additional broth is needed. Cook 10 more minutes, covered. Let stand 5 minutes covered before serving.

CHICKEN AND SHRIMP WITH ARTICHOKES AND CAPERS

Yield: 6 servings

1 pound large shrimp, shelled and deveined
1 (10 ounce) package large mushrooms, sliced
1 shallot or small onion, minced
1 pound chicken tenders, cut into 3 inch pieces
All-purpose flour
Salt
Olive oil
¼ cup dry white wine
2 (6 ounce) jars marinated artichoke hearts
2 tablespoons capers

♦ **Combine** 2 tablespoons flour and ¾ teaspoon salt on waxed paper. Roll chicken pieces to coat.

♦ **Cook** mushrooms in 1 tablespoon of oil until golden in a 12 inch skillet over medium heat. Remove with slotted spoon to a large bowl.

♦ **Cook** shrimp in 2 tablespoon hot oil in the same skillet until shrimp turn opaque. Remove to bowl with mushrooms.

♦ **Cook** chicken in 1 tablespoon hot oil for 2 or 3 minutes or until chicken loses its pink color in the same skillet. Remove to bowl.

♦ **Stir** in 1 tablespoon flour with 1 tablespoon hot oil in the same skillet and cook over medium heat until flour begins to brown lightly. Gradually stir in wine, ½ teaspoon salt and 1½ cups water. Heat over high heat until sauce thickens slightly. Boil 1 minute.

♦ **Return** the chicken mixture to skillet. Stir in capers and artichokes. Add salt and pepper to taste and heat through.

CRAB-STUFFED CHICKEN

Yield: 8 servings

2 tablespoons butter or
  margarine
¼ cup all-purpose flour
¾ cup milk
¾ cup chicken broth
⅓ cup dry white wine
⅓ cup chopped green onion
2 tablespoons butter or
  margarine
1 (6 ounce) package frozen
  crabmeat, thawed and
  drained
1 (8 ounce) package fresh
  mushrooms, sliced
½ cup cracker crumbs
1 tablespoon chopped fresh
  parsley
½ teaspoon salt
¼ teaspoon pepper
8 chicken breasts, boned and
  skinned
1 cup grated Swiss cheese
1 teaspoon paprika
  Hot cooked rice

♦ **Melt** 2 tablespoons butter in a heavy saucepan over low heat. Add flour, stirring until smooth. Cook 1 minute, stirring constantly.

♦ **Combine** milk, broth, and wine; gradually add to flour mixture. Cook over medium heat, stirring constantly, until thickened and bubbly. Set sauce aside.

♦ **Sauté** green onions and mushrooms in 2 tablespoon butter until tender. Stir in crabmeat, cracker crumbs, parsley, salt, and pepper. Stir in 2 tablespoons sauce.

♦ **Place** each chicken breast on a sheet of waxed paper. Flatten chicken to ¼ inch thickness, using a meat mallet or rolling pin.

♦ **Spoon** ¼ cup crabmeat mixture in center of each chicken breast. Fold opposite ends over and place seam side down in a greased 9x13 inch baking dish. Pour remaining sauce over the chicken.

♦ **Cover** and bake at 350° for 1 hour. Sprinkle with cheese and paprika. Bake uncovered an additional minute or until cheese melts. Serve over hot cooked rice.

CHINESE BROILED TURKEY STEAKS

Yield: 6 to 8 servings

6 - 8 turkey steaks
MARINADE
  1 tablespoon grated fresh
    ginger or ground ginger
  1 teaspoon Accent
  1 tablespoon honey
  1 teaspoon dry mustard
  ½ cup soy sauce
  ¼ cup salad oil

♦ **Combine** ingredients for marinade in glass or pottery bowl. Let stand 24 hours at room temperature.
♦ **Pour** marinade over turkey, cover and refrigerate for several hours or overnight.
♦ **Drain** steaks and cook quickly on both sides over hot coals allowing about 8 minutes each side. Brush occasionally with marinade.

SMOTHERED QUAIL

Yield: 4 to 6 servings

  12 quail
  ½ cup butter
    Flour
1 - 2 (10½ ounce) cans consommé
¼ - ½ cup sherry
  2 cups sliced fresh
    mushrooms
    Salt and pepper to taste
  3 cups cooked long grain and
    wild rice

♦ **Clean** quail and dust with flour, salt and pepper. Melt butter in heavy skillet and sauté quail until brown. Remove quail from pan and place in baking dish.
♦ **Add** flour to butter in skillet and stir well. Slowly add consommé and sherry. Cook until slightly thick and bubbly.
♦ **Sauté** mushrooms with a little butter in a small skillet. Add mushrooms to sauce and pour over quail.
♦ **Cover** and bake at 350° for 1 hour. Lower oven to 275° to 300° and bake an additional 45 minutes to 1 hour. Check occasionally and if dry, add more consommé.
♦ **Serve** quail over rice.

GRILLED QUAIL

Yield: 6 to 8 servings

16 whole quail breasts
16 small jalapeño peppers
16 slices bacon
 1 (8 ounce) bottle Italian
   dressing
½ cup white wine
⅓ cup soy sauce
¼ cup lemon juice
¼ teaspoon pepper

♦ **Rinse** quail in cold water. Pat dry. Place a seeded pepper in the cavity. Wrap bacon around and secure with a toothpick. Place in shallow dish.

♦ **Mix** remaining ingredients and pour over quail. Cover and marinate in the refrigerator several hours. Remove, reserve marinade.

♦ **Grill** quail away from the coals. Brush on the marinade during grilling. Cook about 20 to 30 minutes, then put over hot coals for 5 minutes or until bacon crisps.

OILFIELD PHEASANT

Yield: 4 to 6 servings

2 medium pheasants
1 can cream of mushroom
  soup
1 (8 ounce) package fresh
  mushrooms
1½ cups sour cream (may use
   low fat)
1 tablespoon Worcestershire
  sauce
2 tablespoons parsley flakes
½ onion, coarsely chopped
1 teaspoon garlic salt
1½ cups Burgundy wine
   Seasoned salt
   Coarse ground pepper

♦ **Wash** birds and pat dry. Place in deep roasting pan after sprinkling with seasoned salt and coarse ground pepper.

♦ **Mix** remaining ingredients thoroughly and pour the mixture over the pheasant.

♦ **Cook** 1½ hours in a 350° oven. Turn and baste pheasant and cook 1½ hours longer, basting occasionally. Serve with wild or white rice and pan gravy.

ELEGANT SKILLET DUCK

Yield: 4 to 6 servings

4 - 6 duck fillets
1 can cream of mushroom
   soup
¼ cup milk
½ cup flour
   Salt and pepper
2 ounces brandy
1 ounce Curaçao
¼ cup butter

♦ **Marinate** fillets in milk for several hours in refrigerator. Drain well.

♦ **Mix** flour, salt and pepper in a bag. Toss fillets, one at a time, in the bag until well coated.

♦ **Brown** fillets in butter, remove from skillet and drain.

♦ **Add** soup and liquor. Turn heat to low and add fillets. Simmer covered one hour until tender. Add liquid if needed. Serve over wild rice.

CORNISH HENS WITH FRUITED STUFFING

Yield: 4 servings

1½ cups herb-seasoned
   croutons
1 (8¾ ounce) can apricot
   halves, drained and
   chopped
½ cup halved seedless green
   grapes
⅓ cup chopped pecans
2 tablespoons apricot nectar
2 tablespoons melted butter or
   margarine
1 tablespoon capers
1 tablespoon chopped fresh
   parsley
¼ teaspoon salt
¼ teaspoon pepper
4 (1-1½ pound) Cornish hens
⅓ cup apricot nectar
2 tablespoons melted butter or
   margarine
2 teaspoons soy sauce

♦ **Combine** first 10 ingredients. Stir gently and set aside.

♦ **Remove** giblets from hens. Rinse hens in cold water and pat dry.

♦ **Stuff** hens with crouton mixture and close cavities. Secure with toothpicks and truss. Place hens, breast side up, on rack in a shallow roasting pan.

♦ **Combine** ⅓ cup apricot nectar, 2 tablespoons butter or margarine, and 2 teaspoons soy sauce. Brush on hens. Bake at 350° for 1½ hours, basting occasionally with apricot mixture.

SMOKED CHICKEN AND SHRIMP ◦ p.168 WITH PASTA ALFREDO

Yield: 8 servings

1 pound shaped pasta, cooked and drained
½ pound julienne smoked chicken breast
½ pound grilled shrimp
½ cup julienne zucchini
⅓ cup chopped sun-dried tomatoes in olive oil

ALFREDO SAUCE
3 tablespoons butter
3 tablespoons flour
1 clove garlic, crushed
2 cups milk
2 cups heavy cream
½ cup white wine ✓
Salt and coarse black pepper
½ cup grated fresh Parmesan cheese

♦ **Melt** butter in medium saucepan with a clove of crushed garlic. Remove garlic and stir in flour. Cook over medium heat 1 minute.
♦ **Scald** milk and cream. Stir into roux and continue stirring until slightly thickened.
♦ **Stir** in wine, salt, pepper and Parmesan cheese. Stir until cheese is melted and sauce is smooth.
♦ **Toss** hot pasta with chicken, shrimp, zucchini, tomatoes and cream sauce. Serve immediately.

PEPPER SAUSAGE PASTA SAUCE ◦

Yield: 6 servings

3 large red bell peppers, cut in 1 inch pieces
3 tablespoons olive oil
1 onion, chopped
Salt and pepper
1 (15 ounce) can diced tomatoes
1 pound mild Italian sausage, cut in ½ inch pieces
1 pound spaghetti, cooked and drained
Fresh grated Parmesan cheese

♦ **Sauté** onion in 3 tablespoons oil until soft. Add peppers and cook 7 to 8 minutes. Add tomatoes and cook 10 minutes more.
♦ **Cook** sausage in ¼ cup water in heavy skillet over high heat until water is gone. Lower heat to medium and cook sausage until brown and fully cooked. Drain.
♦ **Add** sausage to pepper mixture. Toss with pasta and sprinkle with Parmesan cheese.

LEMON CHICKEN AND PASTA ON GREENS

Yield: 4 to 6 servings

CHICKEN

¼ cup white vinegar
2 tablespoons Dijon mustard
1 teaspoon freshly ground black pepper
4 lemons
⅓ cup olive oil
4 whole chicken breasts

PASTA

1 pound rigatoni pasta
Fresh black pepper
4 lemons
4 tablespoons freshly grated Romano cheese
½ cup freshly grated Parmesan cheese
Dash of crushed red pepper flakes

GREENS

Romaine lettuce
2 tablespoons balsamic vinegar
¼ cup olive oil
1 teaspoon Dijon mustard
1 teaspoon lemon juice

♦ **Pound** out chicken breast halves until even. Mix together first 5 ingredients. Add chicken breasts and marinate at least 4 to 6 hours. Chicken may be marinated in refrigerator up to 2 days.

♦ **Grill** chicken until done (4 to 6 minutes per side), preferably on outdoor grill. (Chicken may be cooked in oven.) Cut chicken into strips and set aside.

♦ **Cook** pasta al dente in boiling water to which 1 tablespoon salt and 1 tablespoon olive oil has been added. Drain. Rinse. Cool. Rinse pasta pan and return cooked pasta to pan.

♦ **Add** cheeses, peppers and juice from lemons. Stir constantly over medium heat 3 to 4 minutes.

♦ **Blend** vinegar, olive oil, Dijon mustard and lemon juice. Toss washed, dried, torn pieces of lettuce with dressing. Top the greens with the grilled chicken and serve the pasta on the side.

Chicken and pasta can be prepared ahead. When ready to serve, heat pasta with lemons, cheeses, and peppers.

WHITE LASAGNA

Yield: 8 servings

5 - 6 boneless, skinless chicken breasts
1 (14½ ounce) can chicken broth plus enough water to equal 3 cups
¼ cup butter
1 pound mushrooms, sliced
½ cup white wine
½ teaspoon tarragon leaves
¼ cup butter
5 tablespoons all-purpose flour
½ - 1 teaspoon salt
¼ teaspoon white pepper
¼ teaspoon ground nutmeg
2 cups half-and-half
9 - 12 lasagna noodles, cooked al dente
¾ pound Swiss or Gruyère cheese, shredded

♦ **Place** chicken in a 4 quart pan, add chicken broth and water, and bring to a boil. Reduce heat, cover, and simmer until chicken is tender, about 20 to 25 minutes. Strain broth and reserve. Shred chicken.

♦ **Melt** butter in a wide frying pan over medium high heat. Add mushrooms and cook.

♦ **Add** wine and tarragon; reduce heat to medium and cook until most of the pan juices are evaporated. Set aside.

♦ **Melt** butter in a 2 quart pan over medium heat. Blend flour, salt, pepper, and nutmeg and cook, stirring until bubbly. Remove from heat. Gradually stir in half & half and 2½ cups reserved broth.

♦ **Return** to heat and stir until smooth and thickened. Stir mushrooms into sauce.

♦ **Butter** a 9x13 inch baking dish. Spread a thin layer of sauce on bottom. Arrange noodles evenly over sauce, next layer chicken, then sauce, and finally cheese. Repeat this layering at least one more time, ending with cheese layer. If made ahead, cover and refrigerate.

♦ **Bake** uncovered in a 350° oven until hot and bubbly (40 to 50 minutes). Cut into squares and serve.

THREE CHEESE SPINACH ROLL-UPS

Yield: 8 servings

8 lasagna noodles
3 tablespoons butter
1 red bell pepper, finely chopped
½ cup chopped onion
2 (10 ounce) packages frozen chopped spinach cooked, squeezed and sautéed briefly in butter
2 cups shredded mozzarella cheese
¾ cup ricotta cheese
¾ cup Parmesan cheese
1 egg, slightly beaten
¼ cup butter
¼ cup all-purpose flour
⅛ teaspoon pepper
½ teaspoon salt
1 cup milk
1 cup light cream or half-and-half

♦ **Cook** lasagna noodles according to package directions. Place in a large bowl of cold water, set aside.

♦ **Sauté** onion and red pepper with 3 tablespoons butter for 5 minutes or until tender.

♦ **Combine** spinach, onion, red pepper, 1½ cups mozzarella cheese, ricotta cheese, ½ cup Parmesan and egg. Set aside.

♦ **Melt** ¼ cup butter in saucepan. Stir in flour. Add salt and pepper. Stir in milk, cream and remaining Parmesan cheese. Bring to a boil, stirring constantly until thickened.

♦ **Remove** noodles from water. Pat dry with paper towels.

♦ **Spread** about ½ cup spinach mixture over each noodle. Roll up jelly roll fashion, starting at short end.

♦ **Spread** a small amount of sauce on bottom of buttered 2 quart rectangular baking dish. Place rolls in dish. Spoon remaining sauce over roll-ups. Sprinkle with remaining shredded mozzarella cheese. Bake 30 to 35 minutes or until hot and bubbly.

VEGETABLE GARDEN PASTA

Yield: 10 servings

1 tablespoon olive oil
1 large onion, diced
½ pound snap peas or Chinese pea pods, stems and strings removed
2 tablespoons olive oil
4 medium carrots, sliced
1 bunch broccoli, cut in small pieces
¼ cup water
1 (16 ounce) package rigatoni macaroni
¼ cup red wine vinegar
1 tablespoon mustard
1 teaspoon sugar
1 teaspoon salt
⅓ cup olive oil
3 small tomatoes, cut in wedges
½ cup fresh basil
¾ cup grated Parmesan cheese

♦ **Heat** 1 tablespoon olive oil over high heat in large (5 quart) pan. Add onion and sauté 2 minutes. Add peas and cook 2 to 3 minutes until tender crisp. Remove to a large bowl.

♦ **Cook** carrots and broccoli in 2 tablespoons hot olive oil. Stir until vegetables are coated with oil.

♦ **Add** ¼ cup water and reduce heat to medium. Cook 3 minutes covered. Uncover and cook 5 more minutes until tender crisp.

♦ **Prepare** rigatoni as directed.

♦ **Mix** vinegar, mustard, sugar, salt and ⅓ cup olive oil in small bowl.

♦ **Toss** vegetables with pasta, dressing, tomatoes, basil and Parmesan cheese. Serve hot or cold.

SPAGHETTI WITH ARTICHOKES

Yield: 4 servings

4 tablespoons butter
½ cup minced onion
4 ounces prosciutto or cooked ham
1 (14½ ounce) can chopped tomatoes and liquid
16 ounces artichoke hearts
2 tablespoons basil
1½ cups whipping cream
½ teaspoon nutmeg
Salt and pepper
1 pound spaghetti, uncooked

♦ **Melt** butter in frying pan. Add onion and ham. Cook, stirring until onion is soft.

♦ **Stir** in tomatoes. Add artichokes, basil, and cream. Bring to a boil and cook until artichokes are tender and juice is reduced.

♦ **Season** with nutmeg, salt and pepper. Serve hot over cooked spaghetti.

PASTA AL RACCOLTO

Yield: 6 servings

3 tablespoons extra-virgin
olive oil
1 large onion, chopped
medium
4 ears fresh early sweet corn,
kernels cut off
2 large cloves garlic, minced
6 sun-dried tomatoes, soaked
and chopped
3 fresh ripe tomatoes,
medium size, roughly
chopped
Fresh ground black pepper
Salt to taste
1 pound dry pasta

♦ **Sauté** onion in olive oil in a
large deep frying pan over
medium heat for 2 minutes.
♦ **Add** corn and garlic and sauté,
stirring frequently, until the
corn begins to look translucent.
♦ **Add** sun-dried tomatoes, sauté
1 minute.
♦ **Add** ripe tomatoes and fresh
ground pepper, stir and reduce
heat to low. Simmer 20
minutes.
♦ **Cook** pasta according to
package directions. Drain and
add directly to frying pan with
sauce. Mix thoroughly, salt if
desired, and serve
immediately.

Substitute butter for olive oil;
after adding ripe tomatoes, add 1
cup heavy cream. Keep heat on
medium for a few minutes till
cream has reduced slightly, then
lower heat. Use white pepper
instead of freshly ground pepper.

*This is an original recipe from
Ransom Wilson, conductor of Solisti
New York Orchestra, resident every
year in Bartlesville at the renowned
OK MOZART International
Festival.*

ASPARAGUS PASTA

Yield: 2 servings

3 tablespoons olive oil
3 cloves garlic, minced
1 bunch asparagus
1 cup white wine
1 tablespoon lemon juice
1 red bell pepper, sliced
Fettuccine

♦ **Trim** ends of asparagus. Sauté garlic and asparagus in olive oil until the asparagus looks glossy (about 5 minutes).
♦ **Add** wine and lemon juice. Cover and simmer 10 minutes.
♦ **Toss** with fettuccine. Grind pepper over pasta and sprinkle with Parmesan cheese. Garnish with sliced red pepper.

FRESH TOMATO FETTUCCINE •

Yield: 4 servings

1 small onion, chopped
1 clove garlic, minced
1 tablespoon olive oil
3 tablespoons butter or margarine
1 pound sliced fresh mushrooms
⅓ cup dry white wine
½ cup fully cooked chopped ham or chicken
2½ cups fresh tomatoes, peeled, seeded and chopped
¼ teaspoon ground nutmeg
8 ounces fettuccine, cooked
¾ cup shredded Parmesan cheese

♦ **Cook** onion and garlic in hot oil and 2 tablespoon margarine over medium-low heat until tender (use a large skillet).
♦ **Add** mushrooms. Cook, uncovered, 10 minutes or until tender, stirring often.
♦ **Stir** in wine and ham. Simmer, uncovered, 10 minutes or until liquid is almost evaporated, stirring occasionally.
♦ **Add** tomatoes and nutmeg. Simmer for 15 minutes more, stirring occasionally.
♦ **Toss** cooked pasta with remaining margarine and half the cheese.
♦ **Transfer** to platter, and ladle tomato sauce over pasta. Sprinkle remaining cheese over pasta.

SUN-DRIED TOMATO PESTO

Yield: ¾ cup

12 sun-dried tomatoes soaked
   in hot water
2 cloves garlic
2 tablespoons chopped
   walnuts
2 tablespoons grated
   Parmesan cheese
¼ cup olive oil
½ cup chicken broth
1 teaspoon salt
½ teaspoon pepper
1 tablespoon lemon juice

♦ **Purée** tomatoes, garlic and walnuts in food processor or blender with a little oil. While blending, add remaining oil, Parmesan, chicken stock, lemon juice, salt and pepper and purée until smooth.

♦ **Place** in an airtight container.

Use about 2 to 3 tablespoons of this concentrated sauce with 12 ounces pasta or serve on ½ inch slices of good French bread that has been toasted. May garnish with black olives, parsley, and more cheese. May be refrigerated up to one month.

SHRIMP ALFREDO • p. 161

Yield: 4 servings

½ cup butter
1 pound medium shrimp,
   peeled and deveined
1 tablespoon minced green
   onions
½ teaspoon minced garlic
9 ounces fettuccine, cooked
   al dente and drained
4 egg yolks ✓
1 cup half-and-half
1 cup freshly grated
   Parmesan cheese
2 teaspoons fresh minced
   parsley
½ teaspoon salt
¼ teaspoon freshly ground
   black pepper

♦ **Melt** butter and sauté shrimp, green onions, and garlic in large skillet over moderate heat for 3 to 4 minutes, or until shrimp are firm and opaque. Remove pan from heat. Stir warm fettuccine into shrimp mixture.

♦ **Beat** egg yolks, half-and-half, and Parmesan cheese in medium bowl. Add egg yolk mixture to shrimp mixture and cook over moderate heat until sauce thickens, about 3 to 4 minutes. Do not boil.

♦ **Stir** in parsley, salt and pepper. Serve immediately.

PASTA WITH SHRIMP AND SALSA

Yield: 4 servings

3 tablespoons olive oil
2 cloves garlic, minced
3 green onions and tops, cut in diagonal pieces
4 ribs celery, cut in diagonal pieces
2 zucchini, sliced
2 red bell peppers, seeded and sliced
1 pound fresh medium shrimp deveined
1 chicken bouillon cube, dissolved in ½ cup hot water
Juice of 1 lemon
¼ cup picante sauce or salsa
1 tablespoon fresh minced cilantro
9 ounces angel hair pasta, cooked

♦ **Sauté** garlic, onions, celery, pepper, and zucchini, in olive oil for 3 minutes (cook in a large skillet or stir fry pan).

♦ **Add** shrimp and broth and stir for 5 minutes or until shrimp are pink.

♦ **Remove** from heat. Add lemon juice, picante sauce, and cilantro. Toss lightly with cooked pasta.

PENNE WITH TUNA

Yield: 8 servings

2 pounds fresh tuna
24 Kalamata olives
4 cloves garlic, minced
2 tablespoons olive oil
¼ cup capers
1 (28 ounce) can crushed tomatoes
Salt and pepper to taste
1 pound dry penne pasta
Grated Parmesan cheese

♦ **Cut** tuna into bite-sized pieces.

♦ **Pit** olives and cut into quarters.

♦ **Sauté** garlic for 1 to 2 minutes in oil. Add tuna, olives and capers. Cook until tuna changes color.

♦ **Add** tomatoes to the pan. Season with salt and pepper and continue cooking at low to medium heat until heated through.

♦ **Cook** and drain penne pasta. Put in a large bowl and top with the sauce.

♦ **Serve** with Parmesan cheese.

Fresh salmon is a good substitution for fresh tuna.

CLAM SAUCE FOR SPAGHETTI

Yield: 4 servings

⅛ cup olive oil
3 cloves garlic, minced
1 (8 ounce) can tomato sauce
3 tablespoons minced parsley
⅔ cup water
1 (10 ounce) can minced clams with juice
Salt and pepper
1 pound spaghetti, cooked and drained
Grated Parmesan cheese

♦ **Sauté** garlic in olive oil on low heat until soft but not brown.
♦ **Combine** tomato sauce and parsley with oil and garlic. Bring to a boil.
♦ **Add** water. Simmer 30 minutes.
♦ **Add** clams and juice and cook 20 minutes longer.
♦ **Season** with salt and pepper. Serve over spaghetti topped with Parmesan cheese.

GRILLED SHRIMP AND ZUCCHINI PASTA

Yield: 4 servings

5 tablespoons lemon juice
2 tablespoons Dijon mustard
⅓ cup plus 2 tablespoons olive oil
½ cup fresh basil leaves or 2 tablespoons dried
1½ pounds uncooked shrimp, peeled
3 zucchini, halved lengthwise
1 pound gnocchi pasta
Parmesan cheese
Salt and pepper

♦ **Combine** 4 tablespoons lemon juice and mustard in small bowl. Mix in ⅓ cup olive oil gradually. Mix in basil.
♦ **Place** shrimp in medium bowl. Drizzle with remaining lemon juice and 2 tablespoons olive oil. Toss to coat. Season with salt and pepper.
♦ **Brush** zucchini on both sides with olive oil. Season with salt and pepper. Grill about 2 minutes per side.
♦ **Cook** pasta according to directions. Drain.
♦ **Grill** shrimp about 2 minutes per side. Transfer to a large bowl.
♦ **Cut** zucchini into bite-size pieces. Add to shrimp. Add pasta and basil mixture. Toss to coat. Serve with Parmesan cheese.

CRAB VERMICELLI

Yield: 6 to 8 servings

2 cups uncooked vermicelli
12 ounces frozen crab
1 can cream of shrimp soup
1 cup mayonnaise
1 cup milk
1 clove garlic, minced
½ cup grated Cheddar cheese

♦ **Break** up vermicelli to make 2 cups.
♦ **Mix** together all remaining ingredients except cheese. Fold into vermicelli. Pour into well greased 9x13 inch baking dish.
♦ **Bake** covered at 350° for 30 minutes. Stir after 15 minutes.
♦ **Add** Cheddar cheese for last 10 minutes.

SAUTÉ OF SHRIMP WITH SHALLOTS AND PINE NUTS

Yield: 4 servings

½ cup chopped shallots
3 tablespoons unsalted butter
1 roasted red bell pepper, sliced
2 tablespoons chopped fresh chives
2 teaspoons white wine vinegar
½ teaspoon crushed hot red pepper flakes, or to taste
Salt and freshly ground pepper to taste
1 tablespoon olive oil
1 pound large raw shrimp, shelled and deveined
2 tablespoons pine nuts, lightly toasted

♦ **Cook** shallots in butter for 5 minutes in a skillet over moderately low heat. Add roasted pepper, 1 tablespoon chives, vinegar and crushed red pepper. Cook stirring for 1 minute over low heat. Season with salt and pepper. Transfer the mixture to a side dish.
♦ **Add** olive oil to the skillet. Increase the heat to moderately high. Add shrimp and cook stirring for 1 minute or until shrimp are just beginning to turn opaque.
♦ **Add** the seasoned shallot and pepper mixture, combining well and continue to cook until the shrimp is cooked through but still succulent, about 2 minutes longer.
♦ **Fold** in the pine nuts and 1 tablespoon chives. Serve hot over rice or noodles.

GRILLED SHRIMP

Yield: 4 servings

½ cup minced fresh dill
3 tablespoons extra-virgin olive oil
1 tablespoon minced garlic
1 teaspoon salt
1 teaspoon crushed red pepper
⅓ cup white wine
1½ pounds medium shrimp, unpeeled

♦ **Rinse** shrimp then combine with dill, oil, garlic, salt and red pepper in a bowl. Cover and refrigerate 2 hours.
♦ **Prepare** grill or preheat broiler 10 minutes.
♦ **Add** wine to shrimp and toss.
♦ **Arrange** shrimp on grill with a slotted spoon. Cook 3 minutes on each side until opaque throughout.
♦ **Serve** immediately.

CAJUN SHRIMP

Yield: 2 servings

½ onion, chopped
½ green pepper, chopped
2 ribs celery, chopped
1 tablespoon butter
2½ tablespoons Tony's Shrimp Boil or Paul Prudhomme's Seasoning
1 pound shrimp in shell

♦ **Melt** butter in a pan. Add shrimp.
♦ **Pour** vegetables and seasoning on top of shrimp and mix with a wooden spoon. Cook over low heat covered for 5 minutes. Stir with wooden spoon.
♦ **Adjust** heat to medium high and cook covered for 8 minutes.
♦ **Remove** from heat and let stand covered for 10 minutes.
♦ **Drain** and pour into a large bowl.

This is every man for himself - definitely a hands-on meal.

Avocado Shrimp Bombay

Yield: 6 servings

1 small onion, chopped
1 small apple, peeled and chopped
2 tablespoons butter
1 (10½ ounce) can cream of chicken soup
Salt to taste
2 teaspoons curry powder
2 cups cooked shrimp, peeled and deveined
3 ripe avocados, peeled and halved
3 cups cooked rice

CONDIMENTS
Raisins
Bacon pieces
Chopped nuts
Green pepper
Toasted coconut
Chutney

♦ **Sauté** onion and apple in butter.
♦ **Stir** in soup, salt and curry powder. Stir over low heat until smooth and heated through.
♦ **Add** shrimp.
♦ **Place** avocado half on bed of rice and fill with shrimp curry.
♦ **Pass** condiments separately.

Shrimp Au Gratin Tiburon °

Yield: 4 to 6 servings

6 tablespoons butter or
   margarine
3 tablespoons finely chopped
   onion
¼ cup flour
¼ teaspoon dry mustard
½ teaspoon salt
⅛ teaspoon white pepper
1½ cups milk
1 cup grated Swiss cheese
2 tablespoons dry white wine
   or vermouth
1½ pounds shrimp, peeled,
   deveined, and cooked
½ pound thinly sliced fresh
   mushrooms
½ cup soft bread crumbs
   Parsley sprigs

♦ **Melt** 3 tablespoons butter in a heavy 12-14 inch skillet or heavy 3-quart saucepan. Sauté onion in the butter over low heat, stirring often for 3 to 4 minutes or until soft and tender.

♦ **Stir** in flour, blending until smooth, and cook over low heat for 3 minutes.

♦ **Add** the mustard, salt and pepper. Cook, stirring constantly over moderate heat until mixture bubbles.

♦ **Add** milk slowly, stirring constantly. Cook over moderate heat stirring until mixture thickens and bubbles.

♦ **Add** ¾ cup Swiss cheese, stirring until melted and blended.

♦ **Add** 2 tablespoons white wine and blend.

♦ **Add** shrimp to the sauce and remove from heat.

♦ **Sauté** mushrooms in 2 tablespoons butter in a heavy 10-12 inch skillet over moderate heat for 3 to 5 minutes or until soft and tender. Remove with a slotted spoon and add to the shrimp sauce.

♦ **Turn** the mixture into a buttered shallow 2-quart baking dish.

♦ **Combine** bread crumbs and ¼ cup Swiss cheese and sprinkle over shrimp mixture. Dot with remaining 1 tablespoon butter.

Continued on next page

♦ **Bake** in a preheated 400° oven for 10 minutes or until sauce is bubbly and top is lightly browned.

♦ **Serve** immediately. Garnish with parsley.

This dish may also be cooked in individual shells or ramekins and served as a first course or luncheon dish.

HERB CRUSTED SALMON WITH DILL SAUCE

Yield: 2 servings

2 (6 ounce) salmon fillets
2 tablespoons chopped fresh rosemary
2 tablespoons chopped fresh tarragon
4 tablespoons chopped fresh parsley
2 tablespoons chopped fresh oregano
4 tablespoons olive oil
2 cloves garlic, minced

DILL SAUCE
½ cup mayonnaise
½ cup sour cream
⅛ cup honey mustard
2 tablespoons chopped onion
1½ teaspoons Worcestershire sauce
1 tablespoon chopped dill
⅛ teaspoon tarragon
⅛ teaspoon basil
¼ teaspoon chopped garlic
Salt and pepper to taste

♦ **Mix** rosemary, tarragon, parsley and oregano together on a dinner plate.

♦ **Heat** olive oil and garlic in a medium sized ovenproof sauté pan over medium heat.

♦ **Press** salmon into herbs on skinless meat side. Sauté in hot oil until golden brown. Turn salmon over and place in a preheated 350° oven for 5 to 7 minutes.

♦ **Mix** all dill sauce ingredients together in a double boiler. Stir often until heated and onion and garlic are softened.

SHRIMP DIJONAISE FOR TWO

Yield: 2 servings

10 - 12 large shrimp, peeled and
  deveined
⅓ cup extra virgin olive oil
¼ cup dry white wine
1 teaspoon fresh cracked
  black pepper
¼ cup whipping cream
¼ cup grated Parmesan cheese
1 tablespoon minced garlic
1 tablespoon Dijon mustard
2 cups cooked white rice

♦ **Combine** olive oil, wine and pepper and simmer in a sauté pan. Add garlic and shrimp and cook on medium high heat for 4 minutes, turning shrimp occasionally.

♦ **Reduce** heat to medium. Add cream, mustard and Parmesan cheese. Blend together and raise heat to high. Reduce sauce until it starts to thicken, stirring constantly.

♦ **Serve** over rice.

Substitute thinly sliced boneless chicken breasts for the shrimp.

BAKED CRAB SUPREME

Yield: 8 to 10 servings

1 cup chopped celery
8 slices French bread, crusts
  removed
3 cups crabmeat
1 yellow onion, chopped
½ cup mayonnaise
½ cup chopped green pepper
4 eggs, beaten
3 cups milk
1 cup canned mushroom
  soup
  Swiss cheese, grated
  Paprika

♦ **Cook** celery slowly in a little water for 10 minutes. Drain.

♦ **Dice** half of bread into 4-quart baking dish.

♦ **Mix** crab, onion, mayonnaise, pepper and celery and spread over bread.

♦ **Dice** remaining bread and place over crab mixture.

♦ **Mix** eggs and milk together and pour over dish.

♦ **Cover** and place in refrigerator overnight.

♦ **Bake** uncovered at 325° for 15 minutes.

♦ **Spoon** soup over the top. Sprinkle with cheese and paprika.

♦ **Bake** one more hour or until golden brown.

GRILLED SALMON FILLETS WITH SPINACH PESTO SAUCE

Yield: 6 servings

3 (2 pound) center cut salmon fillets, with skin on

SALMON MARINADE
½ cup olive oil
Juice of 2 lemons
2 tablespoons chopped fresh dill
2 tablespoons chopped parsley
3 cloves garlic, minced
½ cup white wine
½ teaspoon salt
¼ teaspoon white pepper

SPINACH PESTO
2 cloves garlic, minced
1¼ cups fresh basil leaves
2 cups fresh spinach leaves, well-packed
¼ cup chopped parsley
3 tablespoons pine nuts
½ cup olive oil
¼ teaspoon black pepper
¼ teaspoon salt

SPINACH PESTO SAUCE
¾ cup sour cream
½ cup mayonnaise
½ cup spinach pesto
¾ cup cucumber, peeled, seeded and cubed
¼ teaspoon salt
¼ teaspoon white pepper

♦ **Rinse** salmon fillets and pat dry.

♦ **Combine** salmon marinade ingredients in a large non-metallic dish. Pour over salmon and marinate in refrigerator at least 2 hours or overnight.

♦ **Process** all pesto ingredients (except oil and seasonings) in a food processor until chopped fine. Slowly add olive oil in a fine stream while the blade is running. Process until the oil is absorbed. Add salt and pepper. Pour into a bowl. Cover and refrigerate until ready to use.

♦ **Combine** all spinach pesto sauce ingredients and mix well. Taste for seasonings. Refrigerate until ready for fish.

♦ **Brush** grates of grill with olive oil and heat coals to approximately 350°.

♦ **Grill** fillets 5 to 7 minutes per side until fish flakes easily.

♦ **Transfer** to serving platter and drizzle with spinach pesto sauce. Serve immediately.

EASY LIGHT FISH FILLETS

Yield: 2 servings

1 cup crushed whole grain cereal flakes
1 clove garlic, finely minced
1 tablespoon grated Parmesan cheese
¾ pound fresh fish fillets (haddock, flounder, sole)
½ cup plain lowfat yogurt

♦ **Combine** crushed cereal, garlic and cheese. Put into a pie plate and set aside.
♦ **Dip** fillets in yogurt and roll in cereal mixture until well coated.
♦ **Bake** in a single layer at 425° for 20 minutes or until flaky and crispy.

GRILLED HALIBUT STEAKS WITH FRESH BASIL BUTTER

Yield: 6 servings

¼ cup lightly packed basil leaves
2 tablespoons parsley leaves
1 green onion, coarsely chopped
¼ cup margarine, at room temperature
2 teaspoons lemon juice
⅛ teaspoon ground black pepper
2 tablespoons grated Parmesan cheese
6 (6 ounce) halibut steaks, cut 1 inch thick
Non-stick vegetable spray
Sliced tomatoes (optional)
Fresh basil sprigs (optional)

♦ **Place** basil, parsley and green onion in food processor; pulse on and off until coarsely chopped, about 10 times.
♦ **Add** margarine, lemon juice and pepper. Process until well mixed, about 15 seconds. Reserve ¼ of mixture for basting fish. Add Parmesan cheese to remainder and process until smooth. Set aside.
♦ **Spread** reserved ¼ of basil butter on fish. Place in a fish basket that has been coated with non-stick vegetable spray or directly on a well oiled grill 4 to 5 inches above hot coals. Cover with grill lid or a foil tent. Cook 10 minutes or until fish just flakes when tested with a fork. Turn steaks halfway through cooking time.
♦ **Remove** halibut to hot plates and top each steak with basil butter. Garnish with tomato slices and basil sprigs, if desired.

Orange Roughy Parmesan

Yield: 4-6 servings

2 pounds orange roughy
2 tablespoons fresh lemon juice
½ cup freshly grated Parmesan cheese
4 tablespoons butter, softened
3 tablespoons mayonnaise
3 tablespoons chopped green onions
½ teaspoon salt
Freshly ground black pepper (to taste)
Dash Tabasco

♦ **Place** fillets in a single layer in a buttered baking dish. Brush with lemon juice. Let stand 10 minutes.

♦ **Combine** remaining ingredients in a small bowl.

♦ **Broil** fillets 3 to 4 inches under preheated broiler for 5 minutes or until fish flakes easily with a fork.

♦ **Spread** with cheese mixture and broil until brown and bubbly. Watch closely. Garnish with lemon wedges and parsley.

Sole or any other skinless white fish may be substituted for the orange roughy.

Orange Roughy with Cumin and Capers

Yield: 2 servings

1 tablespoon olive oil
1 medium onion, chopped
1 green pepper, chopped
½ teaspoon cumin
½ teaspoon salt
Zest of 1 orange
1 pound orange roughy
1 tablespoon capers

♦ **Sauté** onion, green pepper, cumin, salt, and orange zest in olive oil. Set aside.

♦ **Bake** orange roughy covered at 400° for 12 minutes.

♦ **Add** onion mixture and bake for 5 minutes more.

♦ **Sprinkle** with capers just before serving.

BAKED OKLAHOMA CATFISH

Yield: 2 servings

2 (¾-1 pound) fresh catfish
fillets, skinned
Salt and pepper
1 teaspoon olive oil
1 teaspoon lemon juice
USE ONE OF THE FOLLOWING:
Chopped parsley, green
onion and fresh basil
Italian herbs and Parmesan
cheese
Cajun seasoning
Cavender's Greek seasoning

◆ **Rub** fillets with olive oil,
lemon juice and salt and
pepper. Sprinkle with your
choice of seasonings.
◆ **Place** on a rack in a 9x13 inch
pan and bake at 400° for 45
minutes.
◆ **Serve** with lemon wedges.

RED SNAPPER WITH LEMON HERB BUTTER

Yield: 4 servings

2 - 3 limes, cut in ¼ inch slices
1½ pounds red snapper fillets
Salt
LEMON HERB BUTTER
½ cup whipped butter
2 tablespoons lemon juice
2 tablespoons minced parsley
2 tablespoons minced chives
2 tablespoons minced
scallions

◆ **Combine** lemon herb butter
ingredients and mix
thoroughly. Shape into a roll
approximately 1½ inches in
diameter. Wrap and freeze at
least 30 minutes.
◆ **Line** a shallow glass baking
dish with a layer of lime slices.
Arrange red snapper fillets on
top in a snug, single layer.
Sprinkle lightly with salt and
top each fillet with 2 slices (½
inch thick) of lemon herb
butter.
◆ **Bake,** uncovered at 350° for 12
to 15 minutes, depending on
the thickness of fish. Transfer
to heated serving platter.

SEAFOOD RISOTTO •

Yield: 4 servings

4 tablespoons olive oil,
  divided
4 cloves garlic, minced,
  divided
½ cup raw shrimp, cut in half
½ cup raw scallops, cut in half
1 cup chopped green onions
1½ cups Arborio rice
1 cup clam broth, heated
1 cup boiling water
2 tablespoons brandy or
  cognac
1 teaspoon salt
⅛ teaspoon pepper
¼ cup chopped parsley

♦ **Sauté** half the garlic in 2
  tablespoons olive oil.
♦ **Add** shrimp and scallops and
  cook for 2 to 4 minutes until
  shrimp is pink. Set aside.
♦ **Sauté** remaining garlic in rest
  of olive oil. Add onions and
  rice to brown. Add broth and
  cook until slightly thickened.
  Add remaining ingredients
  and cook until rice is done.
♦ **Add** seafood to rice mixture.

FRESH MEXICAN SALSA

Yield: 1½ cups

3 ripe tomatoes, finely
  chopped
½ cup onion, chopped
4 - 6 fresh serrano chili peppers,
  seeded and finely chopped
1 tablespoon finely chopped
  fresh cilantro
2 teaspoons salt
2 teaspoons fresh lime juice

♦ **Stir** together the tomatoes,
  onion, chilies, cilantro, salt and
  lime juice. Let stand for 1 hour
  to blend flavors before serving.
♦ **Store** tightly covered in the
  refrigerator for up to 1 week.

BLACK BEAN SALSA

Yield: 3 cups

1 (16 ounce) can black beans,
  drained
1 (12 ounce) jar Mexican-style
  salsa
¼ cup chopped cilantro
1 teaspoon cumin
2 tablespoons fresh lime juice

♦ **Chop** the beans coarsely in a
  food processor, being careful
  not to purée them.
♦ **Stir** in salsa, cilantro, cumin,
  and lime juice.

FESTIVAL SWEET PICKLES

Yield: 1 gallon

1 gallon jar of dill pickles (not garlic or kosher)
4 tablespoons pickling spices
4 cloves garlic, sliced
5 cups sugar

♦ **Drain** all juice from pickles. Cut into thick slices and return to jar.
♦ **Sprinkle** spices over pickles. Add garlic and sugar. Cover with lid.
♦ **Rotate** the jar to distribute the sugar and spices, each day for three weeks. This makes its own juice.

CRANBERRY-APPLE-PEAR SAUCE •

Yield: 6 cups

2 pounds fresh cranberries
4 apples, pared, cored and diced
3 pears, pared, cored and diced
2 cups golden raisins
2 cups sugar
1 cup fresh orange juice
2½ tablespoons orange zest
2 teaspoons cinnamon
¼ teaspoon freshly grated nutmeg
½ cup plus 2 tablespoons orange flavored liqueur

♦ **Place** all ingredients, except liqueur, in a large saucepan. Bring to boil, reduce heat. Simmer, uncovered, for 45 minutes, stirring frequently until mixture thickens.
♦ **Remove** from heat, stir in liqueur, and cool.
♦ **Refrigerate** at least 4 hours. Serve sauce slightly chilled with pork, chicken, or turkey.

FESTIVE CRANBERRY RELISH °

Yield: 25 to 30 servings

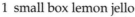

1 small box lemon jello
1 small box orange jello
1 (12 ounce) package fresh √ cranberries
2 red apples (1 peeled, 1 with peel)
2 oranges (1 peeled, 1 with peel)
1 cup crushed pineapple, drained
2 cups sugar
½ - 1 cup chopped pecans

♦ **Dissolve** jello in 3 cups boiling water.
♦ **Process** coarsely in food processor cranberries, apples and oranges.
♦ **Add** fruit to dissolved jello. Add pineapple, sugar and nuts.
♦ **Mix** well and chill several hours in a large serving bowl.

182

DESSERTS

"THE TREE THAT ESCAPED THE
CROWDED FOREST"—That's what
Frank Lloyd Wright said of his only
skyscraper, the Price Tower.

MEN OF VISION

Frank Lloyd Wright called it "the tree that escaped the crowded forest," this conifer-like structure which he originally designed for the environs of New York City. Instead Wright enlivened the Bartlesville skyline with his remarkable Price Tower, completed in 1956. He saw the Oklahoma prairie as the perfect setting for his ideal of environmental architecture. Today the structure stands as a prized example of Wright's work and a tribute to American genius.

Wright designed Price Tower for another man of great vision, H.C. Price. In 1922 Price developed a successful electric welding method for oil pipelines, which was later used during World War II on battlefields and in shipyards. A true pioneer of the oil industry, H.C. Price Company operated internationally for well over 50 years.

STATE FAIR PECAN BARS

Yield: 16 to 24 servings

CRUST
1 yellow cake mix (minus ⅔ cup)
½ cup margarine, softened
1 egg

FILLING
⅔ cup reserved cake mix
½ cup firmly packed brown sugar
1½ cups dark corn syrup
1 teaspoon vanilla
3 eggs
1 cup chopped pecans

♦ **Grease** bottom and sides of a 9x13 inch pan.
♦ **Reserve** ⅔ cup of dry cake mix for filling. In large mixing bowl, combine remaining dry cake mix, butter and one egg. Mix until crumbly. Press into greased pan.
♦ **Bake** at 350° for 15 minutes or until light brown.
♦ **Mix** together all filling ingredients. Pour filling over partially baked crust.
♦ **Sprinkle** pecans over the top. Return to the oven and bake 30 minutes until filling is set. Cool and cut into bars.

COFFEE ALMOND BLONDIES

Yield: 24 squares

2⅓ cups brown sugar, packed
¾ cup butter
3 tablespoons coffee liqueur
5 teaspoons instant espresso powder or coffee powder
3 large eggs
2 cups flour
1½ teaspoons baking powder
½ teaspoon salt
1 cup toasted, coarsely chopped almonds
1 (6 ounce) package chocolate chips

♦ **Grease** a 9x13 inch pan.
♦ **Stir** sugar and butter in large, heavy saucepan over medium-low heat until sugar and butter melt. Add liqueur and espresso powder; whisk to blend; cool.
♦ **Whisk** eggs into sugar mixture. Stir dry ingredients into batter. Add nuts and chocolate chips.
♦ **Bake** in a 350° oven for about 30 minutes or until toothpick comes out with some moist crumbs. Cool. Cut into squares.

PEANUT BUTTER MELT-AWAYS

Yield: 24 to 30 squares

CRUST LAYER
½ cup margarine, softened
1 cup sugar
4 eggs
1½ cups (16 ounces) chocolate
   syrup
1 cup flour
PEANUT BUTTER LAYER
1 cup margarine, softened
3½ cups powdered sugar
1 cup peanut butter
1 teaspoon vanilla
TOPPING
6 tablespoons margarine
1 cup semi-sweet chocolate
   chips

♦ **Cream** together ½ cup margarine and sugar. Add eggs, chocolate syrup, and flour.
♦ **Spread** in a 9x13 inch pan and bake at 350° for 25 to 30 minutes. Cool.
♦ **Cream** together 1 cup margarine, powdered sugar, peanut butter and vanilla. Spread on top of cooled crust layer.
♦ **Melt** 6 tablespoons margarine with chocolate chips. Cool slightly and spread on top of peanut butter layer.

Keep in refrigerator.

BLACK GOLD BROWNIES

Yield: 30 servings

1 package German chocolate
   cake mix
½ cup margarine, melted
⅓ cup evaporated milk
1 tablespoon water
1 package Kraft caramels
⅓ cup evaporated milk
1 (6 ounce) package chocolate
   chips
1 cup chopped nuts

♦ **Mix** cake mix, melted margarine, evaporated milk and water together. Pat half of batter in a 9x13 inch pan. Bake 6 minutes at 350°.
♦ **Melt** caramels with evaporated milk while cake is baking.
♦ **Sprinkle** hot cake with chocolate chips.
♦ **Drizzle** with caramel mixture and sprinkle with nuts.
♦ **Drop** the other half of the batter on the chocolate layer, using a teaspoon. Spread with a spatula.
♦ **Bake** at 350° for 20 minutes. Do not overbake.

Freezes well.

CHOCOLATE MARSHMALLOW SQUARES

Yield: 24 to 30 squares

CAKE

½ cup margarine
3 tablespoons cocoa powder
1 cup sugar
2 eggs
¾ cup flour
¼ teaspoon salt
1 cup chopped pecans
Miniature marshmallows

TOPPING

2 squares unsweetened chocolate
½ cup margarine
½ cup evaporated milk
1 (16 ounce) box powdered sugar, sifted
1 teaspoon vanilla

◆ **Mix** together all cake ingredients (except marshmallows) and bake in a 9x13 inch greased pan at 375° for 15 minutes. Do not overcook.

◆ **Place** a layer of miniature marshmallows on top.

◆ **Resume** baking just long enough to soften marshmallows so they spread easily over entire pan. Do not brown.

◆ **Prepare** topping while cake is baking.

◆ **Mix** chocolate, margarine and evaporated milk together in a saucepan over medium heat, until melted.

◆ **Remove** from heat, add powdered sugar, stir. Add vanilla when mixture becomes smooth.

◆ **Spoon** over marshmallows while they are still warm.

◆ **Refrigerate** overnight and cut into squares the next day.

ENGLISH CARAMEL SQUARES

Yield: 24 squares

SHORTBREAD CRUST
- ¾ cup butter, softened
- ¼ cup sugar
- 2 cups flour

FILLING
- ¼ cup butter
- ½ cup sweetened condensed milk
- ⅔ cup brown sugar
- 6 tablespoons Lyle's Golden Syrup (do not substitute)
- 5 squares semi-sweet chocolate

♦ **Mix** softened butter and sugar. Work in flour with pastry blender. Press into bottom of an ungreased 9x13 inch glass baking pan. Bake at 350° until light golden brown, about 25 minutes. Do not overbake.

♦ **Combine** butter, sweetened condensed milk, brown sugar and Lyle's syrup in a small saucepan. Cook about 10 minutes, stirring constantly. Spread over shortbread crust and cool to touch.

♦ **Melt** semi-sweet chocolate and spread over caramel layer. Chill to set.

Lyle's Golden Syrup has a distinctive flavor and cannot be substituted. It may be found at specialty food stores.

APRICOT ALMOND BARS

Yield: 48 bars

CRUST
- 1 cup butter
- ½ cup sugar
- ½ teaspoon vanilla
- 2 cups flour

TOPPING
- 1 (18 ounce) jar apricot jam
- 2 egg whites at room temperature
- 1 cup powdered sugar
- 1 teaspoon almond flavoring
- 1 package sliced almonds

♦ **Cream** first 3 ingredients till light and fluffy. Mix flour into mixture.

♦ **Spread** in a 10x15 inch jelly roll pan. Pat out with hands.

♦ **Bake** at 350° for 15 minutes. Cool.

♦ **Stir** jam vigorously and spread over crust. Don't spread too close to the edges of crust.

♦ **Beat** egg whites until stiff; gradually add powdered sugar and flavoring. Carefully spread over jam. Top with almonds.

♦ **Bake** at 400° for 20 minutes. Cut while still slightly warm.

CHOCOLATE CHIP PEANUT BUTTER COOKIES

Yield: 3 to 6 dozen

1¼ cups all-purpose flour
½ teaspoon baking soda
½ teaspoon ground cinnamon
½ teaspoon salt
¾ cup butter, softened
½ cup packed brown sugar
½ cup granulated sugar
½ cup creamy peanut butter
1 extra large egg
1 teaspoon vanilla
2 cups semi-sweet chocolate chips
½ cup coarsely chopped pecans

♦ **Combine** flour, soda, cinnamon and salt. Set aside.
♦ **Beat** butter, brown sugar, granulated sugar and peanut butter until creamy in a large mixing bowl.
♦ **Beat** in egg and vanilla. Gradually beat in flour mixture. Stir in chocolate chips and pecans.
♦ **Drop** by either teaspoon or tablespoon (depending on the size you want) onto an ungreased cookie sheet. Press down slightly to flatten.
♦ **Bake** in a preheated 375° oven for 7 to 10 minutes, or until edges are set, but centers are still soft. Let stand for 4 minutes, remove to wire racks to cool completely.

"I CAIN'T SAY NO" CHOCOLATE CHIP COOKIES •

Yield: 8 dozen

1 cup butter
¾ cup sugar
¾ cup light brown sugar
1 tablespoon vanilla
1 tablespoon Tia Maria
1 tablespoon Frangelica
2 eggs
1 teaspoon baking soda
½ teaspoon salt
2½ cups flour
4 cups milk chocolate chips
1 cup walnut halves ✓
½ cup pecan halves ✓
½ cup macadamia nuts ✓

♦ **Cream** butter, sugar, and brown sugar. Add vanilla and liqueurs to eggs. Stir into sugar/butter mixture.
♦ **Add** dry ingredients. Stir.
♦ **Fold** in chocolate chips and nuts. Place in storage container and refrigerate overnight.
♦ **Drop** by teaspoon onto ungreased cookie sheet. Bake at 325° for 10 to 13 minutes. Cool slightly.

Biscotti (Twice Baked Italian Cookies)

Yield: 9 dozen

2 cups sugar
1 cup butter
¼ cup anise seeds
¼ cup anisette
3 tablespoons bourbon or 2 teaspoons vanilla plus 2 tablespoons water
2 cups chopped walnuts
6 large eggs
5½ cups flour
1 tablespoon baking powder

♦ **Mix** first 7 ingredients together.
♦ **Stir** flour and baking powder together and add to butter mixture. Cover and refrigerate 2 to 3 hours.
♦ **Shape** dough on a lightly floured surface into flat loaves ½ inch thick x 2 inches wide x 17 inches long.
♦ **Place** well apart on buttered baking sheets. Bake at 375° for 20 minutes.
♦ **Remove** loaves from oven. When cool to the touch cut into diagonal slices ¾ inch thick. Lay slices cut side down and close together on baking sheets.
♦ **Return** to oven and bake until lightly toasted, about 15 minutes.
♦ **Cool** on racks. Keep in air tight containers.

Hawaiian Cookies

Yield: 5 to 6 dozen

1 cup margarine
1 cup packed brown sugar
1 cup white sugar
2 eggs
1 teaspoon vanilla
2 cups flour
2 teaspoons baking powder
2 teaspoons baking soda
1 teaspoon salt
1½ cups quick oats
2 cups flaked coconut
1 (12 ounce) package butterscotch chips

♦ **Cream** margarine and sugars until light and fluffy. Beat in eggs and vanilla.
♦ **Combine** flour, baking powder, baking soda and salt. Add to creamed mixture. Mix well.
♦ **Stir** in oats, coconut and butterscotch chips.
♦ **Drop** by rounded teaspoonfuls on greased cookie sheets.
♦ **Bake** at 350° for 10 to 12 minutes.

CHOCOLATE BISCOTTI ❧

Yield: 36

⅓ cup butter or margarine
⅔ cup sugar
2 eggs
¼ cup cocoa powder
¼ teaspoon salt
2 teaspoons baking powder
1¾ cups flour
1 cup chocolate chips
1 cup chopped pecans

♦ **Cream** butter and sugar. Add egg and beat well. Add cocoa.
♦ **Add** salt and baking powder to flour and beat in. Add nuts and chips. Combine with butter mixture.
♦ **Divide** dough in half and shape in long loaves about 2 inches wide and 1 inch high. Dough will be soft; dampen hands if necessary to form loaves.
♦ **Bake** at 375° for 25 minutes. Cool and slice diagonally into ½ inch slices.
♦ **Place** slices on ungreased cookie sheet and bake at 325° for 8 minutes. Turn slices over and bake for another 8 minutes. Cool on wire rack.
♦ **Store** in airtight container in freezer or refrigerator.

PRAIRIE WINDMILL COOKIES ❧

Yield: 5 dozen

2 cups margarine
2 cups brown sugar
½ cup sour cream
4½ cups flour
½ teaspoon baking soda
4 teaspoons cinnamon
½ teaspoon nutmeg
½ teaspoon ground cloves
½ cup chopped nuts

♦ **Cream** margarine and brown sugar. Add sour cream, then add remaining ingredients.
♦ **Mix** and shape into rolls. Wrap in plastic wrap, refrigerate or freeze.
♦ **Slice** and bake at 375° for 8 to 12 minutes.

COWBOY BURGER BITES

Yield: 24 servings

1 drop green food coloring
Water
¼ cup flaked coconut
48 vanilla wafers
24 peppermint patties
Sesame seeds

♦ **Combine** 1 drop green food coloring and a few drops water in a small jar lid.

♦ **Add** coconut to the jar. Cover and shake until coconut is tinted green.

♦ **Place** 24 vanilla wafers flat side up on an ungreased cookie sheet. Top each wafer with a peppermint patty. Place in a 350° oven for 1 minute.

♦ **Sprinkle** each peppermint patty with ½ teaspoon green coconut. Top with another vanilla wafer, flat side down.

♦ **Brush** top of wafers with water using a clean paint brush. Sprinkle top with sesame seeds.

Great for a child's party. Looks just like little hamburgers.

OIL BARON'S OATMEAL COOKIES

Yield: 5 dozen cookies

1 cup shortening
1 cup sugar
½ cup brown sugar
2 eggs
1 teaspoon vanilla
1½ cups flour
1 teaspoon cinnamon
¼ teaspoon nutmeg
1 teaspoon baking soda
½ teaspoon salt
1½ cups quick cooking oats
¾ cup nuts, chopped

♦ **Cream** shortening, sugar and eggs. Add vanilla.

♦ **Mix** in dry ingredients, blend thoroughly. Stir in nuts. Chill dough for 1 hour.

♦ **Shape** into small balls and place on a greased cookie sheet.

♦ **Butter** the bottom of a drinking glass, dip into granulated sugar and flatten out dough balls.

♦ **Bake** at 350° for 10 minutes.

SOONER SENSATIONS •

Yield: 7 to 8 dozen

1 cup butter
1 cup sugar
1 cup brown sugar
1 egg
1 cup vegetable oil
1 cup rolled oats
1 cup crushed corn flakes
½ cup flaked coconut
1 cup chopped pecans
3½ cups flour
1 teaspoon soda
1 teaspoon salt
1 teaspoon vanilla
   Powdered sugar

♦ **Cream** butter and sugars until light and fluffy. Add egg and blend.

♦ **Add** oil, stirring until well blended. Add oats, cornflakes, coconut and nuts. Stir until mixed.

♦ **Add** flour, soda, salt and vanilla and mix well.

♦ **Form** into balls about the size of a walnut. Place on an ungreased cookie sheet and flatten with a fork dipped in water. Bake for 12 minutes in a 325° oven.

♦ **Allow** to cool a few minutes before removing. Sprinkle with powdered sugar.

CHRISTMAS PINEAPPLE COOKIES •

Yield: 2 dozen small cookies

COOKIES

½ cup white sugar
½ cup brown sugar
½ cup margarine
½ cup crushed pineapple
   (reserve juice)
½ cup chopped nuts, pecans
   or black walnuts
1 egg
2¼ cups flour
½ teaspoon soda
½ teaspoon salt
½ teaspoon vanilla
   Powdered sugar

♦ **Mix** together all ingredients except powdered sugar and reserved juice.

♦ **Drop** by teaspoon full onto ungreased baking sheet. Bake at 350° for 10 minutes. Do not overbake.

♦ **Prepare** frosting by mixing powdered sugar and reserved juice. Blend and brush on top of cooled cookies.

May use red and green cherry slivers or red hots to add color at Christmas time.

SESAME SEED COOKIES ◦

Yield: 5 dozen cookies

1 pound butter
1½ cups sugar
3 cups flour
1 cup fresh sesame seeds
2 cups coconut
½ cup finely chopped
  almonds

♦ **Cream** together butter and sugar. Add flour. Mix by hand.
♦ **Mix** in sesame seeds, coconut, and chopped almonds.
♦ **Divide** into three parts. Shape into three rolls. Chill and slice. Place on ungreased cookie sheet.
♦ **Bake** at 300° for 30 minutes.

BURIED CHERRY COOKIES ◦

Yield: 35 to 40 cookies

½ cup margarine
1 cup sugar
1 egg
1½ teaspoons vanilla
1½ cups all-purpose flour
½ cup unsweetened cocoa
¼ teaspoon baking soda
¼ teaspoon baking powder
¼ teaspoon salt
1 (10 ounce) jar maraschino
  cherries
1 cup semi-sweet chocolate
  pieces
½ cup sweetened condensed
  milk

♦ **Beat** margarine and sugar in a large bowl until fluffy. Add egg and vanilla.
♦ **Stir** together flour, cocoa, baking soda, baking powder and salt in a medium bowl. Add to sugar mixture. Beat until well mixed.
♦ **Shape** dough into 1 inch balls. Place 2 inches apart on an ungreased cookie sheet. Press down center of each ball with thumb.
♦ **Drain** cherries, reserving juice. Place one cherry in the center of each cookie.
♦ **Combine** sweetened condensed milk and chocolate pieces and cook over low heat until melted. Stir in 4 teaspoons cherry juice.
♦ **Spoon** 1 teaspoon of this frosting mixture over each cookie, spreading to cover cherry. Frosting may be thinned with additional cherry juice if necessary.
♦ **Bake** at 350° for 10 minutes until edges are firm.

"EVERYTHING'S UP TO DATE" ROLLS •

Yield: 4 to 5 dozen

½ cup butter or margarine
½ cup sugar
1 cup (8 ounce package) chopped dates
½ teaspoon vanilla
2 cups crispy rice cereal
1 cup flaked coconut
½ cup chopped nuts
Powdered sugar

♦ **Mix** butter, sugar and dates in a saucepan. Bring to a boil and boil for 3 minutes. Add ½ teaspoon vanilla. Mix well. Remove from heat.

♦ **Combine** rice cereal, coconut and nuts in a large bowl. Pour date mixture over and stir.

♦ **Let** cool. Roll into 1 inch balls, and then roll in powdered sugar.

CHOCOLATE-RASPBERRY TRUFFLES •

Yield: 36 one inch balls

1 (8 ounce) package cream cheese, softened
1 (6 ounce) package chocolate chips, melted
¾ cup crushed vanilla wafers
¼ cup raspberry preserves, heated and strained to eliminate seeds
Finely chopped almonds

♦ **Combine** all ingredients except almonds. Chill.

♦ **Shape** into one inch balls. Roll in finely chopped almonds. Keep refrigerated.

FRENCH CHOCOLATES •

Yield: 60 to 70 pieces

1 (12 ounce) package semi-sweet chocolate pieces
1 cup chopped walnuts or pecans
¾ cup sweetened condensed milk
1 teaspoon vanilla extract (or liqueur of choice)
⅛ teaspoon salt
1 cup chocolate sprinkles or finely chopped slivered almonds

♦ **Melt** chocolate pieces in double boiler over hot, not boiling water. Stir in nuts, sweetened condensed milk, vanilla and salt.

♦ **Cool** mixture about 5 minutes or until easy to shape.

♦ **Shape** mixture into 1 inch balls with buttered hands. Roll each ball immediately in chocolate sprinkles or almonds; or may do half in each, as desired.

These look best when served in decorative petit four cups.

May also be dipped in white dipping chocolate for variety.

SPICY SUGARED PECANS

Yield: 4 cups

1 cup sugar
1 teaspoon cinnamon
½ teaspoon nutmeg
½ teaspoon cloves
½ cup water
4 cups pecans

♦ **Combine** all ingredients except pecans in heavy saucepan. Bring to a boil over medium heat.
♦ **Cook** to soft ball stage. Remove from heat and add pecans.
♦ **Stir** till creamy. Turn out on wax paper. Separate pecans.
♦ **Store** in an airtight container when completely cool.

FRANK LLOYD WRIGHT CHOCOLATE DELIGHT

Yield: one 8-inch pie

1 (8 inch) pastry or crumb crust, baked and cooled
1 (4 ounce) package German sweet chocolate
⅓ cup milk
2 tablespoons sugar
1 (3 ounce) package cream cheese, softened
1 (8 ounce) frozen whipped topping, thawed
½ pint whipping cream
1 teaspoon sugar

♦ **Melt** chocolate with 2 tablespoons of the milk over low heat, stirring frequently.
♦ **Cream** sugar and cream cheese together in a mixing bowl. Add remaining milk and the melted chocolate mixture. Beat until smooth. Fold in whipped topping, blend thoroughly.
♦ **Spoon** into pie shell. Refrigerate or freeze for 4 hours.
♦ **Whip** cream with 1 teaspoon sugar. Top pie with sweetened whipped cream.

Mint pie can be made by adding ½ teaspoon peppermint extract to mixture before folding in the whipped topping. Pour into a chocolate cookie crust.

ENGLISH TOFFEE

Yield: 16 to 20 pieces

1 cup sugar
1 cup butter or margarine
1 tablespoon white corn syrup
3 tablespoons water
¾ cup chopped almonds
1 (4½ ounce) chocolate candy bar, cut fine

♦ **Cook** sugar, butter, syrup and water until hard crack, or until candy thermometer reaches 300°.

♦ **Chop** nuts fine and sprinkle over bottom of pie pan while syrup cooks. Pour hot syrup over nuts, sprinkle with chocolate bar.

♦ **Refrigerate.** When toffee is cool, break into 16 to 20 pieces.

CAPPUCCINO MOUSSE PIE

Yield: 8 servings

1½ cups semi-sweet chocolate chips
16 ounces heavy whipping cream
1½ tablespoons instant coffee granules
2 tablespoons sugar
1 teaspoon vanilla extract
1 (6 ounce) graham cracker crust

♦ **Microwave** chocolate chips on high in a small bowl for 1 to 1½ minutes or until melted.

♦ **Mix** whipping cream, coffee granules, sugar and vanilla until granules dissolve. Beat with an electric mixer on high until stiff peaks form.

♦ **Remove** and reserve 1¼ cups coffee/whipping cream mixture. Set aside.

♦ **Fold** in melted chocolate chips until blended. Spread in crust.

♦ **Spread** and swirl reserved coffee/whipping cream mixture over mousse.

♦ **Chill** 30 minutes in freezer or 1 hour in refrigerator.

GRAND FINALE CHOCOLATE PIE

Yield: one 9 inch pie

CRUST
1 cup sifted flour
½ teaspoon salt
⅓ cup shortening
2 - 4 tablespoons cold water

SECOND LAYER
2 egg whites
½ teaspoon vinegar
¼ teaspoon salt
¼ teaspoon cinnamon
½ cup sugar

THIRD LAYER
1 (6 ounce) package semi-sweet chocolate chips
2 egg yolks
¼ cup water

FOURTH LAYER
1 cup heavy cream
¼ cup sugar
¼ teaspoon cinnamon

♦ **Combine** flour and salt in a mixing bowl. Cut in shortening until it is the consistency of cornmeal. Add water one tablespoon at a time until the batter is moist enough to hold together.

♦ **Roll** out crust to fit a 9 inch pie plate. Pierce many times with a fork. Bake 12 minutes at 450°, until golden brown. Cool to room temperature.

♦ **Beat** together egg whites, vinegar, salt and cinnamon until stiff, but not dry.

♦ **Add** sugar gradually and beat until very stiff. Spread meringue over bottom and up sides of the baked crust.

♦ **Bake** at 325° for 15 to 18 minutes until lightly browned. Cool.

♦ **Melt** semi-sweet chocolate chips over hot (not boiling) water in a double boiler. Blend in egg yolks and water until smooth.

♦ **Spread** 3 to 4 tablespoons chocolate mixture over cooled meringue. Chill remaining chocolate until it begins to thicken.

♦ **Beat** together heavy cream, sugar and cinnamon until thick. Spread one half of whipped cream mixture over chocolate layer in pie shell.

♦ **Fold** chilled chocolate mixture into remaining whipped cream mixture. Spread over whipped cream in pie shell. Chill pie at least four hours before serving.

WOOLAROC PIE

Yield: 12 to 16 servings

CRUST
½ cup margarine
1 cup flour
1 cup chopped pecans
FIRST LAYER
1 (8 ounce) package cream cheese, softened
1 cup powdered sugar
SECOND LAYER
2 small packages chocolate instant pudding mix
3 cups milk
THIRD LAYER
1 large container frozen whipped topping
Sliced almonds

♦ **Mix** margarine, flour and pecans and pat into a 9x13 inch greased pan. Bake at 350° for 15 to 20 minutes, or until lightly browned. Cool.

♦ **Mix** cream cheese with powdered sugar. (If too thick, add a little milk so it will easily spread on pie crust). Spread on crust.

♦ **Beat** 2 packages of instant pudding mix into milk until thick. Spread over cream cheese layer.

♦ **Top** with whipped topping and sprinkle with sliced almonds. Chill and serve.

BOURBON PIE

Yield: 8 servings

CRUST
½ package chocolate wafers
3 tablespoons butter
FILLING
1 (5 ounce) can evaporated milk
21 large marshmallows
½ pint whipping cream
3 tablespoons bourbon

♦ **Roll** chocolate wafers into crumbs and mix with butter. Save ½ cup of crumbs for top. Spread balance of crumbs evenly in a 9 inch pie pan and bake at 350° for 5 minutes. Cool.

♦ **Mix** evaporated milk with marshmallows in a double boiler and heat over hot water (not boiling) until smooth, stirring until mixed. Cool.

♦ **Whip** the cream and add bourbon. Fold into cooled marshmallow mixture, combining well.

♦ **Pour** into prepared pie shell. Sprinkle reserved crumbs on top and chill overnight.

🍵 ALMOND MOCHA PIE

Yield: 8 servings

CRUST

½ cup butter, softened
2 tablespoons sugar
1 cup all-purpose flour

FILLING

⅓ cup chopped shaved
  almonds
1 (6 ounce) package semi-
  sweet chocolate chips
¼ cup light corn syrup
¼ cup water
½ cup sugar
¼ cup water
1 large egg white, room
  temperature
1 teaspoon instant coffee
  granules
1 teaspoon pure vanilla
  extract
1 teaspoon fresh lemon juice
2 cups heavy cream, whipped
3 tablespoons hot fudge
  sauce, warmed (optional)

♦ **Mix** butter and sugar with mixer on lowest speed, in a small bowl. Add flour, stirring until mixture resembles coarse meal.

♦ **Press** all but ⅓ cup flour mixture onto bottom and sides of a buttered 9 inch pie plate. Bake at 375° for 12 to 15 minutes or until light golden brown; cool.

♦ **Spread** reserved crumbs on cookie sheet and bake at 375° for 5 minutes or until golden brown; cool.

♦ **Place** chopped almonds on cookie sheet and toast at 375° for 5 to 7 minutes, watching carefully. Cool.

♦ **Stir** chocolate chips, corn syrup, and ¼ cup water in small saucepan over low heat until chips melt; cool.

♦ **Beat** sugar, ¼ cup water, egg white, coffee granules, vanilla and lemon juice in small bowl until soft peaks form, about 3 to 5 minutes. Fold chocolate mixture, whipped cream and almonds into egg white mixture. Spoon into baked crust.

♦ **Decorate** top with warmed hot fudge sauce by drizzling chocolate in three concentric circles. Pull knife tip from center to edge in several places to create web design. Sprinkle top with reserved toasted crumbs. Freeze until firm, about 4 to 6 hours. Cover if stored longer.

FLUFFY PEANUT BUTTER PIE

Yield: Eight servings

GRAHAM CRACKER CRUST
   2 cups graham cracker
      crumbs
   7 tablespoons butter, melted
   ⅓ cup sugar

FILLING
   1 (8 ounce) package cream
      cheese, softened
   ½ cup peanut butter, smooth
      or crunchy
   1 cup powdered sugar
   ½ cup milk
   1 (9 ounce) carton non-dairy
      topping
   ¼ cup finely chopped roasted
      peanuts

♦ **Combine** graham cracker crumbs, melted butter and sugar. Press into a 10 inch pie plate. Bake at 375° for 6 to 8 minutes. Cool.

♦ **Whip** cream cheese until it is soft and fluffy.

♦ **Beat** in peanut butter and sugar. Slowly add milk, blending thoroughly.

♦ **Fold** in topping. Pour into cooled crust.

♦ **Sprinkle** with peanuts. Freeze until firm.

ALMOND TORTE

Yield: 10 to 12 servings

CRUST
   1 cup flour
   ½ cup butter, softened
   1 tablespoon water
   1 tablespoon sugar
   1 teaspoon vanilla

FILLING
   1 cup sliced almonds
   ¾ cup sugar
   ¾ cup whipping cream
   1 teaspoon almond extract

♦ **Mix** crust ingredients together well and press in either a 10 inch tart pan or springform pan with removable bottom. Build up sides of crust 1 to 1½ inches.

♦ **Bake** at 400° for 10 minutes. Cool for 30 minutes.

♦ **Mix** filling ingredients well and allow to sit for 20 minutes. Pour into crust and bake at 350° 40 to 50 minutes until crust is golden and top of filling is caramelized.

♦ **Cool.** Remove sides of pan. Transfer to serving dish.

BLACK WALNUT CHESS PIE

Yield: 6-8 servings

1 (8 inch) unbaked pie shell
½ cup butter, softened
1 cup sugar
3 tablespoons flour
3 egg yolks
1 (5 ounce) can Milnot
1 teaspoon vanilla
½ cup chopped black walnuts
   (do not substitute)

♦ **Beat** butter and sugar in a medium bowl until well mixed. Add flour, salt, egg yolks and Milnot.
♦ **Beat** with rotary beater until well mixed. Stir in walnuts.
♦ **Pour** mixture into pie shell and bake on low shelf of oven at 350° for 45 minutes or until center is almost set.

FRUIT SALAD PIE

Yield: two 9 inch pies

1 can sour, pitted cherries
1 large can crushed pineapple
1¼ cups sugar
2 heaping tablespoons flour
1 small package orange
   gelatin
4 chopped bananas
1 cup chopped pecans
2 (9 inch) prepared graham
   cracker crusts
   Whipped cream

♦ **Cook** cherries, pineapple, sugar and flour in a large saucepan until thick.
♦ **Remove** from heat and add gelatin. Cool to room temperature.
♦ **Add** bananas and pecans. Pour into two prepared graham cracker pie crusts.
♦ **Chill.** Cover with whipped cream before serving.

SHREDDED APPLE PIE

Yield: one 8 inch pie

1½ cups sugar
1 tablespoon flour
½ cup butter
1 teaspoon vanilla
1 teaspoon cinnamon
2 eggs
1½ cups shredded tart apples
1 (8 inch) unbaked pie crust

♦ **Cream** together first 6 ingredients by hand. Add apples.
♦ **Turn** into pie crust and bake at 350° for 50 minutes.

HAVE-A-TART

Yield: 6 servings

TARTS

1 (15 ounce) package refrigerated pie crust
1 cup fresh raspberries
1 cup fresh blackberries
1 cup fresh whole strawberries
1 cup fresh or canned apricots, halved
2 kiwifruits, peeled and sliced
1 tablespoon sugar, optional

LEMON CREAM SAUCE

1 (11¼ ounce) jar lemon curd
1 cup whipping cream

♦ **Unfold** 1 pie crust and roll on a lightly floured surface into 13 inch circle. Carefully tear 3 (5½ inch) circles, leaving jagged edges. Repeat with remaining pie crust.

♦ **Place** 6 (6 ounce) custard cups upside down on a 10x15 inch jellyroll pan. Lightly grease bottom and sides of cups.

♦ **Drape** a pastry circle over each cup, pinch dough, conforming pastry to shape of cup. Prick bottom and sides with fork.

♦ **Bake** at 425° for 10 minutes or until lightly browned. Transfer to wire racks, cool 5 minutes. Carefully remove pastry from cups, turn right side up and cool completely on wire racks.

♦ **Combine** fruit. Add sugar, if desired. Refrigerate up to 2 hours before serving.

♦ **Combine** lemon curd and whipping cream, beating with a wire whisk until smooth. Refrigerate up to 24 hours before serving.

♦ **To** serve, spoon lemon cream sauce in the bottom of pie crust cups and top with fruits. Add a sprig of mint.

Use extra cream mixture over pound cake.

For a faster variation mix together ½ cup of lemon pie filling and 2 cups ice cream in place of lemon curd. Stir until smooth, but not melted. Prepared pastry tarts may also be used.

⤳ LENZER TORTE

Yield: 8 servings

2 tablespoons fine bread
   crumbs
1 (16 ounce) can pitted tart
   cherries, well drained
2 eggs
1 cup sugar
½ cup unsalted butter, melted
3 tablespoons cocoa
½ teaspoon vanilla
½ cup flour, sifted after
   measuring
1 teaspoon baking powder
½ cup chopped walnuts

♦ **Butter** a 9 inch springform
   pan. Cover bottom evenly with
   bread crumbs.
♦ **Place** cherries on a paper towel
   until needed.
♦ **Beat** eggs and sugar together
   until thick and lemon colored.
   Stir in the butter, cocoa, and
   vanilla. Mix well, then fold in
   flour, baking powder and nuts.
♦ **Scatter** cherries in pan and
   pour batter over. Bake at 325°
   for 50 to 55 minutes or until
   top of cake is completely firm.
♦ **Cool** 10 minutes. Remove sides
   of pan and cool completely.
   Invert onto a plate and remove
   bottom of pan and reverse
   again onto serving plate so
   cake is right side up.
♦ **Dust** with powdered sugar
   and serve with whipped
   cream.

*Line pan bottom with parchment
because cherries sometimes pick up
metallic taste of tin springform pan.*

GREEN TOMATO PIE

Yield: 6 servings

Green tomatoes, unpeeled
   (enough to layer to top of
   crust)
1 cup sugar
1 tablespoon flour
¼ teaspoon nutmeg
¼ teaspoon cinnamon
¼ teaspoon cloves
4 tablespoons vinegar
1 (9 inch) pie crust

♦ **Slice** tomatoes thin and put in
   crust.
♦ **Mix** together sugar, flour,
   nutmeg, cinnamon and cloves.
   Sprinkle over sliced tomatoes
   and dot with butter.
♦ **Pour** vinegar over tomatoes
   and arrange top crust over pie.
♦ **Bake** 15 minutes at 350°. Finish
   at 300° until brown.

"OUT OF MY DREAMS" • LEMON CLOUD PIE

Yield: 8 servings

1 (9 inch) baked pastry shell
¾ cup sugar
3 tablespoons cornstarch
1 cup water
1 teaspoon grated lemon peel
⅓ cup lemon juice
2 egg yolks, slightly beaten
1 (3 ounce) package cream cheese
2 egg whites
¼ cup sugar

♦ **Combine** ¾ cup sugar, cornstarch, water, lemon peel, lemon juice and slightly beaten egg yolks in a saucepan. Beat with rotary beater until well blended.

♦ **Cook** over medium heat, stirring constantly, until thick. Remove from heat.

♦ **Add** cream cheese, stir until well blended. Cool while preparing meringue.

♦ **Beat** egg whites at high speed in a small mixing bowl, until foamy. Add ¼ cup sugar gradually, continuing to beat until meringue stands in stiff, glossy peaks. Fold into lemon mixture.

♦ **Spoon** into baked pastry shell. Chill at least two hours before serving.

PUMPKIN ICE CREAM PIE •

Yield: 8 servings

PIE

1 (9 inch) baked pie crust
1 cup pumpkin
½ cup sugar
1 teaspoon pumpkin pie spices
½ teaspoon vanilla
1 quart vanilla ice cream, softened

TOPPING

4 tablespoons brown sugar
4½ tablespoons butter
3 tablespoons milk
½ cup chopped pecans

♦ **Combine** pumpkin, sugar, spice and vanilla.

♦ **Fold** in softened ice cream

♦ **Pour** into pie shell and freeze

♦ **Cook** topping ingredients until smooth. Add pecans.

♦ **Pour** slowly over pie and return to freezer.

♦ **Take** out 10 minutes before serving

PUMPKIN PECAN PIE

Yield: 8 servings

PUMPKIN LAYER
- ¾ cup canned pumpkin
- 2 tablespoons light brown sugar
- 1 large egg, lightly beaten
- 2 tablespoons sour cream
- ⅛ teaspoon cinnamon
- ⅛ teaspoon nutmeg
- 1 (9 inch) pie shell, chilled

PECAN LAYER
- ¾ cup light corn syrup
- ½ cup light brown sugar
- 3 large eggs, beaten lightly
- 3 tablespoons unsalted butter, melted
- 2 teaspoons vanilla
- ¼ teaspoon grated lemon rind
- 1½ teaspoons lemon juice
- ¼ teaspoon salt
- 1½ cups pecan halves

♦ **Whisk** together pumpkin, brown sugar, egg, sour cream, cinnamon and nutmeg. Spread in pie shell.

♦ **Mix** together ingredients for pecan layer, except pecans.

♦ **Add** pecans. Gently spoon over pumpkin layer.

♦ **Bake** in upper third of 425° oven for 20 minutes. Reduce heat to 350° and bake for 20 to 30 minutes more, until filling is slightly puffed. The center will appear not quite set.

♦ **Cool** on rack.

HEAVENLY RUM CAKE •

Yield: 16 to 18 servings

CAKE
- 1 cup chopped pecans
- 1 butter flavor cake mix
- 1 package vanilla pudding mix
- ½ cup oil
- ½ cup light rum
- 4 eggs
- ½ cup water

GLAZE
- ½ cup butter
- 1 cup sugar
- ¼ cup white rum
- ¼ cup water

♦ **Pour** one cup chopped pecans into the bottom of a greased Bundt pan.

♦ **Mix** next six ingredients together and pour over nuts. Bake at 325° for 50 to 60 minutes.

♦ **Remove** from oven and let cool in pan for ten minutes. Turn out onto long sheet of foil for glazing.

♦ **Combine** glaze ingredients and cook over low heat until thickened (about 30 to 45 minutes), stirring frequently to prevent separation. This can be done while cake is baking. Spoon over warm cake.

Chocolate Mousse Cake

Yield: 8 to 10 servings

CAKE

7 ounces semisweet chocolate
½ cup unsalted butter
7 eggs, separated
¾ cup sugar
1 teaspoon vanilla
⅛ teaspoon cream of tartar
¼ cup sugar

WHIPPED CREAM FROSTING

½ pint whipping cream
⅓ cup powdered sugar
1 teaspoon vanilla

♦ **Melt** chocolate and butter in a small saucepan over low heat.

♦ **Beat** egg yolks and ¾ cup sugar in a large bowl until very light and fluffy, about 5 to 8 minutes. Gradually beat in warm chocolate mixture and vanilla.

♦ **Beat** egg whites with cream of tartar in another large bowl until soft peaks form. Add ¼ cup sugar one tablespoon at a time. Continue beating until stiff. Fold egg whites carefully into chocolate mixture.

♦ **Pour** ¾ of the batter into an ungreased 9 inch springform pan. Cover remaining batter and refrigerate.

♦ **Bake** cake 35 minutes in a 325° oven.

♦ **Prepare** frosting by whipping cream powdered sugar and vanilla. Set aside.

♦ **Remove** cake from oven and cool. Cake will drop as it cools. Remove outside ring of pan.

♦ **Stir** refrigerated batter to soften slightly. Spread on top of cake. Refrigerate until firm.

♦ **Spread** frosting over top and sides. Garnish with chocolate leaves, if desired. Refrigerate several hours or overnight. May be frozen.

RASPBERRY CHOCOLATE MERINGUE ICEBOX CAKE

Yield: 12 servings

MERINGUES
  4 large egg whites
  ¼ teaspoon cream of tartar
  1 cup sugar

GANACHE
  ¼ cup heavy cream
  6 ounces fine-quality bittersweet (not unsweetened) chocolate, chopped

CREAM MIXTURE
  1½ teaspoons unflavored gelatin
  3 tablespoons cold water
  2½ cups heavy cream
  ½ cup sugar
  1½ cups sour cream
  1 teaspoon vanilla
  3 pints fresh raspberries

♦ **Line** 2 baking sheets with parchment paper and trace three 8 inch circles onto paper.

♦ **Beat** egg whites with cream of tartar and a pinch salt until they just hold soft peaks.

♦ **Add** 1 cup sugar gradually, beating. Continue beating meringue until it holds stiff peaks.

♦ **Pipe** or spread meringues onto parchment circles, smoothing with a spatula.

♦ **Bake** meringues 30 minutes in a 250° oven and switch positions of baking sheets in oven. Bake meringues 30 minutes more, or until pale golden and crisp. Cool meringues completely and peel off paper. Meringues may be made one day ahead and kept in turned off oven.

♦ **Bring** ¼ cup heavy cream just to a boil in a saucepan, and remove from heat. Add chocolate and stir mixture until chocolate is melted completely.

♦ **Divide** ganache between two meringue layers and gently spread evenly on each meringue, leaving ½ inch borders. Chill ganache until hardened, about 10 minutes.

♦ **Sprinkle** gelatin over water in a small saucepan and soften 1 minute. Heat mixture over low heat, stirring until gelatin is dissolved and keep warm.

Continued on next page

- **Beat** 2½ cups heavy cream with ½ cup sugar until it just holds stiff peaks; beat in sour cream and vanilla. Add gelatin mixture in a stream, beating until mixture holds stiff peaks.
- **Arrange** 1 ganache-topped meringue on a plate and spread it with about 1½ cups cream mixture, mounding it at the edge.
- **Arrange** one pint raspberries over cream mixture and top with second ganache-topped meringue. Repeat procedure with about 1½ cups more cream mixture and another pint raspberries and top with third meringue.
- **Transfer** about one cup cream mixture to pastry bag fitted with a star tip and reserve for decoration. Frost top and sides of cake with remaining cream mixture.
- **Chill** cake at least 2 hours and up to 8 hours. Remove wax paper carefully and scatter remaining pint raspberries on and around cake. Cut cake into 12 wedges with a serrated or electric knife.

CAPPUCCINO BUTTERCREAM CAKE

Yield: 15 to 20 servings

CRUST

4 whole graham crackers
½ cup chopped walnuts
½ cup blanched slivered almonds
¼ cup sugar
Pinch salt
5 tablespoons unsalted butter, melted and cooled

FUDGE LAYER

2 cups whipping cream
1 pound semi-sweet chocolate, finely chopped
2 tablespoons light corn syrup
½ cup unsalted butter, at room temperature, cut into 8 pieces

CAPPUCCINO BUTTERCREAM LAYER

2½ cups firmly packed golden brown sugar
½ cup water
6 egg yolks
1½ cups unsalted butter, room temperature
1 tablespoon instant espresso powder dissolved in 1 teaspoon hot water
4 ounces unsweetened chocolate, chopped, melted and cooled to lukewarm

COFFEE WHIPPED CREAM

1¼ cups chilled whipped cream
2 teaspoons instant espresso powder
½ teaspoon vanilla extract
2 tablespoons powdered sugar
2 ounces semi-sweet chocolate, grated
Chocolate shavings, optional
Chocolate coffee bean candies, optional

◆ **Butter** a 10 inch springform pan.

◆ **Grind** graham crackers in food processor. Add nuts, sugar, salt and chop coarsely, pulsing on and off. Add butter and process until crumbs are evenly moistened.

◆ **Press** into the bottom of pan. Bake until edges begin to brown, about 15 minutes. Cool.

◆ **Bring** cream to boil in heavy saucepan. Reduce heat to low. Add chocolate and stir until melted. Remove from heat.

◆ **Mix** in corn syrup. Add butter, one piece at a time stirring until smooth. Cool to lukewarm, stirring occasionally.

◆ **Pour** fudge into cooled crust. Refrigerate until firm, about 2 hours.

◆ **Cook** sugar and water in heavy medium saucepan over very low heat, stirring until sugar dissolves; avoid scraping sides of pan. Increase heat to medium and boil mixture 2 minutes.

◆ **Beat** yolks in heavy duty mixer at high speed until thick. With mixer running, gradually pour boiling syrup into yolks; do not scrape pan. Continue to beat until yolk mixture is cool, about 15 minutes.

◆ **Reduce** mixer speed to medium. Mix in butter, one tablespoon at a time. Add Espresso mixture, then melted chocolate.

Continued on next page

♦ **Spread** buttercream over chilled fudge layer. Cover pan loosely with waxed paper. Refrigerate overnight.

♦ **Combine** 1 tablespoon whipping cream, espresso powder and vanilla in small bowl. Stir until powder dissolves. Beat remaining cream in large bowl until beginning to thicken. Mix in coffee mixture and powdered sugar. Beat whipping cream mixture to form peaks.

♦ **Insert** small sharp knife around sides of springform pan to loosen torte. Carefully release sides of pan.

♦ **Spread** most of coffee whipped cream neatly over top and sides of torte. Press grated chocolate around sides. Transfer torte to serving dish.

♦ **Transfer** remaining cream to pastry bag fitted with medium star tip. Pipe cream in rosettes around top edge of torte. Garnish with chocolate shavings and coffee bean candies, if desired.

♦ **Refrigerate**. Let stand at room temperature one hour before serving.

May be prepared 6 to 8 hours ahead.

GERMAN CHOCOLATE UPSIDE DOWN SURPRISE CAKE

Yield 12 to 15 servings

1 cup flaked coconut
1 cup chopped pecans
1 package German chocolate cake mix
1¼ cups water
⅓ cup oil
3 eggs
3½ cups (about one pound) powdered sugar
1 cup margarine or butter, melted
1 (8 ounce) package cream cheese, softened

♦ **Sprinkle** coconut and pecans evenly over the bottom of a 9x13 inch greased pan.

♦ **Combine** cake mix, water, oil and eggs at low speed until moistened, then beat two minutes at high speed. Spoon batter evenly over coconut and pecans.

♦ **Combine** powdered sugar, margarine and cream cheese in another bowl. Beat until smooth and creamy. Spoon evenly over batter to within one inch of edges.

♦ **Bake** at 375° for 40 to 50 minutes or until toothpick inserted comes out clean. Cool completely. Cut into squares. Invert each square onto individual plates. Serve warm or cold. Store in refrigerator.

The cream cheese mixture sinks during baking and forms a creamy layer that you will see when you serve inverted pieces.

BLUE RIBBON CHEESECAKE *

Yield: 12 servings

CRUST
1 box crushed vanilla wafers
½ cup butter melted
1 (4 ounce) package chopped
   pecans

FILLING
3 (8 ounce) packages cream
   cheese
1½ cups sugar   *Jam.*
4 eggs, beaten

TOPPING
1½ cups sugar
1 pint sour cream
   Fresh strawberries

♦ **Mix** crushed wafers, melted butter and pecans in a large bowl. Place in a 10 inch springform pan and flatten to form crust.

♦ **Blend** cream cheese, sugar and eggs thoroughly and pour on top of crust.

♦ **Bake** at 350° for 45 to 50 minutes or until center is firm and lightly browned. Remove from oven and cool.

♦ **Blend** sugar and sour cream. Pour over cooled filling and bake for another 20 to 30 minutes at 350° or until set.

♦ **Place** sliced fresh strawberries on top.

Any fresh fruit such as blueberries, cherries, etc., may be used for topping.

TERRITORY FOLKS' RAW APPLE CAKE

Yield: 15 to 20 servings

¾ cup margarine
1½ cups white sugar
2 eggs, well beaten
2¼ cups flour
1½ teaspoons soda
½ teaspoon salt
¾ cup strong cold coffee
1 teaspoon vanilla
3 cups peeled and chopped
   apples
¾ cup brown sugar
1½ teaspoons cinnamon
¾ cup chopped nuts

♦ **Cream** together margarine, sugar and eggs.

♦ **Add** flour, soda, salt, coffee and vanilla.

♦ **Fold** in apples and pour into a 9x13 inch greased pan.

♦ **Mix** brown sugar, cinnamon and nuts, and sprinkle over top.

♦ **Bake** at 350° for 45 to 50 minutes.

After cake is cool you may drizzle with a glaze, or dust with powdered sugar.

ZINFANDEL DELIGHT

Yield: One large two layer cake

CAKE

2¼ cups sifted flour
2¼ teaspoons baking powder
½ teaspoon cinnamon
½ teaspoon ground cloves
½ teaspoon salt
¼ cup butter or margarine
¼ cup shortening
1 cup sugar
3 tablespoons grated orange rind
⅔ cup California Zinfandel wine
⅓ cup buttermilk
1 tablespoon Grand Marnier
½ cup ground walnuts
4 egg whites
¼ cup sugar

ORANGE CREAM FROSTING

6 tablespoons butter or margarine
2 tablespoons sour cream
1 tablespoon orange juice concentrate
1 tablespoon Grand Marnier
1 (16 ounce) box powdered sugar

GARNISH

Walnut pieces
Orange rind

♦ **Grease** and flour two (9 inch) cake pans.
♦ **Mix** together the first five ingredients. Set aside.
♦ **Cream** the butter and shortening, in a large bowl. Add 1 cup sugar and grated orange rind. Cream until fluffy.
♦ **Combine** Zinfandel, buttermilk and Grand Marnier, in another bowl.
♦ **Add** the flour mixture, walnuts and the Zinfandel mixture to the creamed butter mixture and stir until smooth.
♦ **Whip** the egg whites until foamy. Add gradually, by the spoonful, the ¼ cup of sugar. Beat until the egg whites are stiff. Fold into cake batter lightly.
♦ **Bake** for 25 to 30 minutes in a 375° oven. Cool.
♦ **Prepare** frosting by beating butter and sour cream together. Beat in orange juice concentrate, Grand Marnier, and powdered sugar. Frost cooled cake.

You may ice only the middle and top layer. This looks more interesting if the icing oozes out the middle. Garnish the top with sprinkled walnut pieces and shredded orange peel.

"EVERYTHING'S GOING MY • WAY" CINNAMON CAKE

Yield: 16 to 18 servings

CAKE
- 1 package yellow cake mix with pudding
- ¾ cup oil
- ¾ cup water
- 4 eggs
- 1 teaspoon butter extract
- 1 teaspoon vanilla
- ½ cup chopped pecans

FILLING
- ½ cup sugar
- 4 teaspoons cinnamon

GLAZE
- 1 cup powdered sugar
- 3 tablespoons milk
- ½ teaspoon butter extract
- ½ teaspoon vanilla

♦ **Combine** cake mix, oil and water. Mix well. Add eggs one at a time, mixing continuously. Add flavoring and beat on high speed for 6 to 8 minutes.
♦ **Combine** ½ cup sugar and 4 teaspoons cinnamon for filling.
♦ **Sprinkle** ⅓ of nuts in a greased and floured Bundt pan.
♦ **Spread** in layers over nuts, alternating layers of batter, filling and nuts, ending with batter.
♦ **Bake** at 350° for 40 to 50 minutes. Cool and remove from pan.
♦ **Prepare** glaze by combining powdered sugar, milk, butter extract and vanilla. Glaze cake with a pastry brush.

HOSPITALITY CAKE •

Yield: 12 to 15 servings

CAKE
- 2 cups flour
- 2 cups sugar
- 2 teaspoons soda
- 2 eggs
- 2 teaspoons vanilla
- 1 (20 ounce) can crushed √ pineapple (not drained)

FROSTING
- 1¾ cups powdered sugar
- 1 cup chopped nuts
- 1 (8 ounce) package cream cheese
- ¼ cup butter or margarine
- 1 teaspoon vanilla

♦ **Stir** flour, sugar, soda, eggs, vanilla and pineapple by hand until well mixed. Spread in greased sheet cake pan (10x15 inches).
♦ **Bake** at 350° for 20 to 25 minutes.
♦ **Mix** all frosting ingredients and spread on warm cake. Store cake in refrigerator.

UPSIDE-DOWN GINGER CAKE

Yield: 8 to 9 serving

TOPPING

    4 tablespoons butter, melted
    ½ cup soft brown sugar, not
        packed
        Fresh or canned pears
        Chopped walnuts or pecans

CAKE

    1 cup flour
    ½ teaspoon soda
    ¼ teaspoon salt
    2 teaspoons cinnamon
1 - 2 teaspoons ground ginger
    ¼ teaspoon grated nutmeg
        Pinch ground cloves
    1 beaten egg
    ½ cup soft brown sugar,
        packed
    ⅓ cup dark molasses
    ½ cup soured milk
    4 tablespoons melted butter

◆ **Add** brown sugar to the melted butter and stir for 1 to 2 minutes over gentle heat. Pour into an 8 or 9 inch cake pan.

◆ **Arrange** pears in cake pan flat side down. Surround with nuts.

◆ **Sift** together dry cake ingredients, except sugar, into a bowl.

◆ **Mix** together with an electric mixer egg, sugar, molasses, soured milk and cooled butter. Stir into flour mixture.

◆ **Beat** hard for one minute until smooth and thick. Spoon on top of pears.

◆ **Bake** at 350° for 45 to 50 minutes.

◆ **Turn** out onto a serving plate and serve hot with whipped cream or whipped cream combined with a small carton of plain yogurt.

To reheat, cover with foil and place in 350° oven for 10 minutes.

HUMMINGBIRD CAKE ❖

CAKE
3 cups all-purpose flour
2 cups sugar
1 teaspoon baking soda
1 teaspoon salt
1 teaspoon ground cinnamon
3 eggs, beaten
1 cup vegetable oil
1½ teaspoons vanilla extract
1 (8 ounce) can crushed
  pineapple, undrained
1 cup chopped pecans
2 cups chopped bananas

FROSTING
1 (8 ounce) package cream
  cheese, softened
½ cup butter or margarine,
  softened
1 (16 ounce) package
  powdered sugar, sifted
1 teaspoon vanilla extract
½ cup chopped pecans

♦ **Combine** first 5 ingredients in a large mixing bowl. Add eggs and oil, stirring until dry ingredients are moistened. Do not beat.

♦ **Stir** in vanilla, pineapple, 1 cup chopped pecans and bananas.

♦ **Spoon** batter into three greased and floured 9 inch round cake pans.

♦ **Bake** at 350° for 25 to 30 minutes or until toothpick inserted in center comes out clean. Cool in pans 10 minutes. Remove from pans and cool completely.

♦ **Combine** cream cheese and butter, beating until smooth. Add powdered sugar and vanilla. Beat until light and fluffy.

♦ **Frost** between layers, top and sides of cake. Sprinkle ½ cup chopped pecans on top.

APRICOT NECTAR CAKE •

Yield: 24 servings

CAKE
- 4 eggs, separated
- 1 small package lemon gelatin
- ¾ cup corn oil
- ¾ cup apricot nectar
- 2 teaspoons lemon extract
- 1 box yellow cake mix

ICING
- 1 lemon rind, grated
- Juice of one lemon
- 2 cups powdered sugar, sifted

♦ **Beat** egg whites until stiff and set aside.
♦ **Combine** 4 egg yolks, lemon gelatin, oil, nectar, lemon extract and cake mix in a mixing bowl. Beat for about 5 minutes. Fold in stiffly beaten egg whites.
♦ **Bake** in a greased tube pan for one hour in a 325° oven.
♦ **Prepare** icing by mixing lemon rind, lemon juice and powdered sugar. Icing will be thin.
♦ **Drizzle** icing over cake while still hot.

MOM'S CHERRY CAKE °

Yield: 9 servings

CAKE
- ½ cup butter
- 1 cup sugar
- 1 egg
- ½ cup milk
- 1 cup flour
- 1 teaspoon baking powder
- 1 cup pie cherries, drained, reserving juice
- 1 tablespoon flour
- ½ cup chopped toasted pecans

CHERRY SAUCE
- 1 tablespoon flour
- ½ cup sugar
- 1 cup cherry juice
- Water
- Red food coloring, if needed
- ½ teaspoon almond extract

♦ **Cream** butter and sugar, then add egg and milk.
♦ **Mix** dry ingredients together; mix into creamed mixture.
♦ **Sprinkle** drained cherries with 1 tablespoon flour. Stir cherries and nuts into batter.
♦ **Spread** into a greased and floured 9 inch baking dish. Bake at 350° for 50 to 60 minutes.
♦ **Prepare** sauce by mixing flour and sugar in a saucepan. Add juice (plus water to make one cup). Cook until thick.
♦ **Remove** from heat. Add red food coloring if needed and almond extract. Cool.
♦ **Serve** cake with ice cream topped with cherry sauce.

BOX SUPPER BANANA CAKE °

Yield: 10 to 12 servings

CAKE

¾ cup shortening
1½ cups sugar
2 eggs
1 cup mashed ripe bananas
½ teaspoon salt
2 cups sifted cake flour
1 teaspoon soda
1 teaspoon baking powder
½ cup buttermilk
1 teaspoon vanilla
½ cup chopped pecans
1 cup shredded coconut

FILLING

½ cup sugar
2 tablespoons flour
½ cup cream
2 tablespoons butter
½ cup chopped pecans
¼ teaspoon salt
1 teaspoon vanilla

ICING

1 egg white
¼ cup shortening
¼ cup butter
½ teaspoon vanilla
2 cups powdered sugar

♦ **Cream** together ¾ cup shortening and sugar. Add eggs and beat for two minutes. Add mashed bananas and beat two more minutes.

♦ **Mix** together salt, cake flour, soda and baking powder.

♦ **Add** buttermilk to banana mixture, alternately with dry ingredients. Beat two minutes. Add vanilla and pecans.

♦ **Pour** into two greased and floured 9 inch pans. Sprinkle ½ cup coconut on each cake before baking.

♦ **Bake** at 350° for 25 to 30 minutes. Remove from pans and cool coconut side down.

♦ **Prepare** filling by combining ½ cup sugar, flour, cream and butter in a saucepan and cooking until thick. Cool. Add pecans, salt and vanilla.

♦ **Place** one cake layer coconut side down and cover with filling. Place second cake layer on top, coconut side up.

♦ **Prepare** icing by creaming together egg white, shortening, butter and vanilla. Add powdered sugar gradually. Beat until fluffy.

♦ **Frost** sides of cake first and about one inch around edge of top. There is not enough icing to frost whole cake. Center should show toasted coconut.

CHERRY PUDDING CAKE •

Yield: 24 servings

CAKE

2 cups flour
2 cups sugar
½ teaspoon salt
2 eggs, beaten
1 (16 ounce) can tart pitted cherries, drain and reserve juice
2 tablespoons butter, melted
2 teaspoons soda dissolved in 2 teaspoons water
Pecans

SAUCE

2 cups brown sugar
2 tablespoons flour
¼ teaspoon salt
2 tablespoons butter
2 cups hot water
2 teaspoons vanilla

♦ **Mix** flour, sugar, and salt together.

♦ **Mix** cherry juice (drained from cherries), butter and dissolved soda together. Add eggs.

♦ **Add** dry ingredients to liquid ingredients. Fold in cherries and nuts.

♦ **Bake** in a 9x13 inch pan at 375° for 45 to 50 minutes.

♦ **Prepare** sauce by mixing first 5 sauce ingredients and cooking over low heat until thick. Stir in vanilla.

♦ **Pour** over hot cake and refrigerate immediately.

FLUFFY FROSTING

Yield: Icing for one large layer cake

1 cup sugar
¼ teaspoon cream of tartar
⅛ teaspoon salt
⅓ cup water
1 tablespoon corn syrup
2 egg whites
¼ teaspoon vanilla

♦ **Combine** sugar, cream of tartar, salt, water and corn syrup in a saucepan. Cook, stirring occasionally, until sugar is dissolved; about four minutes.

♦ **Break** egg whites in mixer bowl.

♦ **Add** hot syrup mixture to egg whites, and beat until fluffy.

♦ **Add** vanilla.

HEAVENLY FILLING FOR ANGEL FOOD CAKE

Yield: Filling and icing for one angel food cake

1 package unflavored gelatin
5 egg yolks, beaten
2½ cups milk
1½ cups sugar
2 tablespoons flour
4 tablespoons cold water
1 tablespoon vanilla
1 pint whipping cream, whipped
1 angel food cake

♦ **Dissolve** gelatin in 4 tablespoons of cold water.
♦ **Make** a custard with the beaten egg yolks, milk, sugar and flour in the top of a double boiler, cooking until it thickens.
♦ **Remove** from heat and immediately add the gelatin.
♦ **Add** 1 tablespoon vanilla. Allow to cool well, then refrigerate until very cold.
♦ **Add** 1 pint COLD whipped cream to custard mixture, and fold together.
♦ **Allow** this mixture to cool well, then fill between the layers of angel food cake which has been split into three layers. Ice outside of cake with remaining filling. Keep refrigerated.

Serve topped with fresh fruit or fruit sauce.

SPICED CREAM

Yield: 3 cups

1½ cups whipping cream
⅓ cup powdered sugar, sifted
1 teaspoon ground cinnamon
¼ scant teaspoon ground cloves
1 teaspoon vanilla extract

♦ **Whip** cream slightly and add other ingredients slowly. Continue to beat constantly until soft peaks form.

Use as a topping for warm spice cake or gingerbread, or with fresh strawberries on un-iced chocolate cake.

HOT FUDGE SAUCE •

Yield: 2 cups

5 tablespoons unsalted butter
¼ cup cocoa
2 squares unsweetened chocolate, chopped
¾ cup sugar
⅔ cup evaporated milk
Pinch salt
1 teaspoon vanilla

♦ **Melt** butter in a small saucepan. Remove from heat. Whisk in cocoa until smooth.
♦ **Stir** in the chocolate, sugar and milk. Bring to a boil over medium heat, stirring constantly.
♦ **Remove** from heat at once and stir in salt. Cool slightly and then add vanilla.

Keeps well in refrigerator.

CHOCOLATE SAUCE

Yield: 2 cups

½ cup butter
1 cup chocolate chips
1 (12 ounce) can evaporated milk
2 cups powdered sugar

♦ **Mix** together butter, chocolate chips, evaporated milk and powdered sugar in a saucepan.
♦ **Boil** 8 minutes, stirring constantly.
♦ **Cool** at least 2 hours before serving.

STRAWBERRY ICE CREAM •

Yield: 1 gallon

3 cups sugar
1 (12 ounce) can evaporated milk
½ pint whipping cream
1 large package frozen strawberries, partially thawed
Juice of 4 lemons
Enough milk to make one gallon

♦ **Break** apart partially thawed strawberries with fork.
♦ **Mix** all ingredients. Freeze in ice cream freezer according to manufacturer's directions.

Peaches or other fruit may be substituted for strawberries.

CHERRY STRAWBERRY DESSERT •

Yield: 16 servings

CRUST
    6 egg whites
    ½ teaspoon cream of tartar
    ¼ teaspoon salt
    1½ cups sugar
FILLING
    2 (3 ounce) packages cream
      cheese
    1 cup sugar
    1 teaspoon vanilla
    2 cups whipping cream
    2 cups miniature
      marshmallows
TOPPING
    1 can cherry pie filling
    1 (10 ounce) package frozen
      strawberries, thawed

♦ **Prepare** the night before: Beat egg whites and salt until foamy. Add cream of tartar. Beat until stiff. Gradually add sugar, beating until stiff and glossy.

♦ **Spread** mixture into a greased 9x13 inch pan. Bake at 275° for 60 minutes. (If glass pan, bake at 250° for 60 minutes). Turn oven OFF. Leave pan in oven overnight.

♦ **Whip** cream in a separate bowl. Beat softened cream cheese, sugar and vanilla until fluffy. Fold in the whipped cream and marshmallows. Spread over meringue. Chill 3 to 4 hours.

♦ **Combine** cherry pie filling and strawberries. Spread over cream cheese mixture.

SUPER STRAWBERRY DESSERT

Yield: 18 to 24 servings

    Crushed graham crackers
    ¼ cup butter, melted
    1 quart strawberries, thinly
      sliced
    1 (8 ounce) frozen whipped
      topping
    1 (14 ounce) can sweetened
      condensed milk
    6 tablespoons lemon juice
    1 cup chopped walnuts or
      pecans

♦ **Cover** bottom of a 9x13 inch glass pan with crushed graham crackers.

♦ **Pour** ½ stick of melted butter over crackers.

♦ **Combine** strawberries, frozen whipped topping, condensed milk, lemon juice and nuts. Mix for 2 minutes.

♦ **Pour** strawberry mixture over graham cracker crust. Place in freezer for 30 minutes. Garnish with strawberries and cracker crumbs if desired. Slice and serve. Store in refrigerator.

🍃HEAVENLY SUMMER TRIFLE

Yield: 12 servings

12 ounces fresh raspberries
12 ounces fresh blackberries
  Granulated sugar
2 small packages instant
  pudding mix, French
  vanilla or vanilla
1 quart skim or low-fat milk
3 large ripe nectarines or
  peaches
1 (12 ounce) container frozen
  whipped topping
1 (8 ounce) container low-fat
  sour cream
1 angel food cake, unfrosted,
  plain
6 tablespoons orange flavored
  liqueur

♦ **Place** berries in two separate bowls. Sweeten with sugar; set aside.
♦ **Make** pudding with milk according to package directions. Set aside.
♦ **Mix** 8 ounces of the whipped topping with the sour cream. Set aside. Reserve the remaining 4 ounces of whipped topping.
♦ **Pull** off about ⅓ of the angel food cake and tear into chunks and place in the bottom of a trifle bowl with at least a 3 quart capacity.
♦ **Sprinkle** cake with 2 tablespoons liqueur.
♦ **Slice** nectarines or peaches in a layer on top of cake pieces.
♦ **Repeat** layer of cake sprinkled with liqueur.
♦ **Spoon** ½ the pudding over the cake. Spoon ½ the whipped topping/sour cream mixture on top of the pudding.
♦ **Spoon** the sweetened blackberries on top of topping layer.
♦ **Repeat** layer of cake sprinkled with liqueur.
♦ **Spoon** remaining pudding over cake. Spoon the rest of the whipping topping/sour cream mixture over pudding. If dish is getting too full, use only part of this mixture.
♦ **Spread** the sweetened raspberries on the topping mixture layer.

Continued on next page

♦ **Cover** with plastic wrap and refrigerate for about 8 hours. At serving time, uncover and garnish with reserved whipped topping. Decorate with a few sprigs of mint.

Any variety of fresh summer fruits will make a tasty trifle.

STRAWBERRY PIZZA •

Cookie Crust

Yield: 12 to 16 servings

CRUST
1 cup self-rising flour
½ cup butter, melted
¼ cup powdered sugar

FILLING
1 (8 ounce) package cream cheese
1 can sweetened condensed milk
⅓ cup lemon juice
1 teaspoon vanilla
2 pints fresh strawberries, washed and sliced

GLAZE
¾ cup sugar
1½ tablespoons cornstarch
1 cup water
Red food coloring

♦ **Mix** together crust ingredients and pat into a round pizza pan.
♦ **Bake** at 350° until barely brown.
♦ **Beat** together cream cheese and sweetened condensed milk. Add lemon juice and vanilla. Spread over cooled crust. Arrange strawberries over filling.
♦ **Combine** and boil glaze ingredients until thickened, about 5 minutes. Cool completely. Spoon cooled glaze over strawberries. Slice like a pizza.

May use other fruit combinations - kiwis, bananas, grapes, or pineapple.

RHUBARB CRISP

Yield: 4 to 6 servings

CRISP

1 cup all-purpose flour
¾ cup old fashioned rolled oats
½ cup butter
1 cup packed brown sugar
1 teaspoon cinnamon
4 cups rhubarb, fresh or frozen, drained

GLAZE

1 cup sugar
2 tablespoons cornstarch
1 cup water
1 teaspoon vanilla

♦ **Mix** flour, oats, sugar, cinnamon and butter in a large bowl. Mix till crumbly.
♦ **Put** half of the mixture in an ungreased 9 inch square pan.
♦ **Cover** with rhubarb. May add a drop of red food coloring to rhubarb.
♦ **Prepare** glaze by combining all ingredients in a small saucepan. Cook and stir until bubbly, plus 2 minutes more.
♦ **Remove** from heat, stir in vanilla. Pour over rhubarb already in pan.
♦ **Top** with remaining crumb mixture.
♦ **Bake** at 350° for 50 to 60 minutes.

HARVEST MOON BAKED APPLES •

Yield: 4 servings

4 red delicious apples or any baking apple, cored
4 tablespoons light brown sugar
2 teaspoons cinnamon
2 tablespoons golden raisins
2 tablespoons dried cranberries
2 tablespoons chopped pecans
4 teaspoons butter
4 tablespoons Chambord liqueur
½ cup cranberry or apple juice

♦ **Trim** peeling a quarter of the way down the apple. Trim bottom if necessary, so that apples will sit level.
♦ **Mix** sugar, cinnamon, raisins, cranberries and pecans. Fill core of apples with this mixture. Tightly pack.
♦ **Place** one teaspoon butter on top of each apple and spoon liqueur and juice over.
♦ **Bake** at 350° 30 to 40 minutes or until soft but not falling apart. Baste occasionally while baking. Serve warm with cream.

LEMON BISQUE •

Yield: 12 to 16 servings

CRUST
2½ cups graham cracker
    crumbs
½ cup sugar
⅔ cup margarine
FILLING
1 (12 ounce) can evaporated
    milk
1 (3 ounce) package lemon
    gelatin
¾ cup boiling water
¾ cup sugar
2 tablespoon bottled lemon
    juice, or the juice from 1
    large lemon
    Whipped topping
    Lemon slices

♦ **Melt** margarine and mix with graham cracker crumbs and sugar. Press into a 9x13 inch pan or two 9 inch pie plates.
♦ **Bake** at 375° for 6 to 8 minutes. Cool.
♦ **Chill** evaporated milk thoroughly.
♦ **Dissolve** gelatin in boiling water. Add sugar, cool on counter top.
♦ **Beat** evaporated milk to stiff peaks. Add cooled gelatin mixture gradually. Beat lemon juice into mixture.
♦ **Pour** into graham cracker crust. Chill and garnish with whipped topping and lemon slices.

CHOCOLATE PEPPERMINT DESSERT

Yield: 15 to 18 pieces

2 cups vanilla wafer crumbs
⅔ cup margarine
1 (1 ounce) square
    unsweetened chocolate
2 (2 ounce) squares semi-
    sweet chocolate
3 cups powdered sugar
1 teaspoon vanilla
3 egg whites
¾ cup chopped nuts (optional)
½ gallon peppermint ice
    cream, softened

♦ **Sprinkle** 1 cup of vanilla wafer crumbs in an ungreased 9x13 inch pan.
♦ **Melt** butter and chocolate over low heat. Add sugar and vanilla.
♦ **Beat** egg whites and blend into chocolate mixture. Add nuts if desired. Spread mixture over crumbs.
♦ **Spread** ice cream over chocolate and top with remaining crumbs.
♦ **Cover** with foil and freeze. Cut into squares to serve.

PUMPKIN AND CREAM • CHEESE ROLL-UP

Yield: 10 to 12 servings

CAKE
¾ cup sifted flour
1 teaspoon baking powder
2 teaspoons cinnamon
1 teaspoon pumpkin pie spice
½ teaspoon nutmeg
½ teaspoon salt
3 eggs, slightly beaten
1 cup sugar
⅔ cup canned pumpkin
1 cup chopped nuts

FILLING
1 cup powdered sugar
1 (8 ounce) package cream cheese, softened
6 tablespoons butter
1 teaspoon vanilla

♦ **Grease** a 10x15 inch jelly roll pan; line with wax paper; grease and flour wax paper.
♦ **Sift** together flour, baking powder, cinnamon, pie spice, nutmeg and salt. Set aside.
♦ **Beat** eggs and sugar in large bowl until thick and fluffy. Beat in pumpkin.
♦ **Stir** in dry ingredients all at once. Pour into prepared pan, spread evenly with spatula. Sprinkle with nuts.
♦ **Bake** at 375° for 15 minutes or till center springs back.
♦ **Loosen** cake around edges and invert onto a clean, damp towel, dusted with powdered sugar. Peel off wax paper.
♦ **Trim** ¼ inch from all sides. Roll cake and towel together from short side. Place seam side down on wire rack. Cool completely.
♦ **Prepare** filling by beating together powdered sugar, cream cheese, butter and vanilla until smooth.
♦ **Unroll** cake and spread with cream cheese filling. Reroll cake and refrigerate until ready to serve. Slice and serve.

DRILLERS' DOWNFALL •

Yield: 16 to 24 servings

1 (25 ounce) package brownie mix
2 boxes chocolate mousse mix (Royal Brand - 2 packages, other brands 4 packages).
1 large frozen whipped topping
1 package Bits-O-Brickle (or grind up 2 Heath Bars)
2 - 3 tablespoons Kahlua or amaretto (optional)
½ cup chopped pecans

♦ **Mix** and bake brownie mix according to cake-like directions on box.

♦ **Prepare** mousse mix according to box directions. Set aside.

♦ **Break** up cooled brownies in the bottom of a very large bowl. Drizzle Kahlua over brownies, if desired.

♦ **Spread** prepared mousse over brownies. Spread whipped topping over mousse. sprinkle Bits-O-Brickle over whipped topping.

♦ **Refrigerate** until ready to serve.

Could be layered twice instead of a single layer of each or could be done in individual parfaits.

CHOCOLATE TOFFEE DESSERT

Yield: 16 (2 inch) squares.

CRUST
15 chocolate wafers (1 cup), crushed
3 tablespoons margarine, melted

FILLING
½ cup margarine, softened
½ cup sugar
4 eggs, separated
1 square bitter chocolate, melted
2 teaspoons instant coffee granules (not freeze-dried)
½ teaspoon vanilla
¼ cup sugar
3 (¾ ounce) chocolate covered toffee bars

♦ **Combine** chocolate wafers and melted margarine. Press into an 8 inch baking pan. Refrigerate.

♦ **Cream** margarine and sugar until fluffy. Beat in egg yolks, melted chocolate, instant coffee granules and vanilla.

♦ **Beat** egg whites until soft peaks form. Gradually beat in ¼ cup sugar until stiff peaks form. Fold egg white mixture into chocolate mixture. Spread over chocolate wafer crust.

♦ **Crush** chocolate toffee bars coarsely and sprinkle on top.

♦ **Freeze** for 3 hours. Cut and serve.

CHILLED CHOCOLATE LOAF •

Yield: 8 to 10 servings

8 ounces semi-sweet chocolate chips
¼ cup rum
1 cup unsalted butter, softened
⅓ cup granulated sugar
2 eggs, separated
5 ounces blanched almonds, chopped fine
Pinch salt
12 - 14 Lorna Doone cookies, cut into small chunks
Powdered sugar

♦ **Grease** bottom and sides of a 2 quart pan lightly with oil; invert to drain.

♦ **Melt** chocolate in a heavy pan or double boiler over low heat, stirring constantly. Add rum and cool to room temperature.

♦ **Cream** butter and sugar. Add egg yolks one at a time.

♦ **Combine** almonds and cooled chocolate with butter mixture.

♦ **Beat** egg whites in a separate bowl, to form soft peaks. Fold whites into chocolate mixture, then fold in cookie pieces.

♦ **Spoon** mixture into loaf pan, smooth with spatula and cover tightly with plastic. Refrigerate until loaf is very firm, about 4 hours.

♦ **Invert** loaf an hour before serving. Smooth top and sides with spatula and return to refrigerator.

♦ **Cut** loaf into thin slices and serve with sprinkled powdered sugar over each piece.

MYSTERY MOCHA DESSERT

Yield: 9 servings

¾ cup sugar
1 cup sifted flour
2 teaspoons baking powder
⅛ teaspoon salt
1 square unsweetened chocolate
2 tablespoons butter or margarine
½ cup milk
1 teaspoon vanilla
½ cup chopped pecans
½ cup packed brown sugar
½ cup granulated sugar
4 tablespoons cocoa
1 cup cold strong coffee (may be instant)

♦ **Grease** a 9 inch square pan.
♦ **Sift** together the first four ingredients.
♦ **Melt** together chocolate and butter over hot water in a double boiler, or in a microwave.
♦ **Add** dry ingredients alternating with milk to chocolate mixture. Blend in vanilla and pecans.
♦ **Pour** into a greased 9 inch pan. Combine brown and white sugars and cocoa. Sprinkle over batter. Pour coffee over the top.
♦ **Bake** at 350° for 30 to 40 minutes . Make sure it looks done but not crusty around the edges.
♦ **Serve** by cutting in squares and inverting the serving in a small bowl before topping with ice cream or whipped cream.

This recipe may be doubled and baked in a 9x13 inch pan.

This dessert is not pretty, but is a chocoholic's dream.

MAPLE MOUSSE

Yield: 8 servings

4 egg yolks, beaten until very light
¾ cup maple syrup
1 pint heavy cream, whipped
Roasted, slivered almonds

♦ **Combine** egg yolks and maple syrup in the top of a double boiler. Cook until mixture thickens, stirring constantly. Do not boil. Cool completely.
♦ **Fold** whipped cream into maple syrup mixture.
♦ **Turn** into a mold, or eight sherbet glasses. Freeze for at least four hours.
♦ **Sprinkle** with almonds.

 BAKLAVA

Yield: 50 or more pieces

CRUST
1 (1 pound) box phyllo dough
¾ cup butter, melted
¾ cup margarine, melted
FILLING
2 teaspoons cinnamon
¼ teaspoon ground cloves
1 pound walnuts, ground to a coarse consistency
½ cup sugar
SYRUP
1½ cups water
1½ cups sugar
10 - 12 whole cloves
1 cup honey
1 stick cinnamon, broken
1½ teaspoons lemon juice

♦ **Thaw** phyllo at room temperature in box overnight, then refrigerate. Keep wrapped until ready to use.
♦ **Mix** together filling ingredients in a large bowl. Set aside.
♦ **Combine** syrup ingredients except lemon juice and boil 5 minutes.
♦ **Add** lemon juice to syrup and set pan in a sink of cold water. Set aside.
♦ **Open** phyllo package and unfold dough at center. Keep covered with a damp towel so dough won't dry out.
♦ **Brush** a 16x12x2½ inch metal pan with melted butter and margarine using a large pastry brush or clean paint brush.
♦ **Lay** one sheet phyllo evenly in bottom of pan. Brush with butter and continue adding four more sheets of phyllo, buttering each one.

Continued on next page

- **Spread** ⅓ of filling mixture evenly on top of dough and cover with one flat sheet of buttered phyllo.
- **Lay** subsequent sheets of phyllo with edge of phyllo in center of pan, brush with butter, fold overhanging half back on itself and brush with butter. This will keep edges from being too thick. Always use flat sheet directly on top of nut mixture, however.
- **Repeat** process until all nuts and phyllo are used, and the last layer of phyllo (3 or 4 sheets) is flat.
- **Bend** edges toward center with a knife so that it leaves a neat edge. Butter if necessary.
- **Use** a very sharp knife and carefully cut in diagonal rows and then cut each row in pieces BEFORE BAKING. Should resemble diamond shapes.
- **Bake** uncovered at 350° for approximately 1 hour. Check at 50 minutes, should be golden brown.
- **Remove** from oven. Measure 1 cup syrup, with cloves and cinnamon removed, and pour over hot baklava until all is used. Let cool.
- **Store** unused syrup, with cloves and cinnamon in refrigerator for later use.

DOWN HOME BREAD PUDDING •

Yield: 12 servings

12 slices of French bread,
    crusts removed
5 tablespoons butter, at room
    temperature
5 eggs
4 egg yolks
1 cup sugar
⅛ teaspoon salt
4 cups milk
1 cup heavy cream
1 tablespoon vanilla

♦ **Butter** one side of bread. Line a three quart baking bowl with bread, buttered side up. Set aside.

♦ **Beat** together eggs and egg yolks. Stir in sugar and salt.

♦ **Mix** milk with cream in saucepan and scald. Gradually add hot milk to egg mixture, stirring constantly. Add vanilla.

♦ **Pour** over bread. Bread will float to top.

♦ **Put** the bowl into a larger shallow pan and fill pan with enough hot water to come up sides of bowl 1½ inches.

♦ **Bake** at 350° for 45 to 50 minutes. Center should shimmer when done. Do not overbake.

Pudding should have a creamy custard base with a caramelized bread on top. If it's tough or riddled with holes, it has cooked too long.

INDIAN PUDDING

Yield: 8 servings

5 cups milk
½ cup yellow cornmeal
½ cup sugar
½ cup molasses
4 tablespoons butter
1 teaspoon salt
1 teaspoon pumpkin pie spice

DELAWARE
NATION

♦ **Combine** 2 cups of milk with cornmeal and remaining ingredients in a large heavy saucepan.
♦ **Heat** slowly to boiling, then simmer 5 minutes or until creamy thick, stirring often.
♦ **Pour** into a buttered 8 cup baking dish. Stir in 2 more cups milk.
♦ **Bake** at 325° for one hour. Stir in remaining cup of milk. Bake 2 hours longer or until pudding sets. (The secret is long slow baking.)
♦ **Serve** with cream or ice cream.

CAFFÈ GRANITA

Yield: 4 servings

1 cup water
½ cup sugar
2¼ cups very strong coffee (may be made with 4 teaspoons instant coffee)
½ cup crème de cacao

♦ **Boil** water and sugar for three minutes.
♦ **Add** to coffee and set aside to cool.
♦ **Pour** into shallow dish and freeze for several hours stirring occasionally until crystalline.
♦ **Spoon** ice into serving dishes. Top with Crème de Cacao and add whipped cream, if desired.

CRÈME BRÛLÉE

Yield: 8 servings

4 cups heavy cream
1 vanilla bean
  Pinch salt
8 egg yolks
¾ cup plus 2 tablespoons
  sugar
8 tablespoons light brown
  sugar

♦ **Combine** cream, vanilla bean and salt in a heavy saucepan. Warm over medium heat until surface begins to shimmer, about 5 minutes.

♦ **Stir** egg yolks and sugar with wooden spoon until blended. Pour in hot cream and stir gently to avoid forming air bubbles.

♦ **Strain** the custard into a large measuring cup or pitcher through a thin cloth that has been placed in a strainer and skim off any air bubbles (with a wooden spoon).

♦ **Place** a wet towel in the bottom of a large shallow roaster pan.

♦ **Fill** eight ¾ cup ramekins and place upon the towel in the roaster pan and pour hot water half way up onto ramekins.

♦ **Cover** loosely with foil and bake 1 to 1½ hours until custard is firm around the edges.

♦ **Remove** ramekins from water and let cool. Cover and refrigerate until cold, at least 3 hours. Will keep at this point at least 2 days. If small pools of liquid develop, blot with a paper towel.

♦ **Preheat** broiler. Set ramekins on a baking sheet. Sift 1 tablespoon of brown sugar on top in a thin layer, spreading with a knife to even out.

♦ **Broil** as close to heat as possible until sugar is caramelized. Watch constantly as this burns easily. Takes approximately 2 to 5 seconds.

♦ **Let** cool and serve immediately or refrigerate up to 4 hours.

May garnish with mint leaf and raspberries.

SEASONAL CELEBRATIONS

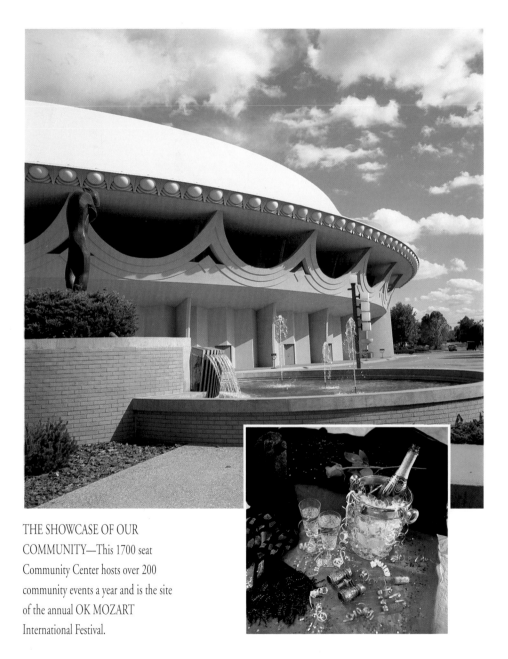

THE SHOWCASE OF OUR
COMMUNITY—This 1700 seat
Community Center hosts over 200
community events a year and is the site
of the annual OK MOZART
International Festival.

A PROUD HERITAGE

The mastery of Frank Lloyd Wright also evidenced itself in one of the city's later architectural gems—the Bartlesville Community Center, designed by the late William Wesley Peters, chief architect of the Frank Lloyd Wright Foundation.

The Center, which boasts one of the most acoustically perfect concert halls in the country, is home to the renowned OK MOZART International Festival, taking place in June. Ransom Wilson conducts Solisti New York, the Festival's orchestra-in-residence. The Festival attracts thousands of people to our special blend of classical music and territorial heritage.

Many other celebrations reflect the wide variety of interests of the city. Sunfest, a three-day arts fair, occurs every spring and attracts artists from the region. Enthusiasts from across the country gather in June for the annual Biplane Expo, hosted by the National Biplane Association. Native American heritage is celebrated each fall during Indian Summer, and in December the city is aglow during the Fantasyland of Lights.

As Bartlesville celebrates its first 100 years, we wonder what the dreamers and visionaries of yesterday would think of the city today. We hope they would be happy to see us still working to improve the quality of life here and proud to know that the generous spirit of old Indian Territory still burns strong.

SPRING FEVER

EASTER SUNDAY

Caviar Mousse   page 25

Chutney Glazed Ham   page 146

Hot or Cold Asparagus   page 115

Orange Ambrosia   page 66

Angel Biscuits   page 47

Raspberry Chocolate Meringue Ice Box Cake   page 205

WILD ONION BRUNCH

Wild Onions and Eggs   page 54

Fried Ham Steaks

Homestead Hominy   page 114

Julia Lookout's Fry Bread   page 43

Indian Pudding   page 233

Rainy Day Supper

Mango Chutney Spread on Crackers page 28

Grilled Hoisin Marinated Leg of Lamb page 149

Almond Pilaf page 110

Honey Plum Dressing Over Seasoned Fruit page 84

Crescent Moon Rolls page 49

Coffee Almond Blondies page 183

From the Sea

Red Snapper on a Bed of Limes page 177

New Potatoes in White Wine page 112

Spinach Salad with Pine Nut Dressing page 65

Cappuccino Buttercream Cake page 208

Mama Mia

Sun Dried Tomato Pesto on
Toasted Slices of Italian Bread   *page 168*

White Lasagna   page 163

Mixed Greens with Easy Vinaigrette   page 82

Italian Bread

Chocolate Toffee Dessert   page 227

Espresso

Friends for Lunch

Toast Points and Assorted Cheeses

Tomato Basil Sorbet   page 122

Lemon Chicken and Pasta on Greens   page 162

English Caramel Squares   page 186

BREEZY DAYS

Oriental Angel Wings   page 14

Seafood Risotto   page 181

Snow Pea Salad   page 69

Hard Rolls

Lemon Bisque   page 225

——————— ◆ ———————

KIDS, KITES AND KITTENS

Crispy Chicken   page 151

Mashed Potato Casserole   page 111

Rancho Baked Beans   page 128

Cowboy Burger Bites   page 190

LAZY SUMMER DAYS

MORNING GLORIES

Orange Mint Spritzer   *page 33*

Italian Herb Bread with Scrambled Eggs   *page 54*

Spinach Fruit Salad   *page 64*

Chocolate Peppermint Dessert   *page 225*

OUT ON THE PORCH

Cold Peach Soup   *page 85*

Home-Grown Tomato Quiche   *page 51*

Roasted Asparagus   *page 115*

Poppy Seed Bread   *page 38*

French Chocolates   *page 193*

FAMILY REUNION

Black Bean Salsa   page 181

Chuck Roast on the Grill   page 132

Corn on the Cob

Gourmet Green Beans   page 114

Hard Rolls

Strawberry Ice Cream   page 220

Oil Baron's Oatmeal Cookies   page 190

DOWN ON THE RANCH

Red Pepper Soup with Fresh Dill   page 95

Stuffed Tenderloin   page 135

Potato Gratin   page 113

Sensational Summer Squash   page 119

Territory Tomatoes   page 70

Angel Biscuits   page 47

Down Home Bread Pudding   page 232

SPARKLERS AND ROCKETS

Chicken with Peach Salsa   page 152

Caesar Margarita Salad   page 63

Pinto Beans Cooked with Jalapeño Peppers

Cold Mexican Beer

Super Strawberry Dessert   page 221

CATCHING FIREFLIES

White Sangria   page 34

Campfire Flank Steak   page 132

Roasted Green Beans with Garlic   page 116

Bleu Cheese Potato Salad   page 70

Heavenly Summer Trifle   page 222

CANNING TIME

Denim and Diamond Steak Salad   page 81

Zucchini Stuffed with Red Pepper Purée   page 120

Spiced Peaches

German Chocolate Upside Down Cake   page 210

HOT! HOT! HOT!

Tomato Basil Soup   page 95

Creamy Nutty Tuna Sandwich   page 103

Minted Orange and Grapefruit Salad   page 66

Almond Mocha Pie   page 198

AUTUMN LEAVES

Indian Summer Supper

Grilled Salmon Fillets with Spinach Pesto Sauce   page 177

Roasted Bell Peppers and Onions   page 123

Rice Pilaf with Saffron and Gruyère Cheese   page 110

French bread

Chocolate Mousse Cake   page 205

Wild Things

Smothered Quail   page 158

Pecan Wild Rice   page 109

Spinach Salad with Pine Nut Dressing   page 65

Rustler's Rolls   page 49

Pumpkin Pecan Pie   page 204

HARVEST MOON HAYRIDE

Scandinavian Roast Pork with Salad   page 144

Marinated Carrots with Walnuts   page 117

Swedish Rye Bread   page 41

Pescatore Wine

Territory Folks' Raw Apple Cake   page 211

Thermos of Strong Hot Coffee

EMPTY NEST SUPPER

Veal with Queen Anne Cherries   page 142

Broccoli Soufflé   page 129

Pears Tarragon   page 65

Crescent Moon Rolls   page 49

Cappuccino Mousse Pie   page 195

FIRESIDE SUPPER

Lemon Veal Scallops with Avocado   page 143

Mixed Greens with Green Goddess Dressing   page 82

Almond Pilaf   page 110

Chilled Chocolate Loaf   page 228

————————— ◆ —————————

THE FROST IS ON THE PUMPKIN

Grilled Marinated Pork Chops   page 147

Rotkraut   page 122

Roasted Green Beans with Garlic   page 116

Pumpkin and Cream Cheese Roll-Up   page 226

BUENOS DIAS

Magnifico Margarita   page 35

Fresh Mexican Salsa with Tortilla Chips   page 181

Rolled Beef Enchiladas   page 140

Oklahoma Rice   page 111

Greens with Avocado Dressing   page 81

Refried Beans

Mexican Beer

Almond Torte   page 199

HARVEST DAYS

French Onion Soup   page 97

Roast Tenderloin of Pork with Plum Sauce   page 144

Szechuan Collard Greens   page 126

Almond Pilaf   page 110

Upside Down Ginger Cake   page 214

WINTER WONDERLAND

COZY KITCHEN LUNCH

Company's Comin' Chicken Sandwiches   *page 105*

Assorted Vegetables with Curry In a Hurry   *page 28*

Chocolate Biscotti   *page 189*

Cafe Latte

———————— ◇ ————————

MONDAY NIGHT FOOTBALL

Black Bart's Vegetarian Chili   *page 101*

Mexican Corn Bread   *page 40*

Sliced Avocado, Oranges and Red Onions

Black Gold Brownies   *page 184*

DREAMS OF MYSTERIOUS PLACES

Chèvre Stuffed Mushrooms   page 21

Lamb Marrakech   page 151

White Rice with Parsley and Cilantro

Drizzled Oranges   page 66

Fantastic Feta Salad   page 67

Zinfandel Delight   page 212

Very Black Coffee

WARMS THE SOUL

Gin Stew   page 138

Buttered Egg Noodles

Mixed Greens with Mustard Vinaigrette   page 84

Wavin' Wheat Cheddar Bread   page 39

"Out of My Dreams" Lemon Cloud Pie   page 203

VALENTINE'S DAY

Shrimp Dijonaise for Two   *page 176*

Steamed Broccoli

Italian Bread

Lenzer Torte   *page 202*

Chardonnay

COMPANY'S COMING

Ten Carrot Soup   *page 94*

Fillet of Beef with Brown Sugar and Poached Pears   *page 136*

Goat Cheese Salad   *page 63*

Mushrooms and Rice   *page 111*

Frank Lloyd Wright Chocolate Delight   *page 194*

TALL GRASS DINNER

Traditional Buffalo Roast   page 135

Fireside Winter Salad   page 69

Green Bean Bundles   page 116

Mashed Potato Casserole   page 111

Black Walnut Chess Pie   page 200

CROCUS DAYS

Chinese Broiled Turkey Steaks   page 158

Curried Rice Salad   page 71

Cranberry Apple Pear Relish   page 182

Cheese Stuffed Zucchini   page 119

Cardamom Bread   page 43

Apricot Nectar Cake   page 216

CONTRIBUTORS

Service League of Bartlesville extends sincere appreciation to those who have contributed to the success of *Taste of the Territory*.

Abeyta, Clare
Adams, Diana
Adams, Louise
Ambler, Sharon
Anderson, Marge
Askew, Alice Ann
Atherton, Susie
*Atkins, Ann
Ayres, Evelyn
Babcock, Cheryl
Bailey, Linda
Ball, Becca
Ball, Shirley
Bandy, Rufus
Barrett, Jan
Barto, Susie
Bartolo, James
Basinger, Ann
Batchelder, Becca
Bates, Jim
Bates, Sharen
Beard, Beth
Beard, Linda
Beard, Martha Mae
Belmont, Linda
*Benz, Jan
Blair, Pat
Blakemore, Nancy
Boesiger, Margaret
*Bohnsack, Denise
Bonifazi, Patti
Bonner, Kris
Bowles, Jesse
Bowles, Ruthie
*Boyce, Peggy
Boyd, Karen
Brady, Carolyn
Bratt, Arlene
Brining, Mary Ann
Brookby, Jean
Bryan, Elgia
Buckles, Cheryl
Burkhart, Martha

Burness, Nancy
Caldwell, Kerry
Campbell, Joyce
Carey, Linda
Carroll, Kathryn
Chandler, Caroline
Clark, Peggy
Clayton, Ann
Coffman, Sunday
Collins, Joan
*Cooper, Janet
Copeland, Donna
Cox, Lynn
*Cozby, Karole
Craig, Sue
Creel, Carol
Cubbage, Catherine
Cubbage, Linda
Cubbage, Marie
Cubbage, Mildred
*Cunningham, Judy
Curd, Kacy
Dalrymple, Betty
Daniels, Charlie
Daniels, Julie
Davis, Keitha
DeFehr, Joyce
DeMartino, Linda
Dickson, Cassandra
Dillard, Pam
Doty, Cheri
*Dreisker, Joan
Drummond, Janet
Elfstrom, Linda
*Emerson, Betsy
Emerson, Frances
Evans, Alvin
Evans, Mary Martha
Eynard, Mary
Farmer, Nancy
Findlay, Ethel
Finney, Helen
Fish, Gayle

Fooshee, Cindy
Ford, Mary
Fouts, Kay
Freiberger, Marie
Friley, Mary
Gaede, LaVonne
Gallery, JoAnn
Garber, Karen
Geissler, Ingrid
Gerhold, Linda
Gorman, Carolyn
Grigsby, Carmen
*Grillot, Ada
Guillory, Gloria
Habiger, Celeste
*Haigh, Doris
Haller, Isabel
Hall, Peggy
Hall, Wendy
Hammond, Pat
Hardin, Betty
Harris, Karen
Heady, Jackie
Henderson, Ruth
Hensley, Susan
Hodges, Bryce
Hodges, Judy
Holliman, Dorsey
Holloway, Suzanne
Houchin, Louise
Houston, Donna
Houston, Judy
Hover, Linda
Howe, Carrie
Howenstine, Barbara
Hughes, John
Hughes, Lorna
Hugo, Helen
Hunziker, Becky
Hurn, Fern
*Jemison, Carole
*Jenneman, Betty
Johnson, Bobbie

Cookbook Committee

251

Johnson, Kyle
*Johnson, Melody
Jones, Betty
Jones, Mary
Kane, Ellen
Kane, Holly
Kane, Jamie
*Keltner, Kaye
Ketchum, Annette
Ketchum, Dee
*Kidd, Amy
Kleinschmidt, Jeanne
Koch, Sharon
Lacey, Sue
Lanckriet, Bertha
Lanning, Margaret
LeBlanc, Shirley
Lemons, Debbie
Leroux, Diane
Lewis, Jo Anne
Lindemood, Sandy
Lindstrom, Cheryl
List, Sue
Loffer, Colleen
Logan, Peggy
Luger, Martha
Macklin, Jodi
*Maddux, Beth
Maddux, Judy
Maddux, Sue
Markel, Kay
Martine, Phyllis
Martinovich, Kathleen
May, Marty
McConnell, Frances
McDonald, Donita
McDonald, Phyllis
*McElroy, Dugan
McFarland, Sylvia
McKinley, Dee
Mecom, Katsy
Miller, Candy
*Mills, Jan
Minter, Betty
Moeller, Sandy
Moore, Sue
Morris, Robbie
Mullendore, Kathleen
Mulva, Miriam
Murphy, Jetta Sue

Musgrave, Adele
Nash, Karen
Nelson, Gail
Newman, Pat
*Olivier, Aggie
Owen, Betty
Pace, Mike
Page, Judie
Pain, Susan
*Pelton, Deanna
Penuel, Marcia
Perkins, Mary
Perryman, Betty
Phillips, Edna
Phillips, Nancy
Pierce, Brenda
Pierce, Jerry
Poole, Janet
Pratt, Claudie
Pregler, Jan
Pritchard, June
Pryor, Nancy
Rawlins, Anne
Reed, Nellie Lou
Riddlebarger, Sue
Robinett, Bruce
*Robinett, Ruth
*Robinson, Beverly
Robinson, Mary Marie
Rogers, Marilyn
Rule, Elizabeth
Ryan, Elaine
Schaffer, Sue
Schoonveld, Lois
Schriber, Rose
Scott, Marilee
Sewell, Georgene
Shadwick, Dianne
Shinn, Becky
Shoffner, Laura
Sigmon, Mary Alice
Siker, Rich
Silas, Theo
Skinner, Sandra
*Skurcenski, Stephanie
Smith, Carolyn
Smith, Mary Lynn
Smith, Mavis
Spencer, Mark
*Staats, Susan

Stables, Gerry
*Standridge, Deedie
Stapp, Linda
*Starcevich, Judy
Starcevich, Matt
Stark, Jimmi Lee
Stayton, Jackie
Stayton, Sara
Stevenson, Lela
Stinson, Louann
*Storer, Kathy
Summers, Frances
Sutherland, Claire
*Swindell, Jeanette
Thomas, Amy
Thomas, Gretchen
Thrasher, Cheryl
Tippeconnic, Lynda
VanAuken, Peggy
Vaughan, Yovene
Waldo, Sandra
*Walthall, Peggy
Wamsley, Marjane
Warren, Garri
*Warren, Suzanne
*Wasemiller, Cindy
Waters, Jane
Watson, Maxine
Webb, Jane
Webster, Ann
Weis, Adrienne
*Welch, Carol
Wertz, Katie
Westfall, Barbara
*Whistler, Betty
White, Norma
*Whitworth, Donna
Williams, Ann
*Williams, Barbara
Williamson, Gail
Wilson, Ransom
Woods, Jan
*Woolrich, Marinel
Worten, Nancy
Young, Mary Jo
Zeiders, Susie
Zervas, Kathy
Zervas, Marcia
*Zimmerman, Jan

Cookbook Committee